# Alexander the Great and the Macedonian Empire

## Professor Kenneth W. Harl

PUBLISHED BY:

THE GREAT COURSES
4840 Westfields Boulevard, Suite 500
Chantilly, Virginia 20151-2299
1-800-TEACH-12
Fax—703-378-3819
www.teach12.com

ISBN 1-59803-654-8

# Kenneth W. Harl, Ph.D.
## Professor of Classical and Byzantine History
### Tulane University

Professor Kenneth W. Harl is Professor of Classical and Byzantine History at Tulane University, where he has taught since 1978. He earned his B.A. from Trinity College and his M.A. and Ph.D. from Yale University.

Professor Harl teaches courses in Greek, Roman, Byzantine, and Crusader history from the freshman to graduate levels. A recognized scholar of coins and classical Anatolia, he takes Tulane students to Turkey on excursions and as assistants on excavations of Hellenistic and Roman sites.

Professor Harl has published numerous articles and is the author of *Civic Coins and Civic Politics in the Roman East, A.D. 180–275* and *Coinage in the Roman Economy, 300 B.C. to A.D. 700*. His current work includes publishing the coins from the excavation of Gordion and a new book on Rome and its Iranian foes.

Professor Harl has received numerous teaching awards at Tulane, including twice receiving the coveted Sheldon Hackney Award for Excellence in Teaching (voted on by both faculty and students). He is also the recipient of Baylor University's nationwide Robert Foster Cherry Award for Great Teaching. In 2007, he was the Lewis P. Jones Visiting Professor in History at Wofford College.

Professor Harl is also a fellow and trustee of the American Numismatic Society. ∎

# Table of Contents

### INTRODUCTION

Professor Biography ........................................................................i
Course Scope............................................................................ 1

### LECTURE GUIDES

**LECTURE 1**
Alexander the Great—Conqueror or Tyrant?.......................................3

**LECTURE 2**
Greece in the Age of Hegemonies.................................................17

**LECTURE 3**
Achaemenid Persia ..................................................................32

**LECTURE 4**
The World of Early Macedon...........................................................45

**LECTURE 5**
Philip II and the Macedonian Way of War..........................................58

**LECTURE 6**
The Third Sacred War ..................................................................71

**LECTURE 7**
The Macedonian Conquest of Greece................................................86

**LECTURE 8**
The League of Corinth..................................................................100

**LECTURE 9**
Alexander, Heir Apparent...............................................................115

**LECTURE 10**
Securing the Inheritance, 336–335 B.C.............................................130

# Table of Contents

**LECTURE 11**
The Invasion of Asia ........................................................................ 145

**LECTURE 12**
The Battle of the Granicus .............................................................. 160

## SUPPLEMENTAL MATERIAL

Timeline ........................................................................................ 175
Glossary ....................................................................................... 192
Biographical Notes ....................................................................... 212
Bibliography .................................................................................. 265

# Alexander the Great and the Macedonian Empire

**Scope:**

Alexander the Great, youthful king of Macedon and the most celebrated conqueror in history, dramatically, unexpectedly, and irrevocably altered the ancient world. This course examines not only the career of Alexander but also the historical conditions that produced this greatest of conquerors as well as Alexander's impact and legacy that endures to the present day. The first quarter of the course deals with the Hellenic world and Persian Empire in the two generations before the birth of Alexander the Great. In particular, Alexander owed so much to his father, King Philip II, hailed the greatest king of Europe in his day, his mother Queen Olympias, and his tutor and mentor Aristotle.

The middle half of the course covers the career of Alexander, with emphasis not only his military genius, but also his impact on the Hellenic world, Near East, and India. Central to this discussion is Alexander's changing perceptions of his destiny that led to clashes with the senior Macedonian nobility, and finally the soldiers themselves who twice protested their king's policies for administering an ever expanding world empire. These same policies steadily alienated his reluctant Greek allies, who, just before the king's death, rose in the rebellion known as the Lamian War. At the same time, his swift victories so awed and stunned the peoples of the Near East that his generals, after their king's death, could wage civil wars over the succession without fear of rebellion. Alexander's aims have thus inspired imitation by later conquerors, and debate among scholars and writers. As a result, each generation has recast the Macedonian king in a guise suitable to its age rather than understood Alexander on his own terms. Such an approach was already true in Antiquity, because each of main surviving accounts, composed by Flavius Arrianus, Plutarch, Diodorus Siculus, and Curtius Rufus, conveys a different image of the Macedonian king. The aim of this course is to put forth the most plausible historical Alexander the Great.

The last quarter of the course deals with the early Hellenistic world wrought by the conquests of Alexander. To be sure, Alexander never possessed a master plan for the Hellenization of the Near East or the creation of a wider unity of mankind. Yet, his actions transformed the face of the Near East. Even though Alexander's generals, the Diadochoi, partitioned Macedonian Empire by 301 B.C., a wider institutional, economic and cultural unity, largely Hellenic in origin and based on the Greek city-state, endured. This resulting Hellenistic world was the foundation upon which Rome, the ultimate heir of Alexander, erected her Mediterranean empire. ■

# Alexander the Great—Conqueror or Tyrant?
## Lecture 1

**Alexander's impact is so wide-ranging. ... He is an epitome, perhaps the best example of how a single individual, for all of the restrictions of his generation, can rapidly, fundamentally, and irrevocably change his world.**

No contemporary account of **Alexander the Great**, has survived, and it is doubtful an objective narrative of Alexander ever existed. Drawing on older contemporary accounts, Greek intellectuals **Arrian** and **Plutarch**, penned two of the four surviving sources. Arrian wrote the *Anabasis* of Alexander the Great based on the account of Ptolemy, companion of Alexander. Arrian gives, in general a favorable account of Alexander the Great, who is to be compared to Arrian's patron and Emperor Trajan.

Plutarch wrote a biography of Alexander, concentrating on details of Alexander's character rather than providing a historical narrative because he sought to draw moral lessons from noble Greeks and Romans. Plutarch, also in part drew on the history of Ptolemy, and so many details about war and politics are consistent with Arrian's version. Plutarch, however, drew on other sources, notably philosophical writers hostile to Alexander who was perceived as a tyrant corrupted by power and wine, and so a slave to his passions.

Writing in Latin in the 1st century A.D., **Curtius Rufus** delighted in exotic details and interpreted Alexander through the prism of Stoicism. **Diodorus Siculus**, writing in c. 50 B.C., devoted an entire book of his universal history to Alexander. Diodorus errs in military details, but he presents many incidents from the perspective of the Greeks or King Darius III of Persia. Perceptions of the career and impact of Alexander, who is arguably the best known secular figure history, have been even more varied. Greeks of Alexander's day resented the youthful conqueror who stripped their cities of freedom and autonomy. Later Greek writers saw Alexander as ushering in an era of great kings, and they too were critical of the Macedonian king's policies. Roman generals and emperors saw Alexander as a model.

To Europeans of the Middle Ages and Renaissance, Alexander epitomized the chivalrous king traversing distant lands populated with monstrous races and fabulous animals. Alexander was the only figure of Classical antiquity who captured the imagination of medieval Islam. The modern image of Alexander, noble conqueror and bearer of Hellenic civilization, was disseminated by the historian W. W. Tarn, who saw in the king's actions the prelude to Victorian Britain's Liberal imperial mission. This was the image transmitted by Western Europeans to the Greek nationalists of the 19th century that created the new nation of Greece. But since WWII, scholars applying the rigorous source criticism of the German acad emy and writing in the shadow of totalitarian dictatorships have recalled into question the greatness and generalship of Alexander. In the works of Badian and Bosworth, Alexander emerges as a cruel and diabolical tyrant, the precursor to the Perhaps, Wilcken, writing two generations ago, has captured best Alexander, a Macedonian king inspired by his sense of destiny and with a longing to perform great heroic deeds. ∎

## Names to Know

**Alexander the Great** (b. 356 B.C.; r. 336–323 B.C.): Argead king of Macedon, son of Philip II. The greatest of generals, he secured Macedon, control over the Greek league, and in 334–324 B.C., Alexander conquered the Persian empire, and transformed the face of the ancient world.

**Arrian** (c. 86–146 A.D.): Lucius Flavius Arrianus Xenophon. Historian and Roman senator. He wrote in Greek the Anabasis or Asian expedition of Alexander the Great based on the account of King Ptolemy I and other eye witness histories.

**Curtius Rufus**: Roman historian writing in Latin during the reigns of Claudius or Vespasian. Composed a history of Alexander in ten books of which only last eight survive. The work is noted for its delight in exotica.

**Diodorus Siculus** (c. 90–30 B.C.): Wrote a universal history in 40 books down to the Gallic Wars of Julius Caesar. His narrative is the prime source on the reign of Philip II.

**Plutarch of Chaeronea**: (c. 46–120 A.D.): Philosopher and biographer, his work is an invaluable source for the leading figures of the 4th century B.C. as well as a wealth of information on the Hellenistic world.

## Suggested Reading

Badian, "Alexander the Great and the Loneliness of Power."

———, "Alexander the Great and the Unity of Mankind."

Bosworth, *Alexander and the East.*

———, *Conquest and Empire.*

Pearson, *The Lost Histories of Alexander the Great.*

Stader, *Arrian of Nicomedia.*

Tarn, *Alexander the Great.*

Wilcken, *Alexander the Great.*

Wood, *In the Footsteps of Alexander the Great.*

———, *In the Footsteps of Alexander the Great.*

## Questions to Consider

1. Why do the surviving sources on Alexander the Great present such major problems of interpretation? What accounts for the differing perspectives of Arrian, Plutarch, Diodorus Siculus, and Curtius Rufus? Was there ever a single objective account of Alexander in antiquity?

2. Why did the heroic images of the young Macedonian king gain such widespread popularity from antiquity to the present? What about the king appealed to Europeans in Middle Ages?

3. How have modern scholarly opinions about Alexander been shaped by events and perceptions of each scholar? Why did Tarn persist in arguing for the idealistic image of Alexander? How have revisions of this portrait contributed to the understanding not only of Alexander, but the entire ancient world?

# Alexander the Great—Conqueror or Tyrant
## Lecture 1—Transcript

My name is Kenneth Harl, and I teach Greek, Roman, and Byzantine History at Tulane University in New Orleans. I shall be giving 36 lectures dealing with a course on Alexander the Great. The scope of this course is much larger than just Alexander; we will deal with the events leading up to Alexander's succession—that will require us to look at his father, Philip II, conditions in Greece and in the Persian Empire—as well as a series of lectures that will be devoted to the impact of Alexander and the world that followed after him. But our main attention will be on this Macedonian king who, perhaps of all the individuals of antiquity, arguably all of the secular figures of history, is the best known. This has been conducted through various tests by interviewing Americans at the mall, that indisputable center of pop culture. It's been carried out particularly by a very dear friend and colleague of mine, Eugene Borza, who is the leading expert on Macedon; he's done a number of these surveys, and he concludes that Alexander is probably the best-known secular figure bar none, although people are generally very vague about the details. Part of our task will be explaining this enduring image of the king and clarifying some of the obscure details.

In contrast to other periods of ancient history, we don't have many contemporary sources on Alexander the Great. We do have accounts from Classical antiquity, but these were written centuries after Alexander's death, and as a result they pose a certain problem in interpretation. It also raises the question whether there was ever any objective account of Alexander, even in ancient times; and the argument is often made that throughout history one gets the Alexander one wants: Each historian writes about Alexander from the perspective of his generation, the conditions in which that historian might have lived, and also how each historian might make use of these earlier sources.

It's necessary, first, to look at what these sources are. We have four narrative accounts and a fifth—I like to call it a half-account—the *Epitome* by Justin. The most important of the four narrative accounts was written in Greek by a historian known as Lucius Flavius Arrianus Xenophon. We usually call him Arrian, which is the anglicized form of the name. He was born in the city of Nicomedia around A.D. 86; he died about A.D. 146. His first language was Greek, although he knew Latin because he was a Roman senator; that is, he was a Greek provincial who attained the highest position within the Roman Empire. His account of Alexander, known as the *Anabasis*, comes down to us in seven books—each of those books represented a papyrus scroll in antiquity—and then he appended an eighth book, the so-called *Indica*, which is his description of India. He draws very heavily on the voyage of Nearchus, who was Alexander's friend and admiral, who returned part of the Macedonian army from India by sailing along the Indian Ocean, and left a very vivid account of that expedition.

Arrian was an experienced cavalry commander; he had fought on the Rhine, the Danube, and the Euphrates. He actually left us a tactical account of how he countered nomadic cavalry—a group of people known as the Alans who burst into Asia Minor around A.D. 135 when Arrian was governor of Cappadocia, which is central Asia Minor today—and that battle line is directly inspired after tactical formations Alexander used in central Asia back in 329 B.C. Arrian had a certain appreciation for Alexander's feat in arms because he himself was an experienced commander.

He also had access to sources that no longer exist. These include important contemporary accounts; he mentions them in the start of his history. The first and foremost was the account of Ptolemy, who later became king in Egypt; he was one of Alexander's boyhood friends. He's known as Ptolemy, Son of Lagus. He established the succession of Macedonian kings who ruled Egypt down to 30 B.C. Ptolemy distinguished himself in central Asia and India, and he left us an eyewitness account that Arrian made use of and only survives in summaries, what Arrian cites, and also what some later historians cite; we do not have the full account of Ptolemy. Arrian also had access to other sources. These included the account of Callisthenes, the great-nephew of Aristotle who was the official court historian on the expedition; the day book, the *Ephemerides* as it's called in Greek; of Eumenes of Cardia, who was the Greek secretary of Alexander; and a number of other contemporary or near-contemporary sources.

Arrian was a very suave and sophisticated writer. He had a very good sense of what a court is like. He tells us that throughout his account, when he ran into discrepancies, he generally preferred Ptolemy over other sources because Ptolemy was a king and it would be inappropriate for a king to lie. That is a comment that has caused certain consternation among historians; but Arrian is being very clever here. He was a close friend to the emperor Hadrian who ruled from A.D. 117–A.D. 138 and is remembered as the Philhellene emperor of the Roman world; he served under and distinguished himself under the Roman emperor Trajan—the great conqueror, the Optimus Princeps, the best of emperors—who made eastern conquests that were compared to the conquests of Alexander; so Arrian is being a bit circumspect here. He probably knew that Ptolemy's account was reliable in at least the military details; it was written at a time where many of the contemporaries were still alive, and Ptolemy could only go so far in distorting military actions conducted by Alexander.

In any case, Arrian's account is regarded by most historians as the best; and Arrian gives us an explanation why he was determined to write this account. Apparently by his day we have these contemporary sources and official documents but no really synthetic historical account of Alexander, and therefore it's quite different from other periods of Greek history where we have contemporary accounts by Herodotus, Thucydides, or Polybius describing affairs in the Greek world; Arrian is almost 450 years after Alexander's death. This is what Arrian writes about the purpose of his history and the reasons why he decided to write this account on the campaigns of Alexander:

> No prose history, no epic poem was written about him [that is, Alexander]; he was not celebrated even in such choral odes as preserve the name and memory of Hiero or Gelo or Thero [these are tyrants of Sicily from the 6th and early 5th century B.C.], or many other men not in the same class as Alexander, with the result that the wonderful story of his life is less familiar today than of the merest nonentities of the ancient world [Arrian's probably exaggerating a bit here; but nonetheless, the point's well taken]. Even the march of the Ten Thousand under Cyrus against Artaxerxes, the fate of Clearchus and his fellow prisoners, and the return under Xenophon's command to the sea, are, thanks to Xenophon's history, much better known than the great achievements of Alexander [this is the

so-called expedition of 401–399 B.C. known as the March of the Ten Thousand; we'll be discussing it later]; yet, unlike Xenophon, Alexander did not hold a mere subordinate command; he was not defeated by the Persian King, or victorious only over the force that tried to stop his march to the sea. On the contrary, there has never been another man in all the world, of Greek or any other blood, who by his own hand succeeded in so many brilliant enterprises. And this is the reason why I have embarked upon the project of writing this history in the belief that I am not unworthy to set clear before men's eyes the story of Alexander's life. No matter who I am that make this claim. I need not declare my name—though it is by no means unheard of in the world [he's a well-known Roman senator and governor]; I need not specify my country and family, or any official position I may have held. Rather let me say this: that this book of mine is, and has been from my youth, more precious than country and kin and public advancement—indeed, for me it is these things. And that is why I venture to claim the first place in Greek literature [a very bold claim], since Alexander, about whom I write, held first place in the profession of arms.

A very important statement, indeed; and Arrian does give us an extremely accurate account of the military exploits of Alexander. I have tended to follow Arrian in many of the essentials when dealing with the military side of Alexander, although we have these other three accounts plus this *Epitome* by Justin and other sources.

The second most important account is by Plutarch of Chaeronea. He, too, was a Greek living in the Roman Empire, born around A.D. 46 and died in A.D. 120. He wrote a number of works that have come down to us, and he was primarily a moral philosopher. He was a practitioner of what we would probably call Middle Platonism; he was devoted to the practices and theories of Plato, and in augment of those theories he wrote a number of important philosophical treatises and works on morality. But he also wrote biographies, and the most important set of biographies are the *Parallel Lives*. In this case, he compares Alexander the Great to Julius Caesar, and this is a combination that he pursues: the life of a famous Greek compared to the life of a famous

Roman. Unfortunately, Plutarch never wrote a life of Philip II, the father of Alexander the Great, one of Plutarch's great omissions.

In any case, Plutarch, too, drew on Ptolemy and the sources that Arrian used, but he also had access to a number of other sources. These included accounts that are often known as the Vulgate tradition—this comes from the Latin word "vulgus" that means "the crowd"—and these were popular stories about Alexander circulating even in Alexander's own lifetime. They included philosophical writers, some of whom were quite hostile to Alexander, thinking that Alexander had degenerated from a conqueror to a tyrant because of his addiction to drink, or, even worse, he became drunk with power. This goes back to a tradition established in Alexander's own lifetime when Callisthenes, the great-nephew of Aristotle, ran afoul of Alexander over the issue of proskynesis and was eventually arrested and died a miserable death. The philosophical schools, the philosophical writers, got wind of this information and that began a tradition of writing hostile interpretations of Alexander's behavior in his later years, and that passed into this common tradition. So Plutarch made use of these philosophical works; sometimes he went to great lengths to correct their opinions about Alexander, notably his drinking and his drunken sense of power. In any case, Plutarch provides anecdotes that we otherwise would not have. Many of the best stories I remembered about Alexander come out of Plutarch's biography of Alexander, as well as a very short moral treatise called "On the Fortune of Alexander."

Plutarch, unlike Arrian, was a biographer; and he makes very clear what his purpose is. Therefore, it's useful to read Plutarch's own words about what the purpose of this life of Alexander is all about. He's writing at the beginning the biography of Alexander, which is then followed by the biography of Julius Caesar; so he's essentially discussing both of these biographies. Plutarch's words:

> My subject in this book is the life of Alexander, the king, and of Julius Caesar, the conqueror of Pompey. The careers of these men embraces such a multitude of events that my preamble shall consist of nothing more than this one plea: if I do not record all their celebrated deeds or describe any of them exhaustively, but merely

summarize for the most part what they accomplished, I ask my readers not to regard this as a fault. For I am writing biography, not history, and the truth is that the most brilliant exploits often will tell us nothing of the virtues or vices of the men who performed them, while on the other hand a chance remark or a joke may reveal far more of a man's character than the mere feat of winning battles in which thousands fall, or of marshalling great armies, or laying siege to cities. When a portrait painter sets out to create a likeness, he relies above all on the face and the expression of the eyes and pays less attention to the other parts of the body; in the same way it is my task to dwell upon those actions which illuminate the workings of the soul [The Greek word here is psuche, from which we get "psychology," and it is part of Plutarch's philosophical training to stress the importance of the soul, the ultimate reality in any being. This goes back to Plato's Timaeus and the philosophical works of Plato], and by this means to create a portrait of each man's life. I leave the story of his greatest struggles and accomplishments to be told by others [notably Arrian].

Plutarch's account is invaluable. On the whole, Plutarch apparently follows more or less the narrative that Arrian writes, and that would be the account of Ptolemy and other contemporary sources on the military side of Alexander; so very often, the Plutarch-Arrian accounts are in sync with each other on many details.

The third source is an unusual source. It's written by Diodorus Siculus. He is a Greek of Sicily, writing at the end of the 1st century B.C.; his work may have been published around 50 B.C. or thereabouts. He had access to a number of different sources, and he wrote a universal history; that is, a history that starts from legendary times and goes down to his own day. Diodorus Siculus is an extremely difficult source to use. He's one of the sources that one employs in studying Classical Greece, particularly the 5th and 4th centuries B.C., and he's not always the best of sources; he's only as good as the sources that he himself uses. In working with Diodorus, particularly on the 5th century B.C., I have reason to believe that at times Diodorus gets his chronologies wrong, that he duplicates events, and that sometimes he gets confused on names; so he has to be used with a certain amount of care. He gives a very different version of the Battle of Granicus and also the siege of Halicarnassus in the opening stages of Alexander's campaign; I tend to follow Arrian's account on those two events.

On the other hand, Diodorus, for his account on Alexander—which is an entire book of his universal history, Book 17—has access to some apparently very interesting sources that we wish would have survived. These include sources written by Greeks who were in the Persian service—that is, the service of the Great King Darius III, the opponent of Alexander—and this account of Diodorus gives us information about those Greeks who were engaged in diplomatic maneuvers to oppose both Philip of Macedon and Alexander the Great. He gives us an insight into the plans of Darius III, particularly on the eve of the Battle of Issus where Darius consulted with his Greek mercenary commander Charidemus, a refugee from Athens who was in his service. He also provides information that we wouldn't otherwise have in these ugly clashes that occurred later in the campaign, particularly the trial and execution of Philotas in 330 B.C., a very important event we'll be discussing. For the reign of King Philip, the reign of Alexander's father, he is the main narrative account because we do not have any contemporary accounts surviving from the time of King Philip or a later version of King Philip's reign similar to what Arrian wrote for Alexander the Great; so Diodorus becomes an all-important account for us.

The fourth account is written in Latin. It's by a Roman author named Curtius Rufus, and we know very little about Rufus. Rufus is obviously, if not a senator, he's certainly sympathetic to the senators. He writes in some ways in the tradition of Cornelius Tacitus, the historian of the early Roman Empire who is a brilliant Roman historian (I actually think Tacitus is more a cynic who does history as a sideline); but he writes in that tradition. He has a very skeptical eye of rulers who can turn into tyrants, and he's very conscious of that; he's undoubtedly a practitioner of the Stoic doctrines that were common in the Roman ruling class. He also gives us information, and we're not at times sure whether this is really accurate to Alexander's day or reflects more Rufus's own day; and that is, Alexander is always consulting with his officers on the eve of the battles. Arrian and Plutarch see Alexander as the great commander, and they don't tell us that much about the subordinates, other than that Parmenion, the second-in-command, is essentially the cautious foil to Alexander and is always being overruled. But in Curtius Rufus, the officers are there in council; it's led some historians to argue, based on Curtius's account, that Alexander really was a heroic cavalry commander and king who inspired the army and it was a group of professional officers who really directed and won the battles. That's a position that I do not subscribe to; I think that's a misreading. In part, Rufus is probably reflecting Roman practice: Roman commanders did carry out such councils of war with their officers even down to the centurion level; so sometimes when I'm reading Curtius's account I'm wondering if I'm really looking more at the practice of the Roman army of the Imperial Age rather than the Macedonian army of Alexander's day.

On the other hand, Rufus has marvelous information on flora and fauna; he delighted in the exotic. In earlier times—in the late 19th and early 20th century, the beginning of modern scholarship on these sources—a lot of these descriptions were just dismissed as fanciful; but some of them have now been borne out, one of them most dramatically in 1993 by Michael Wood who did this idiosyncratic documentary on Alexander the Great, *In the Footsteps of Alexander the Great*, which does not pretend to be an account of Alexander's life but really looking more at the influence that Alexander had. At one point, Curtius Rufus gives us a description of a dry riverbed in northern Iran where Alexander and 500 mounted infantry made a record dash to capture Darius III. It's been dismissed, but Michael Wood has found that dry riverbed; and so Wood has actually very successfully pointed our several cases where Rufus's account is accurate, and it's been a major contribution into appreciating Curtius Rufus as a source.

We do have other sources; the one I want to mention first is a Latin *Epitome*, written at the end of the 2nd, beginning of the 3rd century A.D. by a fellow named Justin. We know little about Justin. He was essentially making the *Reader's Digest* version of a history of Macedon based on an account by a Latin author known as Pompeius Trogus who wrote a very detailed account in Latin about Philip II and Alexander the Great; and that Latin account goes back to contemporary histories, notably a history by Theopompus who wrote on the reign of Philip II. Would that we had Theopompus's account; we don't. What we have is a Latin abbreviation of the Latin version of that history. Nonetheless, Justin does prove important at times.

There was a papyrus fragment discovered and published of a Greek history. It's in Greek, it's very often known as the *Hellenica Oxyrhynchia*; that is, the Greek history from Oxyrhynchus, the town in Egypt. There is a belief of some scholars that this is part of the lost history of Theopompus. It covers events in the early 4th century B.C. before Philip's succession; and actually the account is very good from what we can tell in the narrative that survives. We have the orations of Demosthenes, the virulent opponent of Philip II; as well as orations by Socrates, Aeschines, Hyperides, and other leading figures in Athens. Archaeology, coins, and inscriptions—these would be public decrees put up on stone—add greatly to our knowledge; we'll be drawing on that information as well.

All of these sources together allow us to create not only the career of Alexander but also the world in which Alexander lived; and also the career of Alexander's parents, Philip II and Olympias, who had an immense importance on shaping Alexander, especially the mother Olympias—some would argue Alexander is, in some ways, the original "mama's boy"; he was devoted to his mother—and all of this information has been transmitted to us from antiquity.

Modern scholars have very divergent opinions about Alexander, and it's necessary to look at two important views. One view comes out of a British view in which Alexander the Great is an extremely heroic figure. This goes back into the 19th century, into Victorian Britain, when the British upper classes were trained in their Latin and Greek and they were taught Demosthenes, Thucydides, and all of these authors, and they saw Alexander as a great hero. They also saw the Athenian democracy as equivalent to the British parliamentary order of the 19th century. This goes back to the general history of George Grote, published between 1846 and 1856; and so the Athenians are the good guys and Philip II turns out to be the tyrant. But Alexander gets a pass because of his great exploits; he was held up as a heroic figure, one that was noble and chivalrous.

These 19th-century images, which in part based on not only the images of antiquity but medieval visions of Alexander as a chivalrous knight which was common in Western Europe, were essentially summed up in the biography of W. W. Tarn published in 1948 in two volumes. That vision of Alexander by

Tarn is the heroic, romantic vision that is very common today. It's actually the vision of Alexander the Great shared by most Greeks; it's the vision of Alexander evoked in 1821–1832 in the Greek War of Independence that saw the establishment of the kingdom of Greece out of the Ottoman Empire. Yet this vision of Alexander is overdrawn. Tarn in particular sees Alexander as not only a chivalrous knight but a perfectly good Victorian gentleman who would have tea with the queen, and at times he just dismisses the source out of hand if it doesn't fit that image. Alexander wouldn't do that; it's just not cricket. Actually, Tarn's vision of Alexander at times gets so heroic that there's no way Alex would have survived the violent politics of the Macedonian court.

The other image comes out of the scholarly tradition of German scholars writing in the 19th century; particularly a brilliant scholar, Johann Gustav Droysen, who lived between 1808 and 1884 and penned a very important history of Alexander the Great. That history of Alexander the Great saw Alexander, and also his father Philip II, as builders of nation-states. The Germans appreciated the Macedonian kings in a way that the British did not in the 19th century; and that tradition of the great leader that could fashion a state became the staple of German scholarship. One of the best views of that is written by Ulrich Wilcken, published in the 1930s before the Nazis took power. Wilcken's account of Alexander in some ways is still the best; he understands the pothos, the yearning, and the desire of Alexander to emulate his ancestors. That biography is still translated in English and available.

However, the tradition turned in a direction after the experience of Nazi Germany, and scholars writing after 1945 saw Alexander in a very different light—German scholars saw Alexander as a Hitler figure, sometimes as a Stalin figure—and this has influenced some of the most important works written in English: by Ernst Badian, a professor at Harvard who is a brilliant historian who has written innumerable articles on Alexander; and by an Australian scholar, A.B. Bosworth, whose works on Alexander are important, particularly his work on Alexander in the east. They see Alexander far more as a tyrant, in some cases as a megalomaniac, rather than as a conqueror and hero, and they act as a very good antidote to the vision of Tarn; although they, too, go overboard, and I tend to think that of all the modern scholars, Wilcken may have come closest to understanding Alexander.

It's remarkable that there isn't as widespread a popular image of Alexander. There are the novels of Mary Renault, is clearly a very fine novelist who evoked the Greek world; *Fire from Heaven*, *The Persian Boy*, and *Funeral Games* are all novels in which Alexander figures at least in part. Those novels are good, but they really aren't as good as her earlier novels, notably *The Last of the Wine* and *The King Must Die*, dealing with Classical Athens and the distant Mycenaean/Minoan past. There have been two attempts at movies, big Hollywood screen movies, and those are the 1956 *Alexander the Great*, written and directed by Robert Rossen, and then the more recent Oliver Stone in 2004. Neither epic film captures Alexander very successfully; I think that Rossen's screenplay is better, at least in the early stages. There's a really nice matchup of Richard Burton as the young Alexander and Fredric March as Philip; but the film very quickly degenerates into rather choppy narrative, it really isn't one of the better supporting casts, and on the whole the film doesn't really work. I think there's even less success with Stone's film, even though he went through great efforts to recreate the ancient world—there's a marvelous recreation of Babylon, of the great altars and monuments erected on the Hyphasis after the mutiny in 326 B.C.—but on the whole Stone never really has a sense of who Alexander is, I think the casting was not particularly well done, and so the film essentially comes out as being, in my opinion, boring; for all of the effort, you really walk away with wondering: Who was Alexander the Great?

I think the problem in coming to terms with Alexander is just the scope of his achievements—it cannot be confined into a two- or even four-hour epic film, you'd essentially have to do a miniseries—and that is because Alexander's impact is so wide-ranging. He was devoted to arete (or bravery) in the Greek tradition, which all great heroes such as Achilles—who was Alexander's ancestor—would seek; he was driven by a pothos, a longing or a yearning that Plutarch and Arrian repeatedly stress that causes him to go out and learn as well as to create great deeds; and above all, he is an epitome, perhaps the best example of how a single individual, for all of the restrictions of his generation, can rapidly, fundamentally, and irrevocably change his world. That is what our task is: to see how Alexander did this, and why his memory is so enduring down to this day.

# Greece in the Age of Hegemonies
## Lecture 2

What did the Greek world look like in the time of Alexander the Great? How did Philip of Macedon, to everyone's surprise, emerge as the man who would unite all of Greece within 10 years of coming to the throne?

In 404 B.C., the city-state of Sparta won the Peloponnesian War against Athens by cutting a deal with the Persians. The Spartans had to deliver on a treaty in which the Persian governors of Asia Minor promised to furnish financial and naval support to the Spartan fleet; but in return, the cities of Asia Minor would return to Persian rule. In 401 B.C., Sparta supported **Cyrus the Younger** who sought to seize the Persian throne from his elder brother **Artaxerxes II**. While Cyrus, with the aid of Greek mercenaries, was victorious at the Battle of Cunaxa. Unfortunately, Cyrus was was killed in the battle. and the Greek mercenaries with no paymaster marched out of the Persian Empire.

Out of fear of Sparta, the Artaxerxes II and the other leading city-states Thebes, Athens, Corinth, and Argos forged an alliance against Sparta in the Corinthian War. The Corinthian War ended in a strategic stalemate. Spartan demands over the next decade alienated their allies, and provoked a challenge from Thebes. Athens regained autonomy and wrested control of the Aegean from Sparta. In 377 B.C., Athens organized another naval league, but it proved far weaker than the Delian League a century earlier. Thebes, under Pelopidas and Epaminondas, ended the Spartan hegemony in mainland Greece at the Battle of Leuctra in 371 B.C. The battle was celebrated across the Greek world as a turning point. Some 700 Spartans fell in the battle; dedications were set up across the Greek world announced that Sparta's day as hegemon of Greece had passed.

In 362 B.C., at a second battle between the Spartans and Thebans, the Thebans won a victory at Mantinea, but Epaminondas was killed and with him the hopes for a Theban hegemony. By 360 B.C., the leading Hellenic city-states were politically deadlocked, but Greece was hardly in economic or cultural decline. In 380 B.C., at the Olympic Games, Athenian intellectual Isocrates called for Panhellenic unity and a war against Persia. Isocrates raised a point that Greek identity is no longer necessarily race, but that non-Greeks—who would adopt Greek institutions; live in a city-state; live under the rule of law; have the elected magistrates, assembly, council, or boule of a Greek city-state; could too become Greeks. Unwittingly, in his enthusiasm to end inter-state war and urge a wider Greek alliance, Isocrates created a notion that the Greek city-state could be exported to the Near East; and it would be the Macedonian kings, especially Alexander and his successors, who would do this. ■

## Names to Know

**Cyrus the Younger** (c. 424–401 B.C.): The younger son, Cyrus cooperated with Lysander in defeating Athens in 407–404 B.C. In 401 B.C., he was slain at Cunaxa in a bid to seize the throne from his brother Artaxerxes II.

**Artaxerxes II** (r. 404–358 B.C.): Memnon, king of Persiathe. Defeated and slew his brother Cyrus the Younger at Cunaxa. He raised the Greek coalition that fought Sparta to a stalemate in the Corinthian War.

## Suggested Reading

Buckler, *The Theban Hegemony*.

Cargill, *The Second Athenian League*.

Cartledge, *Agesilaos and the Crisis of Sparta*.

Hamilton, *Agesilaus and the Failure of Spartan Hegemony*.

Hodkinson, *Property and Wealth in Classical Sparta*.

Lewis, *Sparta and Persia*.

Sinclair, *Democracy and Participation in Athens*.

Strauss, *Athens after the Peloponnesian War*..

1.  How successfully did the Spartans rule the Greek world in 404–386 B.C.? How much was owed to King Agesilaus II? Why did the Spartans fail to maintain their hegemony after 386 B.C.? How important was the Corinthian War in redrawing the political map of the Greek world?

2.  What accounted for the success of Thebes under Epaminondas and Pelopidas? Why did the federal league of Boeotia prove unequal to the position of hegemon of mainland Greece? Did Theban success rest primarily on charismatic leaders rather than institutions and resources?

3.  What accounted for the remarkable recovery of Athens in the 4th century B.C.? Why did the Athenians fail to assert their naval domination in the Aegean world? How did the Second Naval Confederacy restrict Athenian imperial ambitions?

4.  Why did general prosperity in the Greek world fail to produce a wider political unity? In what ways did wars and mercenary service foster economic growth? What other forces monetized markets and promoted commerce in the Greek world?

# Greece in the Age of Hegemonies
## Lecture 2—Transcript

In this lecture, I plan to introduce the Greek world. That is more than just modern Greece: The Greek world in the time of Alexander the Great, who was born in 356 B.C. and died in 323 B.C., is a much wider geographical range than it is today. Both sides of the Aegean were inhabited by Greeks—that includes the western shores of Asia Minor today, Asiatic Turkey; the northern shores of the Aegean, Greek colonies were in southern Italy, Sicily; there were Greek colonies all along the shores of the Black Sea; in eastern Libya; the island of Cyprus was part of this Greek world—and so what we want to look at is what the Greek world was like in these generations just before Alexander the Great; essentially, what happened to Greece after the Peloponnesian War in 404 B.C.? We will follow up with lectures on Persia and Macedon; and as will become clear, Macedon is not synonymous with Greece, Macedon is part of a wider Greek world, but we'll reserve Macedon for later on.

What we wish to do here is to explain: How did the city-states of Greece, by 316 B.C., end up in a political stalemate—almost a case of diplomatic and military exhaustion—which is sometimes compared to what happened to Europe between 1914 and 1945? That is, the Greeks had fought a long series of wars in the 5th century and early 4th century B.C., so that when Philip of Macedon came to the throne in 359 B.C., to everyone's surprise, Philip within 10 years would emerge as the man who would unite Greece. No one would have anticipated this: that Macedon, ruled by a series of kings from the so-called Argead Dynasty would unite the city-states of Greece under their control. The way the Greek city-states responded to Philip II, and to some extent to Alexander the Great in the first two years of his reign, is really quite at odds with the way the Greeks had rallied against the Persian threat in the early 5th century B.C.—that is, the invasion of Xerxes in 480–479 B.C.—in which the Great King of Persia threatened to subject the Greek city-states to the Persian Empire. To answer this question, we really have to look at the results of that Peloponnesian War.

In 404 B.C., the city-state of Sparta won the Peloponnesian War. This is sometimes difficult for many Classical historians to accept, because sympathies generally rest with democratic Athens. But Sparta in 404 B.C. was in a very good position to provide a unity to the wider Greek world, at least in the Aegean world; maybe not to the western Greeks in Sicily and Italy, but at least in the Greek homeland and the associated areas in the eastern Mediterranean and Black Sea. Sparta had many virtues, and in the course of battling Athens between 412 B.C. and 404 B.C. in the later stages of the Peloponnesian War, the Spartans, in my opinion, forged the types of institutions necessary to provide a wider unity to the quarrelsome Greek city-states.

As I've stressed in lectures I've done with The Teaching Company before, Greek political identity was based on the polis, the city-state (the plural of that is poleis); that is the institution that really resonated with Greek citizens, and these poleis were often quite small with citizen bodies of only 5,000 adult men. The city-state was very much a face-to-face society in which the political institutions were administered by the citizens themselves meeting in an Assembly, which elected magistrates as well as an advisory council— the so-called Boule—and these were the institutions that had made Greek civilization go. What Sparta offered was a series of alliances, not only to her traditional allies in central and southern Greece—particularly the so-called Peloponnesus, the southern peninsula of Greece; and very often the original Spartan alliance system is known as the Peloponnesian League—but also to the many other Greek city-states that had been freed from Athenian oppression or had concluded alliances with Sparta in the later stages of the Peloponnesian War.

For one, the Spartans had a tradition of leadership of various Greek city-states, and had evolved a system of commanders under various titles (admirals, known as a navarc) that could command coalition forces—of Spartan citizens, various allies, a class of people known as *perioikoi* (these are the free residents of the Spartan state who are not full citizens)—as well as mercenaries, and weld these forces into an effective professional army and navy. In 404 B.C., by anyone's estimation, the Spartans had somewhere between 50,000 and 60,000 men under arms; and down to 386 B.C., the Spartan state maintained a professional mercenary army of about 20,000 hoplites (those are the heavily-armed infantry), 2,000 cavalry, and a navy of 200 warships, the so-called trireme. This was an enormous expense—it would have cost the Spartan state, by my estimation, 1,760 talents for a campaigning season of six months; a talent is a huge sum of money—and certainly by the standards of the ancient world this is an enormous expenditure on an essentially standing army and standing fleet. The Spartans had the resources—they had the whole former Athenian Empire of the Aegean plus their many Peloponnesian allies; they were collecting taxes, especially import/export duties in the Aegean world; they were collecting contributions from their allies, most of this paid in Athenian coin of the 5th century B.C.—and under the command of Spartan officers, these forces were drilled to professional standard.

Many historians think that Sparta in many ways obtained a bitter victory; that is, in defeating Athens, her social and economic institutions were essentially undermined. These are premised on views of Sparta as some type of oppressive slave society, which is greatly overdrawn in the sources—I've argued this in previous courses with The Teaching Company—and instead Sparta in, say, 400 B.C. in many ways looked like early Rome. She stood at a head of alliances that extended from the southern Peloponnesus all the way to northern Greece, centering on the Gulf of Corinth; they were Spartan citizens, her free residents, the *perioikoi* (that is, people living in southern Peloponnesus who were members of the Spartan state but were not full citizens); and she had many allies. In this way, her political structure resembled very much Rome in the 4th century B.C., with citizens, Latin allies, and Italian allies, all commanded by excellent officers who owed their loyalty to a Spartan state, to a system of education, that in many ways produced some of the finest soldiers and athletes in Greece.

Furthermore, the Spartans had known nothing but a string of victories—they had defeated the Athenians on their own element the sea—and above all, the Spartans really were committed to consulting their allies when they made war; quite in contrast to the Athenians who ran their alliance structure very much as an empire, and when Athens was defeated in 404 B.C., few states wept for the defeat of Athens which had come to be regarded as a tyrant city. So Sparta from 404–386 B.C., in my opinion, had an opportunity to forge wider unity for the Greek world.

The king at the time—you have to remember Sparta had two kings from two separate families, the Eurypontid and the Agiad families—was a man named Agesilaus II who came to the throne in 400 B.C. and died in 360 B.C. This king experienced the rise and fall of the Spartan hegemony, where Sparta was essentially hegemon—that is, the leader—of the various Greek states. Agesilaus was a charismatic and dynamic king; he knew how to command these coalition armies, he carried out important fiscal reforms, and in some ways Agesilaus was almost a model for the type of charismatic warrior-kings you get in the Hellenistic Age.

Sparta had won the Peloponnesian War against Athens by cutting a deal with the Persians. The Great King of Persia at the time, a man named Darius II, and then later his son Artaxerxes II, were very concerned in controlling the western half of the Persian Empire; that is, the regions that were west of the Euphrates, and particularly the troublesome cities of the Greeks of Asia Minor. These cities had been liberated by the Athenians in the 5th century B.C. and incorporated into a naval league or empire, and in 404 B.C. the Spartans had to deliver on a treaty they concluded back in 412 B.C. in which the Persian governors of Asia Minor—and there were two of them at the time—promised to furnish financial support and naval support to the Spartan fleet in the war against Athens; but in return, the cities of Asia Minor that had been liberated by Sparta and Athens back in 479–477 B.C. would have to return to Persian rule. Both the Spartans and Persians had concluded this alliance out of cynical pragmatism; and when the war was over, the Spartans were really ill at ease in turning the Greeks over to Persian rule. In fact, the Spartans went to war against Athens proclaiming freedom of the Greeks, and they took that claim very seriously.

Soon after the war, the Spartans supported a man named Cyrus the Younger who was the brother to the then-reigning king Artaxerxes II. Cyrus, as the younger son of a Persian king, knew that his options were rather limited; he could easily be disposed of by his elder brother, and what he did was he (Cyrus) recruited some 13,000 Greek mercenaries with the blessings of Sparta, and to these forces he added his own levies, and he made a dash in 401 B.C. to seize the throne of Persia. He marched from the city of Sardis— in western Turkey today—almost to Babylon, and on September 3, 401 B.C., his army won a smashing victory at Cunaxa in which the Greek mercenaries played a decisive role; and we'll be discussing this battle later on in the development of Greek warfare. Those mercenaries gave Cyrus the decisive edge to beat his brother. Unfortunately, Cyrus was killed in the battle; and you have this rather peculiar situation where the Great King of Persia lost the battle, his brother won the battle but was killed, and the Greek mercenaries had no paymaster or reason to be there and they therefore essentially marched out of the Persian Empire on their own. King Artaxerxes had managed to murder the primary leaders of this mercenary force, but the Greeks simply elected new leaders, including Xenophon who wrote an *Anabasis*—"a march upcountry" is the Greek word—that is, the retreat to the Black Sea and eventually back to the Greek world.

Xenophon's *Anabasis* is important for several reasons. One, it's virtually a manual on how to conquer the Persian Empire; and many would think that Alexander the Great had read this and had a pretty good idea of how weak and divided the Persian Empire was. Second, it was a remarkable indication of how important Greek heavy infantry were; and from this point on, Greek mercenaries were in high demand among the Great King of Persia, his governors (known as satraps), and even his rebel governors or the pharaoh in Egypt who had rebelled from Persian rule in 404 B.C. Greeks in the thousands were now employed in Persian and Egyptian armies.

In any case, this effort to unseat Artaxerxes II was part of a policy by the Spartans to keep control of those Greek city-states of Asia Minor; they were not going to hand them back under the terms of the Treaty of Miletus in 412 B.C. The result was that Artaxerxes essentially was at war with Sparta; and while he was preoccupied fighting his brother Cyrus and the repercussions of that rebellion, the Spartans had sent armies into Asia Minor under various commanders. The first one was a man named Thibron who freed a number of the cities, he was followed by another commander called Dercyllidas, and then finally King Agesilaus himself undertook an expedition to Asia Minor. These forces drove back the Persian satraps, Agesilaus got onto the plateau of Asia Minor, and Artaxerxes really had no choice but to fight Sparta and the various Ionian city-states, and he did it by diplomacy rather than by war. Agents were sent into the Greek world—to Athens, to Thebes, to Corinth, and Argos, the other leading Greek city-states, all technically in alliance with Sparta—and these four city-states rose up to fight the Spartans in what is known as the Corinthian War, which raged from essentially 395 down to 386 B.C. when it was settled by a general peace very often known as the King's Peace or the Peace of Antalcidas, who was the Spartan diplomat who negotiated the settlement.

The Corinthian War was important for several reasons. First: As soon as the war erupted in Greece, Agesilaus had no choice but to be recalled to Sparta; he had to bring his expedition back to the Peloponnesus, and a series of complicated battles were fought around the Isthmus of Corinth—that is, the isthmus that connects the Peloponnesus to central Greece—and it ended in a stalemate. There were some very significant innovations and tactics, but neither the Spartans nor the coalition of the other four states could achieve a decisive victory, and eventually the war was settled by diplomatic means.

Second: Athens, which had been defeated in 404 B.C., gained Persian money; rebuilt her city walls and long walls; received a fleet from one of the Athenian generals, Conan, who had fled to Persia at the end of Peloponnesian War; and with that fleet had defeated a Peloponnesian fleet off the city of Cnidus in 394 B.C. and reestablished an Athenian presence in the Aegean. Athens hoped to regain something of her hegemony in the Aegean world as a result of the Corinthian War. They did gain some significant advances—they got a hold of some of the northern islands in the Aegean, they concluded alliances with former members of the Athenian Empire—but on the whole, the Athenians were really rather disappointed with the outcome of the Corinthian War.

Thebes, Argos, and Corinth each aspired to supplant Sparta as the hegemon, or the leader, of mainland Greece. They, too, were disappointed by this war, because in 386 B.C. all of the participants, along with King Artaxerxes II of Persia, agreed to a general peace. It is known in Greek as a *koine eirene*, a general peace that ended all outstanding issues and had some very, very simple provisions. Athens was independent, but that was about it; the Athenians really didn't regain much in the way of territory, but the Athenians were at least freed from Spartan control. Sparta gave the Ionian Greeks—the Greeks of Asia—back to Artaxerxes II; those cities were relinquished, cities that had been liberated almost 100 years earlier.

Sparta, on the other hand, was essentially hegemon of Greece; the Spartans were put in the position of interpreting the freedom and autonomy of the Greek city-states, and they used this settlement in 386 B.C. to knock down any potential rival in mainland Greece. Peloponnesian allies were reorganized essentially into tax districts by King Agesilaus II. Spartans issued orders to cities, and if they didn't obey they took direct action. In 382 B.C., a Spartan army under a commander called Phoebidas was moving towards northern Greece against the city of Olympus to break up a league there, in the process seized the city of Thebes and garrisoned it, and broke up Thebes and the local regional league, the Boeotian League, which was put under Spartan control.

Spartan actions became so high-handed that by 378 B.C., the Spartans were resented and disliked even more than the Athenians; and many of the Peloponnesian allies—the Thebans, who were now under Spartan control; cities such as Argos and Corinth in the Peloponnesus—would welcome any effort to knock down Spartan power. In 379 B.C. and 378 B.C., events brought this about; and very quickly, the Spartans found themselves taxed and unable to maintain that hegemony over mainland Greece. In Thebes, there was a democratic rising. In 378 B.C., after less than three years garrisoning the city, the Peloponnesian garrison was butchered and Theban democrats led by a man named Pelopidas threw out not only Spartan rule but reunited the cities of Boeotia—11 of them—into a democratic federal system and declared their independence. Olympus and the Chalcidian League in northern Greece reconstituted itself; it had been defeated by Sparta and had been broken up, it was now reassembled as a rival league. Thessaly, in north central Greece, an area that was also under Spartan influence, was united by a figure known as Jason of Pherae, who was elected tagos or league commander of the Thessalian League. He organized a mercenary army and the 2,000 federal cavalry into another regional league to oppose Sparta. All of a sudden, Sparta found herself facing three major federal leagues in central and north Greece opposed to her aspirations as hegemon of Greece.

The Spartans had also offended the Athenians. A Spartan commander by the name of Sphodrias tried to seize the Athenian port at the Piraeus and botched it; and in 379 B.C., the Athenians responded by not only supporting the Thebans, but also issuing an invitation to her many former members of the old Delian League—that is, the naval league Athens had organized in the 5<sup>th</sup> century B.C.—to hook up with Athens and establish yet a new alliance structure. The Athenians had limited success. The cities in Asia Minor could not join because they were under Persian rule; many of the former allies of Athens were very wary of the Athenians, they knew the Athenians had a tendency to boss them around, to impose tribute; but nonetheless, by 378 B.C., Sparta now found herself facing four large regional confederations—a naval league under Athens and three inland leagues headed by Thebes, Olympus, and Thessaly—opposed to Spartan ambitions.

The Spartans really could not maintain their position for very long; and at 371 B.C., the Spartan army, under the then senior Agiad king, Cleombrotus I, went down in a decisive defeat at the battle of Leuctra, a town in central Greece. That battle was important for several reasons: One was militarily, and we'll discuss that in a coming lecture; but politically, the Spartan army had been decisively defeated on its own element by the Theban army. This was a result of the tactics and inspired generalship of a man named Epaminondas, a Theban commander who had organized the Thebans and their allies into an effective hoplite force and to a large extent were using Spartan tactics. The battle was celebrated across the Greek world as a turning point. Some 700 Spartans fell in the battle (these would be Spartans and *perioikoi*); dedications were set up across the Greek world including Adelphi. There is an epigram that has been found that celebrates this (this is a poem) that reads:

> When the Spartan spear held sway, then it fell
> to Xenokrates' lot to carry the trophy in honour of Zeus,
> fearing neither the army from Eurotas [that's the river near Sparta]
>     nor the Laconian
> shield [that's the district of Sparta]. "Thebans (are) superior in
>     battle"
> proclaims the trophy at Leuctra that announces the victory won by
>     the spear,
>
> nor did we run second to Epameinondas.

This epigram—which is put up on a trophy, a memorial—to the victory at Leuctra was one of many that announced that Sparta's day as hegemon of Greece had passed; but Thebes wasn't really in a position to replace it. The Thebans, in 370 B.C.—that is, the year after Leuctra—under Epaminondas invaded the Peloponnesus. They could not capture Sparta, but they did set up a series of alliances with Argos, the traditional enemy of Sparta; with a new Arcadian League in central Peloponnesus, where they built a federal capital called Megalopolis, which simply means "big city"; and the city-state of Messene, which had been subject to the Spartans for almost 400 years and was liberated in southwestern Peloponnesus; and this band of allies across central Peloponnesus restricted Sparta to her immediate homeland. Thereafter, the Spartans would have a very tough job in trying to reassert their hegemony.

The Thebans, however, really didn't have any kind of systems to forge a wider unity. In 362 B.C., at a second battle between the Spartans and Thebans, the Thebans won a victory at Mantinea in central Peloponnesus, but Epaminondas was killed. The Athenians at this point were actually allied to the Spartans—they had come to fear Theban power, which had grown so quickly—so that in 362 B.C., when the Thebans and Spartans had fought themselves essentially to a stalemate, the Athenians were beginning to reorganize a new naval league. But Athens was much too weak to take any kind of advantage out of this clash between Sparta and Thebes; and by 360 B.C., Athens, Sparta, and Thebes had essentially fought each other to a stalemate.

The Athenians found that their new naval league really was more of a burden than an advantage. The allies put all sorts of restrictions on Athenian actions. The Athenians could not collect tribute, *phoros*; the allies made voluntary contributions, *syntaxis* is the Greek word. The Athenians found themselves with many able generals, but these generals faced two major restrictions: One, the Athenian citizen body was smaller and far more reluctant to undertake military service, unlike the 5th century B.C.; and second, these generals had to recruit, and in addition find the money, for mercenary armies as well as sailors for the fleet. Athens was habitually short of funds in order to pay these mercenary armies; and while their generals were really quite extraordinary as tacticians—the general Iphicrates in particular innovated on light arm tactics; there were several others, Chares and Charidemus who were regarded as very able generals in the 4th century B.C. and actually both of them found employment with the Great King of Persia when Athens didn't have use for them—nonetheless, these generals did not have the resources and means to mount a recovery of the Athenian Empire. Athens, really by 355 B.C.—and we'll get to this in a coming lecture—was not in a position to play the role she had once done in the 5th century B.C. By 360 B.C., literally, the traditional powers of Greece were essentially politically and diplomatically deadlocked. None of them had the resources and means to assert a wider hegemony and unite the Greek world the way Sparta and Athens had done in the 5th century B.C.

This political deadlock has often been taken as an indication of the decline of the city-state. In one way, that's true; that is, the patriotism that motivated citizens to fight against the Persians in the 5th century B.C. and to fight in the great Peloponnesian War was probably no longer there. All of the Greek city-states increasingly turned to mercenaries; they turned their citizens evermore into taxpayers rather than into citizen warriors; and to some extent these wars had sapped the patriotism, loyalty, and sacrifice that had characterized city-states in the 5th century B.C. That goes to some extent towards explaining why the Greek city-states didn't offer the same kind of united resistance to Philip of Macedon, and later Alexander the Great, the way they did to King Xerxes of Persia.

On the other hand, to then go and argue that it means that the city-state as an institution was in decline economically and socially is going too far. This has often been argued in the literature, that political decline was accompanied by economic and social decline; that Greek city-states were essentially divided between the haves and the have-nots. There was constant class warfare; the Greek term for this is stasis, a standing apart. The propertied classes were constantly at war with the lower classes or the so-called demos, which is the Greek word for the general political citizen body, that is, the democrats. This case has been overdrawn. Furthermore, the complicated wars of the 4th century B.C. in some ways stimulated economic growth. Warfare forced city-states to come up with new means of taxation, to build city walls, to make innovations in armament and equipment, naval warfare changed dramatically; all of this put money into circulation.

Furthermore, the Athenians in the 5th century B.C. had set the standard of what a Greek city-state should look like. There were an enormous number of building programs across the Greek world at cities such as Olympus, the capital of the federal league in the Chalcidice in northern Greece; Megalopolis, the city that was the capital of the federal league in Peloponnesus, of the Arcadians. These cities are laid out as rational, organized towns according to the town planning first pioneered by Hippodamus of Miletus. There was a vast construction at the great international sanctuaries at Olympia; also at Delphi, where the great Oracle was located. So building programs, social and festival activities both within cities and the wider Greek world all increased; and there is a good argument to be made that Greece in some ways was wealthier in the 4th century B.C. than in the 5th century B.C. The problem was, this wealth was not at the disposal of a Sparta, a Thebes, or an Athens that could use it to carry out a political unification of the Greek city-states; but the wealth was certainly there.

Finally, there was another very important development besides what I think was the economic growth, and that was new concepts of defining Greeks. I would like to close with this thought because it's extremely important for the upcoming lectures and accounts for some of the success of Philip II and Alexander the Great. In 380 B.C., at the Olympic Games, an Athenian intellectual known as Isocrates—who died in 338 B.C., was born in 436 B.C., and essentially lived through a good deal of the late 5th and 4th century B.C.—announced what later comes to be called Panhellenism. He urged Sparta and Athens at the time to sink their differences and lead a coalition of Greek city-states to conquer Asia Minor from the Persians and settle it. That was a project that the Macedonian kings will be eager to do; but in addition, Isocrates raises a point that Greek identity is no longer necessarily race, but the barbarians—that is, the non-Greeks—who would adopt Greek institutions; live in a city-state; live under the rule of law; have the elected magistrates, assembly, council, or boule of a Greek city-state; could too become Greeks.

Unwittingly, in his enthusiasm to end inter-state war and urge a wider Greek alliance, Isocrates created a notion that the Greek city-state could be exported to the Near East; and it would be the Macedonian kings, especially Alexander and his successors, who would do this, and this would be the means by which Hellenic civilization would be carried to the Near East. But in 360 B.C., this was in the distant future; and no one expected that the Macedonians would bring unity to Greece.

# Achaemenid Persia

## Lecture 3

> When Artaxerxes II came to the throne in 404 B.C., ... the Persian Empire was a vast empire. ... It stretched perhaps some 3,000 miles from the Aegean to the Hindu Kush, by anyone's estimate a minimum of between 35 million and 40 million residents.

King Artaxerxes II by adroit diplomacy and subsidies promoted war among the leading Greek city-states so that under the Peace of Antalcidas, he regained the Ionian cities of Asia Minor. Artaxerxes II ruled the most impressive empire of Eurasia stretching from the Aegean to the Hindu Kush, but in military power and financial resources the later Achaemenid kings ruled an empire lesser than that organized by Darius I.

Persian rule over the Indus Valley had lapsed in the 5th century B.C. Artaxerxes II fought to impose royal authority over satraps, who gained hereditary power in the satrapies or provinces, and the rebel pharaohs of Egypt. Twice, Greek attacks revealed Persian military weakness. In 401 B.C. at the Battle of Cunaxa when Cyrus the Younger and Greek mercenaries challenged his brother Artaxerxes; Cyrus was victorious but was killed during the battle.

The surviving Ten Thousand Greeks, without a paymaster, simply marched out the Persian Empire, and many enlisted in the Spartan mercenary army. This celebrated march of the Ten Thousand, recorded by the Athenian captain Xenophon as Anabasis, was a veritable guide to the conquest of the Persian Empire. In 396–395 B.C., Agesilaus II of Sparta invaded Asia Minor, and his army penetrated to Gordion in central Asia Minor.

Persian diplomatic success in the Corinthian War could not reverse imperial decline. Repeatedly, between 366 and 353 B.C., Persian satraps and native dynasts in Asia Minor and the Levant rebelled from the Great King. In southwestern Asia Minor, even the loyal Mausolus of Caria carved out a veritably independent state. Artaxerxes III ended rebellions in the western satrapies, and reconquered Egypt but this restored Persian Empire was in no position to face a power in the Aegean world: the kingdom of Macedon. ■

## Suggested Reading

Briant, *From Cyrus to Alexander: A History of the Persian Empire.*

*The Cambridge History of Iran.* vol. 2

Cook, *The Persian Empire.*

Dandamaev and Lukonin, *The Culture and Social Institutions of Ancient Iran.*

Lewis, *Sparta and Persia.*

Olmstead, *History of the Persian Empire.*

Xenophon. *The Persian Expedition.*

## Questions to Consider

1. Was the Persian Empire in a state of decline under Artaxerxes II and Artaxerxes III?

2. What accounted for so many insurrections in Asia Minor, Phoenicia, and Cyprus in the 4th century B.C.? Why did the independent pharaohs of Egypt pose a threat to the king of Persia?

3. How did Xenophon and King Agesilaus anticipate Alexander the Great? What lessons about the Persian Empire would Alexander the Great have drawn in reading Xenophon's *Anabasis*?

4. Did the Persian kings after the King's Peace in 386 B.C. commit a strategic error in not interfering more actively in the Aegean world? Could such Persian intervention have prevented the rise of Philip II of Macedon and Alexander the Great?

# Achaemenid Persia
## Lecture 3—Transcript

In this lecture, I plan to introduce Persia in the 4th century B.C. This would be during the reigns of the two Achaemenid kings, Artaxerxes II, who ruled from 404–358 B.C., and then his son and successor Artaxerxes III, who ruled from 358–338 B.C.; that is, he died at the time of the Battle of Chaeronea, the great battle in which Philip of Macedon achieved his mastery of the Greek city-states. This lecture will explain the conditions in the Persian Empire in the two generations before Alexander the Great, and also what the situation was in Persia when in 334 B.C. Alexander crossed from Europe to Asia and began his career of conquest.

The Persian Empire in the early 4th century B.C. had declined from the position it once held at the end of the 6th century B.C. Cyrus the Great, or sometimes known as Cyrus the Conqueror, who ruled as king of Persia from 559–530 B.C., had founded the empire. His career was one of remarkable conquests; and at the time the Greeks were impressed, they thought of Cyrus as one of the great conquerors of all time. Alexander's career would simply completely outclass that of Cyrus. His successor—not his son Cambyses, but the third Persian king, the ultimate successor—Darius I, who ruled from 521–486 B.C., was the king who organized the Persian Empire and gave it the royal institutions that were still in existence when Alexander crossed to Asia in 334 B.C. Darius I was a great organizer; and it is best to look at the empire in its administrative and fiscal organization, and then we can look at the political and military situation in the 4th century B.C.

Artaxerxes II, when he came to the throne in 404 B.C., essentially inherited the administrative system of Darius I. The Persian Empire was a vast empire that stretched from the Aegean to the Hindu Kush. In Artaxerxes's time, there had been some territorial losses. In the time of King Darius I, the Persians ruled possessions in Europe—the lands between the Danube and the northern Aegean—they also controlled the Greeks of Asia Minor, and there were extremely wealthy Indian satrapies in the upper Indus Valley and its tributaries, and in the lower Indus today, the region known as the Sindh. All those areas had been lost by the time that Artaxerxes came to the throne. Even so, it was still an enormous empire; it stretched perhaps some 3,000 miles from the Aegean to the Hindu Kush, by anyone's estimate between 35 million and 40 million residents. At the time that Artaxerxes came to the throne there was a rebellion that had just erupted in Egypt; we'll be talking about that and the importance of Egypt later in this lecture. But for the moment, let's look at the empire that Artaxerxes II inherited.

First, Persian royal power was centered in what is today southwestern Iran. Persia is approximately the same, as far as province; Farsi is essentially the modern Iranian word for the language Persian, which goes back to the Classical Period. There were several different capitals that the Great Kings of Persia used. First and foremost, the cultural and financial capital was probably Babylon; that is, the great city in Mesopotamia on the Euphrates that had been the commercial, political, and cultural center of the Near East since the middle Bronze Age, going back to the time of Hammurabi. It was still regarded as a capital in the sense that it was the cultural and commercial capital—many of the important Babylonian bankers lived there and lent money to the various Persian nobility—and that link between southern Iraq and Iran, which still persists today, goes back to the Achaemenid Period; that is, the period of the Achaemenid kings, the family of Persian kings that rules this empire, and Achaemenid refers to the common ancestor Achaemenes who gave rise to the name of the dynasty. Babylon was a great, fun place for young Persian lords to have a great time, learn a smattering of culture, and also visit the fleshpots; one thinks of the British nobility going off to Paris for a certain time in order to learn a smattering of civilization before they go out and govern the British Empire.

The other important capital was Susa, which is today very far inland from the Persian Gulf. It's centered in the ancient land of Elam; these were people who lived in the region long before the Persians had arrived. In antiquity, it was in close contact with the sea because the coastline of the Persian Gulf came much farther up than it does today. Susa was the administrative capital; it was conveniently located near Babylon, and very often this was where Greek envoys arrived when they went to talk to the Great King of Persia.

There were also two ritual capitals to the east in Persia proper. One was Pasargadae, which had been founded by King Cyrus I, and that's where Cyrus was buried; but the more important one was Persepolis, constructed by Darius I. We have a number of building tablets that explain the hiring of all the labors, engineers, and artists from the entire Persian Empire. It is a magnificent site today. It was only occupied during part of the year. It really was used for the collection of tribute from the various subject peoples. The capital has a remarkable lack of religious iconography. The only religious symbol is a winged sun emblem that comes out of Babylonian art that apparently designates Ahura Mazda. While the Persians were not strict Zoroastrians the way they would be in later times, they tended not to depict their gods in human form, there was just a reluctance to do that; so the emphasis at the capital is on the Great King, and when the Greeks spoke of the Great King—Ho Basileus in Greek—they meant the Persian king. The Macedonian kings, the two constitutional monarchs in Sparta, they didn't count. Darius had constructed a vast complex—a palace and subsidiary chambers for the collection of tribute—and the reliefs are marvelous that have survived to us because they show the various subject peoples rendering tribute, and it was clearly a palace structure built to impress. But again, it was only occupied during parts of the year.

There was a final capital known as Ecbatana—today, essentially Hamadan, the great caravan city in northwestern Iran—and it had been the capital of Media. The Medes were a related people to the Persians; they had actually ruled over Iran before the Persians. Their conquest by Cyrus in 550 B.C. marked the emergence of the Persian Empire; and the Medes and the Persians essentially had a partnership in running this empire. Very often the Greeks could not tell the distinction between the two peoples; and oddly enough, the Greek word to "medize"—to go over to the Medes—meant to go over to the Great King of Persia. The Greeks essentially saw them as two branches of the same people. Ecbatana had been the meeting capital, and it was conveniently located to escape the summer heat; it often acted as the summer palace and retreat for the Great King of Persia. From these five great cities, the Persian kings administered this empire.

The Persians, however, were very well aware of the need to build upon existing institutions—they were remarkably tolerant and effective rulers that way—and they were successful in part because they didn't ask for too much. The Persian Empire was divided into a group of provinces known as satrapies—this goes back to Darius I—and a satrap governed those provinces.

Each satrap had authority within the province; he was directly answerable to the Great King and he could be replaced by the Great King. By the time of Artaxerxes's reign—say in 400 B.C., or 404 B.C. when Artaxerxes comes to the throne—those satraps had essentially in many cases become hereditary rulers. There was already a rather dangerous policy being pursued in Asia Minor at least of elevating local dynasts—the most notable is a fellow named Mausolus of Caria—to the level of satrap; so essentially native rulers were being entrusted with their home regions under the Persian title satrap. There were also garrisons in certain satrapies—the satrapy of Egypt, for instance, was heavily garrisoned—and those garrison commanders were directly answerable to the king, not to the satrap. There were financial officials who supervised the tribute to the Great King that would be collected and rendered at Persepolis, and they, too, were directly answerable to the Great King. That is, military, financial, and administrative arrangements in the satrapy were divided; authority was divided among the individuals, and the idea was to check any kind of rebellion.

The system worked quite well in the 6th and early 5th century B.C., but already there were difficulties by the end of the 5th century B.C. and the opening of the 4th century of B.C. In part, the satraps were becoming hereditary; they had established links among the landed families of their areas; and in the regions west of the Euphrates—Asia Minor, the Levant; that would encompass today Syria, Israel, Jordan, and Lebanon; and Egypt—there was the danger of rebellions, either by native elites or Persian colonial elites with ties to their locale, and this became a constant problem for both Artaxerxes II and Artaxerxes III. Even so, in 400 B.C. the Persian Empire was a mighty structure. It was the most successful of the ancient Near Eastern empires. Even in 400 B.C., the Great King of Persia had at least an annual income of 10,000 or 12,000 talents; this far outclassed the income of any Greek city-state and even of the kingdom of Macedon in the time of Philip and Alexander. To give you a sense of what that money is: 12,000 talents a year is twice the annual revenue of Athens at its height. A talent represents 6,000 drachma—that is, coin, silver money in the Greek world—and a drachma is a very generous wage for a soldier; a third of a drachma would be a daily wage in the Greek world. This is an enormous amount of money.

He also ruled a very diverse empire, and an empire from which he could call great armies: fleets from the maritime peoples of Phoenicia, Cyprus, Egypt, and Asia Minor; enormous amounts of Iranian cavalry; chariots from Mesopotamia. It was a formidable empire indeed; and yet, by the time of Artaxerxes's succession, it was facing some very, very serious crises.

Very shortly, when Artaxerxes came to the throne, he had to deal with a challenge from his younger brother. His brother's name was Cyrus—he's known as Cyrus the Younger—and he's extremely popular among the Greeks. Cyrus the Younger had been appointed *karanos*, or lord of the western satrapies in Asia Minor, to direct Persian interests in the final stages of the Peloponnesian War. Cyrus was on extremely good terms with the Spartans when the war ended in 404 B.C., and Cyrus realized that his days were numbered once his dear brother came to the throne because he was a younger, extra brother and a possible danger. What Cyrus did was use his position in Asia Minor to recruit large numbers of Greek mercenaries, and also to gain the backing of Sparta who was now the dominant state in the Greek world.

In 401 B.C., Cyrus was ready to move. He had some 13,000 Greek mercenaries—at least 11,500 were hoplites, men of the heavy arms; there were additional light arm and cavalry units—and he marched these hoplites and his native levies, an army of about some 35,000 strong, in less than six months from Sardis in western Asia to a place known as Cunaxa, some 60 miles north of Babylon. On September 3, 401 B.C., he clashed with the armies of his brother Artaxerxes II. Artaxerxes fielded a larger army— perhaps 50,000 or 45,000 strong—but in the course of the battle (which we'll be discussing in a later lecture), the Greeks who were holding Cyrus's right wing drove all opposition before them, they sustained almost no losses, and essentially won the battle. However, Cyrus had attacked his brother in the center and was killed in a cavalry engagement. The Greeks who had pursued the Persian left wing that had broken returned to the battlefield late in the day; they chased Artaxerxes and his army off the field, so the Greeks held the field but their paymaster was dead.

Artaxerxes attempted to rectify the situation by negotiation. He murdered the Greek officers—or actually had them seized and executed is what he would say—the five leading Greek officers of these mercenary contingents. The Greeks simply elected new officers including an Athenian named Xenophon, a student of Socrates, and the Greeks marched out of the Persian Empire. This is known as the Anabasis, the March Upcountry, and these 10,000 Greeks eventually reached the sea at Trapezus—today Trabzon on the Black Sea—made their way to the Aegean world, and some 6,000 of them in 399 B.C. hired on with the Spartans to fight the Persians in Asia Minor. The March of the Ten Thousand, which is told in Xenophon's account, is essentially a how-to book. I'm sure Alexander the Great read it; it would explain how to conquer the Persian Empire and it revealed the political weaknesses within imperial structures of Persia, notably in the western half of the empire, the non-Iranian areas. The Greeks could simply move at will, and there was very little that the Persian satraps could do to stop them.

The March of the Ten Thousand and the example of Cyrus rebelling from his brother were very, very chilling and dangerous precedents for the satraps of western Asia Minor, and above all to the Egyptians and other subject peoples in the western provinces. In the winter of 405–404 B.C., the Egyptians had already risen in revolt under a native pharaoh, a fellow named Amyrtaeus in Greek, and they had broken away from the Persian Empire. There were dangers of satraps in Asia Minor doing the same. Furthermore, much to the dismay of King Artaxerxes II, the alliance with Sparta, which went back to 412 B.C., had proved not to be exactly what the Great King wanted. The idea in 412 B.C. was for the Persians to give naval and financial support so that Sparta could defeat Athens. The Spartans would then give the Greeks of Asia Minor—these are the Ionian cities on the shores of western Turkey today—back to the Persian king; these were cities liberated back in 479 B.C. and 477 B.C. when King Xerxes had been defeated by the Greek coalition at the Battle of Salamis and subsequent battles.

However, the Spartans really didn't want to do this. They had declared war on Athens on behalf of freedom of the Greeks, and they took the slogan seriously; so they backed Cyrus in his bid for the throne because Cyrus was willing to let the Greek cities of Asia remain in the Spartan alliance and so free and autonomous. King Artaxerxes could not allow this, and the March of the Ten Thousand meant immediately war with Sparta; and the Spartans understood this. They sent a professional mercenary army into Asia Minor. There was a succession of three commanders; the first two were leading Spartan officers, Thibron and then Dercyllidas. Finally in 396 B.C., King Agesilaus II arrived with a very large force; and he is the charismatic king who made the Spartan hegemony. Agesilaus wins some significant victories: He smashes Persian armies in western Asia Minor; at one point he marches onto the plateau into Phrygia; he puts the city of Gordion under siege; there's an embarrassing Persian defeat outside of Sardis, which is the capital of Lydia and of the western satrapy of the Persian Empire.

Artaxerxes has a problem: He has a rebellion raging in Egypt that could easily spill over into Phoenicia, Cyprus, and the western satrapies in Asia Minor; there's a Spartan army on the loose in the center of Asia Minor; and the only way that Artaxerxes II can counter this threat is by diplomacy. He sends money and agents into Greece; they convince the Athenians, Corinthians, Argives, and the Thebans to form a coalition; and the four states declare war on Sparta in 395 B.C. The result is the Corinthian War. From 395–386 B.C., there is a military stalemate at the Isthmus of Corinth. The Spartans have to recall Agesilaus from Asia Minor, and the result is that Sparta fights the other four leading states of Greece. Argos and Corinth actually go into a political union, Thebes reorganizes the federal league, and Athens has aspirations of resurrecting her position in the Aegean.

Artaxerxes II actually came out of this war the victor, and Sparta came out of the war the second victor. In 387–386 B.C., the war was ended by negotiation, and the terms are extremely significant (and I've discussed them in connection with the Greek world). From the Great King's perspective, it couldn't have been better. The various Greek belligerents agreed to a common peace; that is, they stopped fighting and agreed to settle issues by negotiation. Sparta, in effect, was made the master of Greece. Athens was given independence, and as a result the Athenians jettisoned their allies—Corinth, Argos, and Thebes—and they were rewarded with not only independence but several of their cleruchies in the Aegean. The cities of Asia—the Greek cities of Asia Minor—went back to the Great King, and that was to Artaxerxes's benefit. Furthermore, this treaty, known as the King's Peace or the Peace of Antalcidas, essentially allowed Artaxerxes to impose a peace in Greece through the agency of the Spartans and recruit mercenaries.

Artaxerxes had learned at the Battle of Cunaxa that the only way to win wars was to hire Greek heavy infantry; and the only way to conquer Egypt was to have Greek infantry, since the Egyptian pharaoh was hiring the same types of mercenaries, and the Phoenician fleet. It was hoped by settling affairs in Greece—by imposing this order in Greece—that essentially Greece could be turned into this great mercenary market, there would be no need to conquer Greece as his ancestor Xerxes had attempted, and the reconquest of Egypt would secure Artaxerxes's position as Great King and bring peace and prosperity once again.

Artaxerxes did mount an expedition against the rebel Egyptian pharaoh—at that time it was the pharaoh known as Nectanebo I—and unfortunately that expedition did not go off very well. Artaxerxes did get his mercenaries, at least some 12,000 signed on; he also hired the services of the Athenian commander Iphicrates, a tactician who had distinguished himself in the Corinthian War, especially in the use of light armed infantry; he had one of his most respected satraps, Pharnabazus, a man who had been in touch with the Greeks for several decades, he had been a satrap in Asia Minor; and he had the Phoenician fleet at his disposal. This army and fleet invaded the Nile Delta, unfortunately found the Delta entrances blocked, and defenses built along the easternmost branch of the Nile based on the fortress of Pelusium and actually defended by Greek mercenaries including Athenians in the service of the pharaoh. The expedition ended in a fiasco; Iphicrates and Pharnabazus got into a dispute, and the defeat of that Egyptian expedition in 373 B.C., the example of Cyrus, and the continuing independence of the pharaohs of Egypt resulted in rebellions erupting across the western satrapies.

Between 366 B.C. and 360 B.C. the satrap Datames of Cappadocia in central Turkey today—well-known to tourists for its rugs and its pottery—and the satrap of Orontes and Armenia both made a bid for independence, and each seemed to aspire for the throne of Great King. They were followed by a number of lesser satraps; there were rebellions in Phoenicia among the Phoenician cities. Fortunately, the king of Cyprus didn't join this general insurrection in the 360s B.C. which is known as the Satrap's Revolt, but he enjoyed essentially an independent position on Cyprus to bring the Cypriot Greeks under control, and he's technically a vassal or satrap of the king.

By 360 B.C., this revolt of the satraps had collapsed; however, there were dangerous precedents. The satraps had issued Greek-style money; they had hired enormous numbers of mercenaries; for a time, they controlled most of the eastern Mediterranean ports; and they really mounted a serious challenge to the Great King in Susa. Furthermore, there would be other rebellions: Shortly after the death of Artaxerxes II, his son, Artaxerxes III, faced another rebellion in Asia Minor by a satrap known as Artabazus, one of the senior members of the Achaemenid Dynasty. He remained in rebellion down to 353 B.C. He had an expert Greek mercenary general mentor whose brother was Memnon; they're two brothers from Rhodes who were expert mercenary commanders. Memnon, the younger brother, ends up being an opponent of Alexander. In 353 B.C., actually, Artabazus and his family had to flee to the court at Pella—the court of Philip II—and eventually made its peace with Darius III, the new king in 336 B.C., and returns to Persian service. But that was yet another dangerous insurrection in Asia Minor.

Even those satraps that remained loyal ended up essentially carving out independent positions. That included Mausolus of Caria, a local dynast who essentially gained control of southwestern Asia Minor. He built marvelous Greek-style temples at Mylasa and Labranda, eventually occupied the Greek city of Halicarnassus, and turned it into his capital; that's where he built his tomb, the Mausoleum. It included the Greek king of Salamis on the island of Cyprus. Some of the Phoenician city-states, notably Tyre, negotiated more or less an independent status within the Persian Empire. Artaxerxes II and Artaxerxes III both secured those western satrapies essentially by coming to terms with the local and colonial elites in these regions.

Above all, Egypt proved the greatest danger; and it's important to dwell for a moment on Egypt because of its importance in the ancient world. Egypt was a rival monarchy to the Persian king. The Persian king in effect ruled Babylon, he was a successor to the Mesopotamian traditions, and this war or this tension between Egypt and the Near East went back to the Assyrian and Babylonian kings. To the Egyptians, the Persians were just the newest installment of a Mesopotamian opponent. The Egyptian Valley was extremely wealthy; to the Greek world it was fabulously wealthy. It was one of the sources of grain to feed the hungry cities of the Aegean world; the other was the lands around the Black Sea. There was an old-time connection going back to the 6th century B.C., between Egyptian pharaohs and Greeks, and Greeks came to Egypt as tourists; as visitors like Herodotus, absolutely in complete wonderment of the country; mercenaries, that is hoplite infantry; and above all merchants. There was a Greek community known as Naucratis, which was a Greek colony in the Delta, which acted as the entre peaux, moving grain and other products from the Nile Valley to the Aegean and bringing in silver—notably silver coins—olive oil, fine tableware, and the other products of the Aegean world. There's a very important trade connection. The Greeks had a great respect for the Egyptian pharaohs; and above all, the Egyptian pharaoh was a rival monarch to the Great King.

Sometime in the winter of 405–404 B.C., Amyrtaeus, who was the pharaoh backed by the Libyan military elite in the Delta, declared independence. Amyrtaeus established Dynasty 28; he was to be followed by pharaohs of two other families known as Dynasty 29 and Dynasty 30; and these last three native dynasties of Egypt led to a revival of Egyptian power. All of these pharaohs beautified the temples and shrines of the Nile Valley; they could play the historic role as the son of Horus, as the favorite of Amon-Ra, as Osiris in death. Furthermore, they had the means to hire large numbers of Greek mercenaries.

Repeatedly, Artaxerxes II and Artaxerxes III had to mount expeditions to retake Egypt. After the failure of the expedition in 373 B.C., there were several others. The final one that worked was in 343–342 B.C., and this one worked for several reasons: First, the king, Artaxerxes III, led it in person. He was also accompanied by a large force of Greek mercenaries, expert commanders; and they had the Phoenician fleet. The last Egyptian pharaoh, Nectanebo II, just didn't have nearly the number of mercenaries, and the Greek mercenaries deserted in the course of the expedition. The Persians managed to outflank the defenses at Pelusium, occupy the Delta and then Memphis, and move up the Nile. Nectanebo fled to what today is the Sudan into Nubia and by 342 B.C. the Nile Valley was once again under Persian control. It was a very important reconquest and it kept the career of Artaxerxes III so when he died several years later in 338 B.C. he ruled an empire that at least outwardly looked like the same empire in 400 B.C. with all of its territorial boundaries restored, except, that restoration was very tentative. Many of the western satraps ruled as semi-independent vassals. The Egyptians resented Persian rule deeply. The reports that we get are more one-sided rather than exaggerated, but the Persians were never popular in Egypt. Cambyses, who had conquered Egypt back in 525–522 B.C., had desecrated Egyptian temples and shrines. There are later reports that later Persian armies would slaughter the bull Apis—this is the sacred animal of Osiris at Memphis—or they had injured it. There are even outlandish stories that the Persians held barbeque roasts with the sacred animals. All of this incensed the Egyptians and led to very serious resistance. Repeatedly in the 4th century B.C. the Egyptians fought to overthrow Persian rule.

Artaxerxes III and his successor, Darius III, ruled over Egypt, which had a long tradition of opposing Persian rule, and a long tradition of summoning in allies from the Greek world, or mercenaries, to assist them. Alexander the Great, when he entered Egypt, he entered a land that had only come under Persian rule a little over 10 years earlier. Nonetheless, when Artaxerxes died in 338 B.C., he could with some sense of satisfaction look at his career as a restoration of Persian power. For all of its weaknesses, it was still a remarkable state. Yet, the Persian Empire had been weakened, and it really wasn't in a position to face a new opponent, an opponent at this point which was really quite unimaginable, and that is the young king of Macedon, Alexander the Great, who now had an army that could achieve a conquest of the Persian Empire in a way that no one could anticipate.

# The World of Early Macedon
## Lecture 4

In 360 B.C., when the Greek city-states had fought themselves to exhaustion and the Great King of Persia was desperately attempting to bring his rebel satraps and the pharaoh of Egypt under his control, none of the contemporaries would have given much consideration to Macedon.

In 359 B.C., Macedon was an unstable barbarian kingdom on the fringes of the Hellenic world. Macedon's kings, members of the Argead dynasty, claimed Greek descent and ruled over a mix of different peoples including Macedonians, but many others as well, none of whom were regarded as Hellenes, or members of the Greek national race. To Greeks, the Macedonians were regarded as "barbarians." Instead, most Greeks feared **Mausolus**, Hecatomnid dynast of Caria, who had turned his Anatolian state into a Hellenized power.

Archaeology has revealed that the Macedonians never participated in the material culture of the Greek world since the Late Bronze Age. Greek immigrants and goods were welcomed, but Macedonians remained a distinct, speaking a language unintelligible to Greek. King Archelaus adopted Attic Greek as the court language, built roads, and established market towns, but his subjects remained in habits far closer to their Balkan neighbors Illyrians, Paeonians, and Thracians.

Macedonian kings ruled by force over proud lords and vassal kings. Despite natural resources and manpower, the Argead kings of Macedon could never impose effective authority over their unruly vassals. Hence, the leading Greek powers each in turn promoted civil war and rebellion within Macedon. In 359 B.C., King Perdiccas III and 4,000 Macedonians fell fighting the Illyrians, the Macedonians acclaimed as king his brother and successor, Philip, who transformed Macedon into the greatest kingdom in Europe. ∎

## Suggested Reading

Adams and Borza, *Philip II, Alexander the Great and the Macedonian Heritage.*

Borza, *In the Shadow of Olympus.*

Hammond and Griffith, *A History of Macedonia.*

## Questions to Consider

1. Why did the Greeks in the Classical age not consider the Macedonians Hellenes? Were the political institutions and social mores significantly different between Greeks and Macedonians?

2. What was the relationship between Greeks and neighboring peoples such as Macedonians and Carians? How important were the institutions of the city-state in defining Greek identity?

3. How did the Macedonian kings resemble the heroic kings of the Homeric epic? What were the practical limits to their power? Why did the Argead kings struggle so long to turn their vassals and diverse subjects into loyal Macedonians?

4. What perceptions of Macedon did Athens, Sparta, and Thebes share in the early 4th century B.C.? Why would Mausolus appear far more formidable a foe? Did the Greek states underestimate Philip II?

5. Why did Philip II succeed in forging the Macedonian kingdom? Why did his reign prove so decisive?

# The World of Early Macedon
## Lecture 4—Transcript

In this lecture, I plan to deal with the world of early Macedon. Macedon is the homeland of Alexander the Great and, of course, his father King Philip II; although Alexander's mom, Olympias, came from what today is northwestern Greece, from the region of Epirus, and Epirus was actually considered part of the Greek world. This lecture is important to bring out several points, the role that Macedon played between the Greek world and the Persian Empire.

In 360 B.C., when the Greek city-states had fought themselves to exhaustion and the Great King of Persia was desperately attempting to bring his rebel satraps and the pharaoh of Egypt under his control, none of the contemporaries would have given much consideration to Macedon. For the longest time, it had been considered essentially on the periphery of the Greek world. Its kings, members of the Argead Dynasty, claimed Greek descent—this was eventually accepted as true—and ruled over a mix of different peoples including Macedonians, but many others as well, none of whom were regarded as Hellenes, or members of the Greek national race, the question that we'll get into that is very controversial in the modern state of Greece today.

To Greeks of the Classical world, the Macedonians would have been regarded as "barbarians," and there are a number of reasons for that. First: Macedon, in its climate and geography, is really just part of the Balkan Peninsula; it really isn't part of the Mediterranean world. When I speak of Macedon in antiquity, as opposed to the way the term is used today, much of what is known as Lower Macedon—which is today the heart of northern Greece—was centered on the valleys of the Axius and Loudas Rivers; these are alluvial rivers that rise in the Balkans and bring rich soil and deposit this soil and build up a delta in what is known as the Thermaic Gulf. Very close to the shores were two capital cities: one at Aegeae, modern Vergina, where the kings were traditionally buried, and there are important tombs that were found there by Greek archaeologists in the 1970s (we'll speak about them in a coming lecture); the other was Pella, the political capital, long the political capital of the Argead kings.

These cities, in many ways, were not really Greek cities at all. In the time of 360 B.C., just before Philip II came to the throne, they did not have the institutions of a Greek city-state (a polis); they were royal capitals. There were no independent organs of government such as an assembly, a council, or elected magistrates. In some ways, the cities by 360 B.C. would have had the trappings of Greek civilization: The royal family built its palaces in a Greek style; they decorated them with mosaics, and some marvelous Greek-style mosaics have come to light from the 4th century B.C.; they bought a lot of Greek wares and goods; and in some ways, in manners, the Macedonian nobles and royal family would approximate their Greek contemporaries, at least the Greek aristocrats.

But in many other ways, the Macedonians were really not Greeks at all: First, the kingdom was a hodgepodge of regions in what is today northern Greece that were brought under control by the Macedonian kings between the 8th and the 6th century B.C. They included some very important districts to the west: these western districts like Lyncestris, Eordaea, and Orestis particularly were home to proud nobles, essentially feudal barons, who only gave their loyalty to the kings of Pella if those kings were strong. It really was to the credit of Philip II, and later Alexander the Great, that these noble families were won over and turned into the servants of the Argead monarchy and furnished many of the leading generals of both Philip and Alexander. To the east, particularly to the regions immediately north of the peninsula of the Chalcidice—that three-pronged peninsula in northern Greece today that was home to many Greek city-states founded in the Archaic Age (7th and 6th centuries B.C.) by Greeks coming from the central islands of the Aegean—just north of these city-states were a variety of local peoples living in regions like Mygdonia, Bisaltia, and other districts inhabited by people whose origins are really still unknown to us.

The Macedonians proper, the Makedones—the "tall ones" is apparently what the name means—lived in what is today northern Greece, the regions around Pella and Vergina, in the plains, and they do not seem to have been part of that Greek nationality for several reasons: First, these regions of Macedon were not part of the Greek civilization of the Bronze Age; and it is increasingly clear from archaeology that between 1600 and 1200 B.C., the Bronze Age civilization of Greece, centered on the great palaces of southern Greece, the so-called Mycenaean or Achaean palaces, were really the beginning of at least Greek civilization, maybe not political institutions but the religious, cultural, and economic institutions. Macedon is not part of that Bronze Age world.

In the ensuing centuries, when this Bronze Age collapse occurred in Greece, Macedon seems to have been little affected by the migrations that led to the rearrangements of Greek dialects and Greek populations in the Greek homeland. The Macedonians, as far as we can tell—and this is a surmise that has been the result of two generations of work by philologists (experts in language), archaeologists, and historians, notably Professor Eugene Borza whose work on Macedon is really a turning point in scholarship; I owe a great deal to his work *In the Shadow of Olympus* for this lecture, and Professor Borza and I have been friends for many years—as he points out, the Macedonian language, as far as we can tell, was unintelligible to the Greeks. There are a number of indications of this: the most famous is in 328 B.C. when Alexander gets into a drunken brawl with one of his officers, Cleitus, and calls for his guard to arrest Cleitus, and we're told by Plutarch speaks in the Macedonian language because there were Greeks present and Alexander did not want these Greeks to understand what he had just shouted.

There are other indications that the inscriptions set up in Macedon in the time of Alexander the Great and earlier were done by Greek stonecutters, and the dialect of Greek—and Greek is divided into a series of different dialects—in these inscriptions is the dialect of the stonecutter (there's Dorian, Ionic, there's even I gather a couple of Thessalian and Neolic inscriptions) and what it indicates is there isn't any kind of Macedonian Greek dialect as far as we can tell. Most of the information we have on the Macedonian languages is very limited—it's personal names and certain technical terms—but there seems a good reason to believe that Macedonian, while remotely related to Greek (it goes back to a common Indo-European ancestor) in the time of Philip and Alexander was essentially unintelligible to most Greeks.

Furthermore, Greeks found the Macedonian kings an anomaly. Those Greek intellectuals such as Socrates, the Pan-Hellenist, and figures such as Aeschines and Philocrates who are political figures in Athens in the time of Philip II who urged accommodation with Philip would call the royal family

"Greek," and they would then quality it "a new Greek king's ruling over a barbarian people." It was inconceivable to Greeks that any Greek would put himself willingly under a king. There were kings in Sparta, but these were constitutional rulers, essentially hereditary military commanders, and there were two of them; and in Sparta, both kings—the Argead and Eurypontid kings—simply hated each other and never cooperated, and the Spartans lived under the rule of law, they lived under the institutions of a polis.

So from the viewpoint of the Greek world, the Macedonians were just not Greeks. They didn't have the political institutions, their language was unintelligible, and above all their burial customs and mores were absolutely dreadful to the Greeks. For one, the Macedonians drank unmixed wine; any well-trained Greek knows that at a symposium (at a drinking event) you drank wine cut with water—in fact, it was usually a one-to-one ratio if you were a good host—whereas in Macedon they drank the stuff "neat." There's lots of reports about Macedonian kings having these long, all-night drinking sessions—Philip II excelled in them—but this was just standard fare for the Macedonians. Furthermore, any Greek coming to the court at Pella, the political capital of Macedon, and invited to participate in this symposium would find it quite different from what you would find in a Greek city-state. In a city such as Athens, a symposium was an occasion for learned disputation: Political matters might be discussed—that is, democracy is no good, we should have an oligarchy; that was very common in certain circles in Athens—or literary and intellectual topics; many of Plato's dialogues are set where Socrates is talking to Alcibiades, that marvelous, irreverent figure of Athenian politics. Whereas a drinking party at the court of Pella probably was a combination of the old Homeric strong-arm drinking parties you would have of these bellicose warriors who had very little regard for anything intellectual and was sort of a preview to the Viking age and Hell's Angels. I'm sure that most Greeks were horrified at what went on at the court of Pella, and there were some really extraordinary events that are reported in the sources.

In their burial customs, the Macedonians, who lived in close proximity to peoples known as the Thracians to the east, in what is now Bulgaria, and to the Illyrians to the north and northwest—these are people who are decidedly non-Greek—there are a great deal of similarities; archaeology has revealed this. Finally, the Macedonians, who did not live in a city-state and were ruled by kings, did not have the conceit that they were separated from the rest of the world because they lived under the rule of law. Greeks—or "Hellenes," to use the name that they would use—always saw themselves as distinct from the rest of the world because they lived under the rule of law (eunomia); that the citizens voted various laws into actions, these were implemented by the citizens through juries, courts, and elected magistrates, and officials were held to an account.

It also meant that the Greeks did not tend to intermarry with foreign peoples; and it was a major breakthrough by the Athenian electoral and Socrates to admit the fact that barbarians—and "barbarian" simply means "non-Greek speaker"—or foreigners (perhaps a better term) could become Hellenes if they adopted the Greek language and Greek political institutions and lived in a polis. That was a major concession in the 4$^{th}$ century B. C. In the case of the Macedonian ruling house and its nobility, the policy of the Argead kings was to not only beat your rivals on the battlefield but to marry them. Every time Philip went to war he picked up an extra wife, and many of these women were Illyrians, Thracians; some were Greeks, such as Thessalians— Alexander's mother Olympias was Greek; she was from the royal family of Epirus that was marginally Greek but still regarded as Greek—and the Macedonians had no such bar. This explains Alexander's attitude toward the Persian aristocracy when he conquered the Persian Empire: In his mind, marrying highborn Persian women was perfectly acceptable. The Greeks would be aghast at this; but this was common policy in the Macedonian world. They were, essentially, monarchists: They believed in a monarchy; the nobility and the peasants gave their loyalty to the Argead house; and this is a very, very non-Greek way in governing yourselves and it's an important point that must be stressed.

Today, there is a Republic of Macedonia in the Balkans; it's a breakaway from Yugoslavia. That region represents in antiquity what would have been known as Upper Macedon; that is, the non-Macedonian regions brought into the kingdom of Macedon. It's an unfortunate use of the term because it essentially approximates a Byzantine province of the early Middle Ages, of the 7$^{th}$ or 8$^{th}$ century A.D., and the people living there speak a south Slavic language related to Bulgarian but apparently distinct from Bulgarian, and these Macedonian Slavs—maybe 2.5 million strong—represent in large part people who had moved in there in the early Middle Ages. They have laid claim to Alexander and Philip as their kings; who knows what any of these claims mean in the modern world, some of these Macedonian Slavs may well have ancestry going back to the ancient Macedonians as well as everyone else who's gone through the Balkans. The modern state of Greece is understandably concerned that these irredentist claims might lead to claims by the Slavic Republic of Macedon on places like northern Greece that were part of Ancient Macedon.

The Greeks themselves have inherited this nationalist view best expressed in W. W. Tarn—the historian I mentioned in the first lecture who summed up the heroic image of Alexander coming out of the 19th and early 20th century—and see Alexander the Great as their king, as a Greek king, as a man who conquered the Persian Empire to spread Greek civilization. They even went so far as to issue coins to demonstrate that Macedon is Greek and always Greek; I believe it's a 100 drachma piece. On the obverse is the head of Alexander the Great based on an ancient coin with Alexander's portrait and the horn of Zeus Amman which is Alexander as a deified king; and on the reverse is the inscription "*demokratia Hellenica*" ("Hellenic democracy") which is totally illogical; Alexander had no tolerance for democracy one way or the other. He tolerated it if the Greeks wanted to run it that way, but to him it was just a ridiculous form of government; and the fact that Alexander spoke Greek and in some ways was culturally Greek did not make him politically Greek.

These territorial claims between modern Greece and the Republic of Macedon really have very little to do with antiquity. They are very, very sensitive and controversial issues—I know they will spark all sorts of claims and criticisms—but fundamentally, as a historian who has absolutely no interest either way on what the modern situation is, as far as we can tell, the Macedonians were a non-Greek people who came under very, very heavy Greek influence culturally starting in the 6th century B.C., and then in the reign of their king Alexander I who ruled about 498–454 B.C. The kings of Macedon—and this is a remarkable story in Herodotus—applied to the judges at Olympia, claiming that they were descended from none other than Heracles (the Roman Hercules); they also threw in King Perseus of Argos for good measure. It was accepted that the Macedonian kings were Greek. We don't know if these claims were real or not—the Macedonian royal family did have some Greek ancestors; they intermarried with certain Greek aristocrats—and from that point onward, the Greeks regarded the Macedonians (their kings) as Greeks. That did not extend to the rest of the Macedonian population. As I said, even the strongest supporters of Philip and Alexander might call "Phil" and "Alex" Greeks, but they ruled essentially over a barbarian people, the Macedonians, who drink their wine unmixed and who you can't understand no matter what they say.On the other hand, the royal family made a real effort to project themselves as Hellenes in certain ways. King Perdiccas II, who was the king during the Peloponnesian war, and his son and successor Archelaus, who was particularly important (he ruled from 413–399 B.C.) made every effort to turn Pella and Vergina—that is, the religious capital is at Vergina; it's the ancient city of Aegeae—into Greek-looking cities. They brought in Greek artists; they started publishing public inscriptions in the Greek language; and Attic Greek—that is, the language of Athens—was officially adopted as the language of the Macedonian court by King Archelaus.

That is a very significant point; and if one is looking for a very rough analogy, one could think of the Russian aristocracy of the late 18th and early 19th century that used French but was definitely Russian. One thinks of Czar Alexander I—who, by the way, given his name, liked to style himself as a follower of Alexander the Great, and he has a lot of company historically—who loved to correct the spelling and punctuation of Napoleon because Alexander I spoke better French than Napoleon who came from Corsica. That didn't mean that Alexander I or any of his nobility were French, even though they were French in many ways linguistically and culturally; and I think you should think of the Macedonian royal family and eventually the aristocracy along those lines: that they bought Greek products and goods; that they used Greek in diplomatic and other types of correspondence; they assimilated their gods to the Greek equivalents; and they eventually began to use the Greek title "Basileus" to describe their monarch (we don't really know what the Macedonian title "king" is but it probably was not Basileus in earlier ages. it comes to be used in the time of Alexander and later); and as I mentioned in an earlier lecture, in some ways, the Argead kings of Macedon should be compared to other non-Greek peoples who came under very, very strong Greek influence in which their kings or dynasts—sometimes they didn't have the title "king" but they ruled as monarchs or strong men—were known as "philhellenes"; that is, they loved things Greek.

The most telling example of that in the 4$^{th}$ century B.C. comes from Mausolus. Mausolus is the son of a local dynast in Caria; Caria's in southwestern Turkey today. The Carians are a native Anatolian people; it is now clear that they spoke a language that goes into the Bronze Age and they are descended from an Anatolian people from the Hittite Age in the Bronze Age. They were in close association with the Greeks, particularly the Greeks settled on the shores of Asia Minor. In earliest times, Herodotus tells us that Greeks and Carians intermarried; the Carians used an alphabet that was similar to the Greek alphabet, modified for their language; but they were a distinct Anatolian people. Mausolus, in 377 B.C., achieved a position of dominance in southwestern Asia Minor, and he ruled to his death in 353 B.C. He came to control not only Caria but a region known as Lycia to the southeast of Caria, various cities of Asia Minor. In some ways, he was seen as a far greater threat than Philip II, who was his contemporary; and the Athenians were extremely concerned that Mausolus would extend his control over the islands of Greece, notably over the naval republic of Rhodes. Mausolus actually backed dissident Athenian allies in a war known as the Social War, which raged from 357–355 B.C. ("Social" is an unfortunate term; it means "allied," it comes from the Latin *socius* which means "ally," so it doesn't mean social as we understand the word, as a society, social institutions, sociology, the way we would use it today in modern English).

In any event, Mausolus really conducted himself as a Philhellene king: His court used Greek; he remodeled the shrines of Caria along Greek lines—the most spectacular is Labranda, which is atop a mountain near the ancient city of Mylasa in which there was a very active building program him by him, his wife, and his brothers who follow him to turn the shrine into a Greek-looking shrine—he consults the Oracle of Delphi; he issues coins that are Greek-inspired with Greek inscriptions; and he hires large numbers of Greek mercenaries. He moves his capital to Halicarnassus, the hometown of Herodotus, a Greek city, and sets up his court in Halicarnassus. He commissions the Great Mausoleum, one of the seven wonders of the ancient world, which is built in a Greek style. But he remains, first and foremost, an Anatolian monarch; he has Greek trappings, he uses the Greek language, and he uses Greek mercenaries, but there's no question that he's a Carian dynast. He also doubles as a satrap for the Great King of Persia, Artaxerxes II, and proves a very loyal and able satrap who extends his position into essentially an almost virtually independent monarch in southwestern Asia Minor. He is at the head of what is known as the Hecatomnid Dynasty; that is a family that is descended from a common ancestor. The last Hecatomnid dynast was a queen, Ada, who was ruling in Caria at the time Alexander the Great shows up; he favors her, puts her in control of Caria, she adopts him—that is, Alexander—as her son and heir, and in 326 B.C., when she dies, Caria essentially passes to Alexander.

Mausolus, in many ways, is similar to Philip II of Macedon, who will be appearing in the coming lectures: He is not from the Greek race; he is a monarch both in name and disposition; but he comes to embrace Greek civilization, use Greek institutions, use Greek military technology and mercenaries to make himself one of the most effective kings in the Aegean world. That's what the kings of Macedon themselves aspired to; that is what, essentially, Philip II achieved, and it's important to stress that the Athenians in the 350s B.C.—Philip comes to the throne in 359 B.C.—saw Mausolus as a far more dangerous rival than they saw Philip II. They didn't realize what "Phil" had in store for them, and by the time they recognized Philip it was too late, in my opinion. The kingdom of Macedon is, then, part of the wider Greek world; it's heavily influenced by Greek civilization, but it still technically is not really Greece.

The Argead kings themselves, from the Greek viewpoint in 360 B.C., didn't seem to pose much of a threat. For the longest time, the kings of Macedon were really quite weak. The western barons in Lyncestris, Orestis, and Elimea were essentially virtual independent kings; any king who came to the throne in Pella had to bring these proud nobles, who were virtually kings in all but name, back under control. The kings in Pella and Aegae at the time lived very close to the sea; today those cities are very far inland because of the silting up of the Axius River. They were subject to easy coercion by first the Athenians, and later by the Spartans and the Thebans. It would be very, very easy for the Athenians to back a pretender to the throne of Macedon and land an army on the shores of Macedon, and really complicate the succession of the Argead family. Throughout the entire 5th century B.C.—first king Perdiccas II and then his son Archelaus—lived in fear that the Athenians could raise up pretenders with no problem, provide them with money and mercenaries, and overthrow the monarch in Pella.

To the north and to the east were powerful barbarian peoples, above all the Thracians. The Adresian kings of Thrace were seen for the longest time as a far greater opponent than any of the Macedonian kings, and the Thracians and Illyrians repeatedly would attack the border regions of Macedon to the north and east, plunder these regions, carry off cattle, livestock, peasants, women, you name it; and throughout the 5$^{th}$ and early 4$^{th}$ centuries B.C., the Argead kings were really not in much of a position to challenge these neighbors, who in many instances were wild and far more barbaric and dreaded than the Macedonians themselves who had come under a certain amount of Greek influence.

Finally, the Macedonian kings, really in the whole political game of the 5$^{th}$ century B.C., were not particularly impressive. Their king, Amyntas, submitted to Persian rule; when Xerxes marched through Macedon in 480 B.C., King Alexander I—the man who got certified to be a Greek king of Macedon—did everything in his power to hurry the Persian army through Macedon and played a rather dubious role in the entire war in 480–479 B.C. that saw the defeat of the Persians in Greece. Alexander I's prime concern was preserving his throne, and he really rather admired the Great King of Persia; after all, it would be really great if the Argead king could be the equivalent of the Great King of Persia and issue orders to his nobles that sometimes might even be paid attention to.

Furthermore, the kings of Macedon found themselves without the kind of military power that their neighbors had. Until the military reforms of Philip II, the Macedonian army wasn't much to look at. The population was large: In 359 B.C., when Philip II comes to the throne, the population of the kingdom of Macedon may be twice that of Athens—Athens was regarded as the most populous city-state in the Aegean world—maybe there were 500,000 residents in the kingdom of Macedon, somewhere between 100,000–150,000 men who could be armed. But until Philip II, this army didn't amount to much. Macedonian kings depended very heavily on Greek mercenaries for infantry, because the infantry in Macedon was nothing more than peasant levies. They did very little service on the battlefield; actually, most of the time they got in the way of the Macedonian cavalry, and there's several instances where the Macedonian cavalry would ride over their own peasants in order to close with the enemy. The cavalry was excellent, but it comprised various nobles and sub-kings from different parts of Macedon who styled themselves as great heroic figures rather than fighting as a disciplined cavalry. This, too, would have to be changed by Philip who would train the Macedonian nobility to fight as professional soldiers rather than a bunch of heroes out of the *Iliad*.

In terms of military potential, the Macedonians, while they had the manpower—they had excellent horses, Macedon was home to great amounts of timber, hides, and metals—it really was very, very difficult for these kings to utilize these resources, to equip an effective army, and even more difficult was to inculcate some sort of loyalty in this army where it could be used as an effective royal instrument. In 360 B.C., there really wasn't much concern that Macedon represented a distant threat; and therefore, in 360 B.C.—the year I chose to state that everyone in the Greek world at that point realized that Athens, Sparta, and Thebes had essentially fought themselves to a standstill—Macedon was of very little account. In the next year, 359 B.C., news would have been received by the Greek city-states that the then–ruling king of Macedon, a fellow named Perdiccas III, had been killed in a battle against the Illyrians; that some 4,000 Macedonians had fallen in the battle; that the Illyrians had plundered northern Macedon, driving off livestock and peasants; that the Thracians had overrun certain regions of Macedon; that at least two different pretenders appeared, one of them backed by the Athenians; the lords of western Macedon refused to recognize Pella; and the man who was elected or chosen king, Philip II, who was the brother of Perdiccas III, was just one more Macedonian king and this was politics as usual. Macedonian kings always faced these difficulties when they came to the throne; they faced rivals in western Macedon, Barbarians on the frontiers, pretenders back by Athens, or whoever was the leading Greek city-state. They gave very little concern to this. Little did they know that the king who came to the throne in 359 B.C. would build on Macedonian institutions, royal institutions going back into the 5th century B.C., would forge a whole new army that required a virtual social and economic rewrite of Macedon, and would make himself the greatest king of Europe, and unite Greece.

# Philip II and the Macedonian Way of War
## Lecture 5

**Philip, within a year of coming to the throne, began to evolve a new Macedonian way of war; and one of Philip's great contributions was to create the army with which Alexander conquered the Persian Empire.**

King **Philip II** devised a distinct Macedonian way of war premised on a battle of encirclement and annihilation. In so doing, he forged an effective kingdom and forever influenced Western warfare.

In his first battle against the Illyrians in 358 B.C., Philip commanded in the center the heavy infantry (composed of Greek mercenary hoplites) that pinned the foe, while flanking attacks by the superb Macedonian cavalry converged and destroyed the foe. Philip created this strategy of "hammer and anvil," and he was not, as often argued, inspired by the tactics of Epaminondas and the Boeotian phalanx. The Boeotians, just like other Greek armies, depended on the shock of a infantry attack to break a foe's line rather than to encircle and destroy the foe.

Philip expanded his army by recruiting and drilling Macedonian peasants into territorial regiments under royal officers. Each infantry regiment of phalangites was trained to stand 16 deep, and to wield a sarissa, a pike of 18 to 21 feet in length. The cavalry, armed as lancers, fought in squadron. Subject peoples and allies were incorporated was specialized units such as Thessalian cavalry, Agrianian peltasts, and Thracian light cavalry.

In creating a new army, Philip transformed Macedonian society. Proud nobles of Lower Macedon and kings of Orestis and Lyncestris were attracted to the court of Pella, and turned into royal generals. Aristocrats were rewarded with estates in return for service in the cavalry. Philip founded colonies, built roads, and encouraged trade whereby turning tough Macedonians peasants into veteran soldiers devoted to the Argead house. It was only at the Battle of Chaeronea, in 338 B.C., when the Greek world learned of the power of this Macedonian army. ∎

**Philip II** (r. 359–336 B.C.): Argead king; he transformed Macedon into the leading Hellenic power. He defeated the coalition army of Athens and Thebes, and so united the Greek city-states into the League of Corinth.

## Suggested Reading

Anderson, *Military Theory and Practice in the Age of Xenophon.*

Borza, *In the Shadow of Olympus: The Emergence of Macedon.*

Buckler and Beck, *Central Greece and the Politics of Power in the Fourth Century B.C.*

Ellis, *Philip II and Macedonian Imperialism.*

Engels, *Alexander the Great and the Logistics of the Macedonian Army.*

Hammond and Griffith, *A History of Macedonia.*

Hanson, *The Western Way of War: Infantry Combat in Classical Greece.*

———, *Hoplites.*

Marsden, Greek and Roman Artillery.

## Questions to Consider

1. How Greek hoplite warfare rest on the institutions of the city-state (polis)? Why were the advantages of this style of fighting? Why did mercenaries play an ever more decisive role in Greek warfare since the late 5th century B.C.

2. How did Philip II use his new army as a means to forge a nation out of his diverse subjects? In what ways did the Macedonian royal army act as a political and social institution?

3. What were the bonds between Philip II and his subjects? Why did the Macedonians come to regard the Argead house as their own? How was Philip II the epitome of a Macedonian king?

# Philip II and the Macedonian Way of War
## Lecture 5—Transcript

In this lecture, I wish to introduce Philip II of Macedon; I referred to him in the last lecture as coming to the throne after a colossal defeat suffered by his brother and king, Perdiccas III. Philip, within a year of coming to the throne, began to evolve a new Macedonian way of war; and one of Philip's great contributions was to create the army with which Alexander conquered the Persian Empire. We have very limited information about how Philip did this. The literary sources all agree that he was the first Macedonian king to rearm the Macedonian infantry with a *sarissa*, which is the Macedonian version of a pike that may have been between 18 and 21 feet long; some scholars think it was a bit shorter, but this weapon was at least twice—maybe two-and-a-half times—the length of the usual spear carried by Greek heavy infantry known as hoplites. In rearming the Macedonian army, Philip had to do two things: First, he had to devise new systems of tactics; and in many ways the weapons and the armaments of this new model army of Philip reflected a decisive change in tactics that changed the face of warfare, really until the arrival of the Roman legions in the eastern Mediterranean when essentially the legion replaced the Macedonian phalanx. The second aspect about this: To create this army, Philip literally had to pull off a social-economic revolution in Macedon, because it required the rearming and disciplining of the infantry, as well as a reorganization and a complete refocusing of the ethos of the cavalry forces provided by the nobility of Macedon.

What I wish to do in this lecture is to deal initially with those reforms and describe briefly what we think the army of Philip II looked like by the time he died in 336 B.C. and Alexander took over this army. Alexander made a number of important changes of his own, but that will come later. Then, I want to look at three decisive battles in the 4th century: These are the battles of Cunaxa in 401 B.C., fought between the Persian pretender Cyrus the Younger and his older brother King Artaxerxes of Persia; and that battle shows a classic Greek hoplite phalanx in operation. It is essentially the type of battle the Spartans would wage; the Greek mercenaries in Cyrus's pay were overwhelmingly Peloponnesians—there were some Thessalians—and the senior commander, Clearchus, was a Spartan who had long experience in the Peloponnesian War.

The second battle: We'll look at the Battle of Leuctra; I've mentioned this battle as well. That is a battle in which the Thebans, heading up their federal forces at Boeotia, decisively defeated the Spartans. It's the first time a Spartan army was defeated in a clear win; a great hoplite battle. They had not been destroyed in detail, it hadn't been a question of ambush or attacks made from the rear; this is another decisive battle in the 4th century B.C. that marks a change. The reason I've selected this battle is because to some extent it's often regarded that Philip got his ideas from the Battle of Leuctra, which I do not believe is the case. Then I'll conclude with the Battle of Chaeronea in 338 B.C. where Philip and the Macedonian army showed itself to the Greek world. That battle, which is usually dated to August 2, 338 B.C. or thereabouts, fought in late summer, not only ended Greek liberties—it essentially made Philip master of Greece—but it forever changed the face of warfare in the Greek world.

Let's briefly look at Philip's reforms and what he had done. I said that to carry this out he essentially had to affect a social-economic revolution in the kingdom of Macedon, because he needed to create a body of infantry and a cavalry force comprised of nobility who were devoted to the Argead royal house and would serve at a professional level and not as the sort of ragtag army that characterized earlier Macedonian forces. In this regard, he was remembered fondly throughout the reign of Alexander the Great, and I think one of the best indications of what happened actually comes not from sources in Philip's reign, but from a speech that Arrian attributes to Alexander in 324 B.C. at Opis near Babylon, pretty close to the end of Alexander's career, where the Macedonian soldiers have mutinied. Alexander goes among those forces—he mounts a great tribunal—and he calls these men back to a sense of duty, discipline, and devotion to himself and to the Argead family by appealing to his father, Philip. We'll be talking about some of these issues later on. It begins this way:

> First then I shall begin my speech with my father Philip, as is right and proper. For Philip found you vagabonds and helpless, most of you clothed with sheepskins, pasturing a few sheep on the mountain sides, and fighting for these, with ill success, against Illyrians and Triballians, and the Thracians on your borders; Philip gave you cloaks to wear, in place of sheepskins, brought you down from the

hills to the plains, made you doughty opponents of your neighbouring enemies, so that you trusted now not so much to the natural strength of your villages as to your own courage. Nay, he made you dwellers of cities, and civilized you with good laws and customs.

The word being *nomoi*, "the law of citizens"; it's almost the quality of a Greek city-state, is what Philip did. That is, to create this army, he had to build cities, put in roads, create colonies on the frontiers; the Macedonians would be recruited into infantry regiments, regionally put under royal officers; and the army would become a way of refocusing the loyalties of the Macedonians away from their distinct region to the royal officer and ultimately to Philip himself. These ties were absolutely powerful and carried that army through the conquest of Greece under Philip, and then the conquest of the Persian Empire under Alexander. Alexander elaborates in this speech, talking about all the victories they achieved, first under Philip and then himself; and he concludes with the following:

> So what is left for myself from all these toils save the purple and this diadem? [These are the emblems of royal Persian authority that he has assumed over the last several years; and the "toils" refers to the conquest of the Persian Empire.] I have taken nothing to myself, nor can anyone show treasures of mine, save these possessions of yours, or what is being safeguarded for you. For there is nothing as concerns myself for which I should reserve them, since I eat the same food that you eat, and have such sleep as you have—and yet I hardly think that I can eat the same food as some of you, who live delicately; I know, moreover, that I wake before you, that you may sleep quietly in your beds.

This is within the tradition of Macedonian royal authority of commanding by example; and Alexander was very much the same way as Philip: He served and shared the toils with his soldiers. The army as reorganized by Philip broke down into three important components: First was the cavalry arm; and this was rearming the Macedonian cavalry with heavy armor—helmets, body armor, breastplate, back plate, greaves to protect the lower quarters of the legs—and giving the army a long thrusting spear and teaching it to fight in tight formations. Essentially, the Macedonian heavy cavalry were turned into lancers. They were taught to fight in squadrons—in *ile*, or the plural *ilai* were the various squadrons of some 200 men or so—and "squadron" is an approximate translation, and it fits it pretty well; it's essentially comparable to the 18th-century squadron in European armies. The army of cavalry—the force of cavalry—were known as "the companions," the *hetairoi*; a term that had originally been extended to the close friends of the king and now extended to the entire cavalry arm. We think that the Macedonian cavalry by the death of Philip in 336 B.C. may have numbered some 4,000 men.

There was also a cavalry force from Thessaly—that is, in northern Greece—that was later added to the Macedonian army, and that force is usually comparable in size to the Macedonian. It, too, fought as heavy cavalry in squadrons, or perhaps hipparch, to use a different term that was used to designate these units. This cavalry was the striking force; it was the hammer in an anvil-hammer attack. Its function was to flank and take the enemy army in the rear. Sometimes this would be a single envelopment on the right wing; if possible, the idea was to envelop the enemy forces on both the right and the left. In doing so, the nobility of Macedon were transformed from local barons and lords into professional soldiers who served at the capital, who served in the cavalry, were promoted, married into the royal household, their sons were trained with the crown prince Alexander, and they were turned into an aristocracy of service devoted to the Argead house and also thoroughly professional on the battlefield.

Then there were the two infantry components. Here, Philip made a very important innovation; it's already clear that he's doing this as early as 358 B.C. in a vaguely described battle against the Illyrians, the northern peoples who had given the Macedonians so much trouble. The infantry itself was organized into two components: One was the phalanx. These men were organized into—the Greek term is a *taxeis*—a force of some 1,536 men, on at least paper strength. That is because they stood 16 deep, and these *taxeis*—which often are translated either as "regiment" or "battalion"—were named after their commanders, the royal officer, even though they were recruited regionally, and they stood shoulder to shoulder with this 18–20-foot *sarissa*. They did not carry the heavy body armor of Greek infantry—they were largely equipped with metal helmets, leather jackets, and a small shield that they slung over their shoulder—and they stood in close formation, the first six ranks, their spears pointed out, and then the back 10 ranks held their spears at a diagonal that actually acted as a way of knocking away arrows, slings, and javelins that might be hurtled at the infantry formation. This force would pin the enemy front while the cavalry would encircle and you would have what is called a "battle of encirclement," a classic battle of annihilation. The objective of the Macedonian army was to destroy the enemy on the battlefield, not to break it and pursue it which was the technique in Greek warfare.

There was a third component, which we believe goes back to Philip, known as the hypaspists. The hypaspists apparently are phalangites—that is, "men of the phalanx"—similarly armed but tougher and braver men. They probably carried the *sarissa*; they were originally 1,500 strong, later 3,000 strong; and they stood between the phalanx and the cavalry on the right flank, and they acted as the link between the heavy infantry and the cavalry force. Essentially, you had this marvelous infantry force that could pin the enemy front, some six or seven battalions of phalanx, the hypaspists, and then the cavalry concentrated on the right would sweep around. There were other forces that were recruited along the way—Thessalian cavalry, lots of light-armed troops including javelin men, archers, slingers, many Greek mercenary and later Greek allied forces—but the core of the army was Macedonian, and that army had been forged to fight a distinct way of war that, while it owed something to the Greek tradition, was distinct and apparently original; Philip had come up with it on his own. That leads us to the second part of this lecture: How did this new model army forged by Philip represent such a decisive break in warfare in the Greek world? That requires us, I think, to look at three key battles, which some historians would call battles that resulted in paradigm shifts; that is, the battle was so significant in the types of tactics that were used and the outcome that thereafter warfare would never be the same. That requires us to look at these battles in a bit of detail, and I've chosen the three battles that function as that paradigm shift.

The first one is the Battle of Cunaxa, fought probably on September 3, 401 B.C. To refresh everyone's memory, since I've mentioned this battle twice before, this is the battle between a Persian pretender—Cyrus the Younger, the younger son of the former king of Persia—against his brother Artaxerxes II. The battle was fought some 60 miles north of Babylon, and the army of Cyrus was essentially advancing with the Euphrates River on its right flank.

The Greek mercenary infantry essentially occupied the right wing, and they included some 12,000 or 13,000 Greek mercenaries, of whom over 10,000 were heavily armed hoplites, men equipped in body armor with an eight-foot thrusting spear, organized according to their regional contingents, and apparently recognized as the senior commander a man named Clearchus, a Spartan officer. Essentially, this is a version of the classic hoplite battles long fought in the Greek world based along the Spartan model. That meant the decisive attack would be delivered on the right wing, and the idea was to shatter the enemy line on the opposite side—and the enemy's side would essentially be the left wing—and that right wing would pursue and drive the enemy off the battlefield and so win the battle. Cavalry played, in the Greek tradition, a rather subordinate role; whereas cavalry was all-important in the Persian army.

When this battle opened up, probably about one in the afternoon, Cyrus's army may have numbered some 35,000 against an opposing force that was perhaps 45,000–50,000. The Greek mercenary infantry gave him his decisive edge. As the battle opened and the two lines neared each other, Cyrus wanted the Greek infantry to shift towards the center and support Cyrus who was with his household cavalry. The Greeks essentially ignored this—Clearchus pressed forward—the Great King ordered his forces to engage, and on the Great King's left, his cavalry actually got behind the Greeks but ended up sacking the baggage train, whereas the chariots and infantry on the Persian left essentially broke and ran and were pursued by the Greek infantry for some two-and-a-half miles. Essentially, the Greek army won the battle without actually coming to clash with the Persians, and pursued them off the field. Meanwhile, the Persian army attacked their opponents on the other side, and Cyrus led his cavalry in the center in attack against his brother—an ill-advised attack—and he was killed in the fighting. The Persian king Artaxerxes was apparently wounded; and again, the Persians pushed Cyrus's center and left off the field and sacked the camp.

At about three o'clock or three-thirty in the afternoon, the Greeks returned; they broke off their pursuit; they had only suffered one casualty; and they found the Persian cavalry having a grand time sacking their camp. As soon as the Persians saw the Greeks, the Greeks reformed and essentially the Persians quit the field; they were not about to take on this infantry. This was a classic hoplite attack on the right wing, and it broke the enemy line; and the idea of encircling and destroying the enemy force really wasn't part of Greek warfare. Greek warfare essentially was break the enemy on the wing, drive it off the battlefield, and then the cavalry might pursue the stragglers; but essentially, the idea was to control the field, set up a trophy, and force your opponent to acknowledge your victory and you would return his dead under treaty.

This formation at the Battle of Cunaxa meant that Greek mercenary infantry were henceforth used by Persian kings and satraps. It was also the type of fighting that had characterized Greek warfare probably since the 6th century B.C., and the Spartans were the best at it; and Cunaxa is essentially a Spartan victory, at least on the tactical level. What Cunaxa represented was the height of Spartan military discipline and training.

That gets us to the second battle, in 371 B.C., the Battle of Leuctra. This battle was the first battle that engaged the Spartan army under King Cleombrotus I and the reorganized Theban army and the lesser cities of Boeotia—that is, the so-called Boeotian Federal Army—commanded by Epaminondas. Also, the Theban army had a crack infantry unit known as the Sacred Band, 300 strong, which represented 150 male homosexual couples who were regarded as the best soldiers in the Theban army. One would not abandon his lover on the battlefield; and the Sacred Band had been reorganized and drilled over the last six or seven years by Pelopidas, the political leader of the Boeotian alliance, and Epaminondas. The variation at Leuctra was significant.

German authors writing in the 19th century argue that Leuctra was a showpiece that Philip of Macedon learned while he was a hostage at Thebes between 368 B.C. and 365 B.C., or somewhere in there; Philip was a hostage on good behavior for his kingdom. Philip was not at Leuctra, he was not at later Boeotian victories, and there's no direct evidence that Philip really took this stuff over from the Theban army; and if we look at the sources on the battle, the Battle of Leuctra is a Theban variation of the Spartan attack. The Thebans and Boeotians—and the Thebans refer to the principal city of the Boeotian League, which is the majority of the army; but there are 10 lesser states of Boeotia that also contribute forces to this federal army—the Theban army essentially was a version of the Spartan; they had been members of the Peloponnesian League.

What Epaminondas decided to do—and the author Polyanus, who writes about military anecdotes in Roman Age said—that Epaminondas concentrated his best forces not on the right wing, but on the left wing; and he attributes to Epaminondas the remark that, "I will destroy the serpent's head and therefore destroy the Spartan army." In classic hoplite battles, the best heavy infantry was on the right, the exposes side of the infantrymen, and the right wing was always the decisive attack. In this particular battle, the Spartans had fielded over a thousand Spartans, including 700 full citizens, the king was present, and the Spartan army lined up in classic formation with its main forces on the right. Opposed to it was the Theban army headed up by the Sacred Band, and according to sources drawn back 50 deep; not 8 deep, but 50 deep, with enormous weight.

There was very little cavalry; the Spartan cavalry apparently attacked the Theban cavalry that was drawn up in front of the infantry and not on the flanks. The Thebans drove the Spartan cavalry off and into the Spartan right wing. King Cleombrotus had attempted to shift his army right to flank the Theban infantry and it was botched. The Spartans did not have the same drill they had had at previous battles; and the Spartans moved too far to the right, opened up a gap between their right and center wing, and in barreled Pelopidas with the Sacred Band followed by the full Boeotian force. They flanked the Spartan center, crushed the Spartan army in general; something like 400 Spartan citizens fell on the battlefield, and the king was mortally wounded. The cavalry played a decisively limited role; it essentially pursued stragglers and had not really been a significant force in the battle. This was, in a sense, simply a Theban variation on a theme that was long practiced by the Spartans: Shift your best forces to your left wing, and if you can exploit a gap in the infantry line or flank it, you crush the enemy right rather than the enemy left. Again, the pursuit that followed was always one-sided—that is, the pursuing forces were cut down in great numbers—but this was not a battle of encirclement as understood by military theoreticians of the 19th century or by Philip himself.

That gets us to the third battle, the Battle of Chaeronea, fought in August of 338 B.C. Chaeronea, which comes essentially a generation after Leuctra, really does not show a Theban version of the hoplite battle. This battle was unusual in several ways, but it does point out the essentials of the Macedonian way of war. This battle climaxed a long struggle against Athens and Thebes, and it essentially decided that Philip would be master of Greece. Even the ancient authors tended to dwell upon the political outcome of this battle rather than the actual details. Fortunately, we know where the battle was located—it is in Boeotia in central Greece at a small town of Chaeronea; that's actually the hometown of Plutarch—and the Greek and Theban and other allied Greek city-states were able to assume positions, very good defensive positions, on a slightly raised ground between two rivers, the Haemon on the left and Cephissus on the right. The right wing was held by the Theban army, and particularly the Sacred Band; and then the various allies were put in the center, and the Athenians held the left wing.

We hear very little about Greek cavalry forces, it may have numbered a couple of thousand. What we do hear about is light-armed infantry known as peltasts (javelin men) who occupied the left wing of the Greek allied army, the rough ground; and so acted as an anchor supporting the hoplite, the heavy infantry, so they couldn't easily be flanked from the left. On the right, the Sacred Band stood right up against the river, the Cephissus River, and its marshes; and so essentially the Greek idea was to force a defensive battle on a plain, with the Greeks holding somewhat higher ground, and just allow the Macedonians to charge against this position and break themselves. The Athenian commander was a fellow by the name Chares, a well-experienced mercenary officer, and he had a lot of success in fighting these kinds of classic battles.

But there were several problems with this coalition: First, the Athenians and Thebans had not fought together, nor had any of the others; and so what you had in the Greek ranks was a series of independent hoplite forces—on the left, the center, and the right—the best, by far, the Thebans. Against them stood a Macedonian army; and from all accounts, the armies were probably comparable in size. The Macedonian army was probably some 30,000 infantry, 2,000 cavalry or so; the allied Greek army was approximately the same, it would've been weaker in the cavalry forces. The strength of the Macedonian army was in its discipline, its 20 years of experience, its new tactics and drill, and the commander, Philip, himself.

Philip drew up his army as if he were to wage a battle of encirclement. He placed most of his cavalry apparently on his left wing—that is, along the Cephissus bank—so that it would attack essentially the Thebans, who held the strongest position in the Greek army. He also then had his infantry divided into two wings: a left-wing commanded by Alexander—then 18 years of age and obviously the heir apparent—and Philip on the right wing. Philip concentrated his specialized light-arm forces on his right; they matched the light-arm Greek forces in the rough ground; again, it was to prevent flanking. Then he ordered his army into motion; and the Macedonian army marched with perfect discipline and drill. This was the first time a Greek citizen army—Thebes and Athens, two of the great states of Greece; the Spartans weren't present—now faced the Royal Macedonian army; this was the showdown of the 4th century B.C.

That Greek army awaited for the attack, and they must have been in awe as these huge infantry formations closed, deeper than usual Greek positions—that is, the Macedonians generally came in at 16 deep, not at 8 deep—their spears projecting twice the length, held by two hands by the Macedonians, the back spears held at an angle so that any arrows shot into this formation were deflected; and as that Macedonian army moved with perfect discipline, Philip ordered it to halt briefly, and then on his right wing his phalanx and his light infantry began to retire. They moved backwards, holding their ranks, but it looked as if they were backing off and retreating. This was common in infantry combat; very often the forces did not come into contact, one side would look at the opposing side and say, "We really don't want to do this; they look tougher than we are." The Athenians, who saw this, concluded that Philip's forces were falling back in disarray, and the Athenian commanders eagerly ordered their forces forward towards the Macedonian army, which was falling back on the Haemon River. However, to do this, they shifted their forces left; and so the Greek army started to move not forward but at a diagonal to the left. The Athenians were going to pursue and get these Macedonians. In doing so, the whole Greek army shifted, including their center—which was held by Corinthians, Achaeans, Megarians; some of the lesser states—and part of the Boeotian army. The Sacred Band, on the far right, held its position; that was their task, and that's what they would do.

What happened was two problems emerged in the Greek army: A gap opened up between the Sacred Band and the bulk of the Greek army; and Alexander, with the left-wing infantry, charged into the gap, broke through at that point, the Macedonian cavalry poured through, and carried out an encircling movement that destroyed the Greek army on the left side. The Sacred Band got isolated and was cut down to a man; and that point on the battlefield is still represented by a multiple burial, a monument, where the Sacred Band was buried. They all fought, none of them fled, they were cut down to a man. The Macedonian right wing, the Greek left wing, the Athenians began to move up the Haemon Valley and the rough ground, and what happened is the Macedonians in perfect discipline turned around, reformed, launched an attack at the disorderly citizen hoplites, and drove them back off the field, back down the Haemon, and then flanked the Greek army with its infantry—both its phalanx and its light infantry—on the Greek left side. Essentially, what happened is Philip had lured the Greeks into an ill-advised maneuver that had put the Athenian army in disarray on the left flank, opened a gap on the Greek right flank, and through these two positions the Macedonians moved in, got around the Greek army, and encircled and destroyed it.

This, in part, was necessitated because the battle was fought between two rivers in the cavalry could not deploy; and so the breakthrough had to be achieved by the infantry. But this is a classic Macedonian attack, hammer and anvil; that is, the heavy infantry in the center acts as the base from which the light infantry and the cavalry encircle and destroy the opposing force. The results were overwhelming: Some 2,000 Athenians were captured; at least 3,000 Boeotians; the Sacred Band was wiped out; Demosthenes himself—the orator who had urged the alliance—threw his shield and fled the battle. After the Battle of Chaeronea there was no question that the Macedonian phalanx and this new battle of annihilation would dictate the course of military history; and it did so down until the 2nd century B.C. when a new opponent arrived: the Romans. But this is the type of army Alexander took with him to Asia, and his refinement on these tactics would win Alexander the ancient world.

# The Third Sacred War
## Lecture 6

"In this flight Philip, king of the Macedonians, is reported to have said, 'I have not fled, but I have retired, as rams do, in order that I may make a more vigorous attack next time.'" —Polyanus

In 359–357 B.C., a clash between the Boeotian League, headed by Thebes, and the Phocians escalated in into the Third Sacred War, pitting the leading states of Greece against each other, and provided Philip II the opportunity to turn Macedon into the arbiter of the Aegean world.

In defiance of Theban demands, **Philomelus**, leader of the Phocians, seized the treasuries of Delphi, and hired a mercenary army. The Thebans and Thessalians declared a sacred war. The Phocians were supported by Athens and Sparta, each jealous of Theban hegemony. Desultory fighting in central Greece ended in a stalemate between Phocis and Thebes.

At war with Athens over Amphipolis, Philip II intervened in the sacred war on the side of Delphi. In 352 B.C., Philip II crushed the Phocian mercenary army at Crocus Plain, and so was elected archon of the Thessalian League. The Athenian orator **Demosthenes** henceforth saw Philip II as the greater threat, and urged an end to the war and an alliance against the Macedonian king.

In 349–347 B.C., Philip conquered the Chalcidice. Athenian aid to the league's capital Olynthus was too little, and arrived too late. In 346 B.C., the Greek powers agreed to a general peace. Under the Peace of Philocretes, the Phocians were punished for their sacrilege, but otherwise the belligerents agreed to the status quo ante bellum. Philip was the true victor with control of Thessaly, the conquest of the Chalcidice, and a matrimonial alliance with the Epirote King Neoptolemus. The Greek cities henceforth faced their greatest threat from a foreign king since the invasion of Xerxes of Persia in 480 B.C. ■

**Demosthenes:** (384–322 B.C.): Athenian orator; his speeches are masterful invective and Attic prose, advocating alliances against Philip II, and later Alexander the Great.

**Philomelus** (d. 354 B.C.): The supreme general of the Phocians in the Third Sacred War. In summer 356 B.C., countered an ultimatum from the Boeotians and Thessalians by occupying Delphi and using the treasures to hire 5,000 mercenaries. Philomelus was defeated and killed at the Battle of Neon.

**Suggested Reading**

Borza, *In the Shadow of Olympus.*

Buckler, *Philip II and the Sacred War.*

Buckler and Beck, *Central Greece and the Politics of Power.*

Cawkwell, *Philip of Macedon.*

Ellis, J. K., *Philip II and Macedonian Imperialism.*

Hammond and Griffith, *A History of Macedonia.*

Sealey, *Demosthenes and His Time.*

Worthington, *Philip II of Macedonia.*

**Questions to Consider**

1. How did the Third Sacred War alter the political landscape of the Greek world?

2. What were the initial aims of Philip II in 359–357 B.C.? Why was Amphipolis so crucial to him and to Athens? At what point, did Philip shift from a defensive policy to one of imperial expansion?

3. What were the weaknesses of Athens, Thebes, and Sparta in 359–346 B.C.? Why did they fail to cooperate against Philip II as a common foe whereas their ancestors had united to oppose Xerxes of Persia in 480 B.C.? Did Philip II pose a threat to the autonomy and freedom of the Greek city-states?

4. Did Demosthenes offer an effective policy against Philip II? How misleading were his orations First Philippic and Olynthiacs? Why did the Athenians and Olynthians underestimate Philip and the Macedonian army in 349–347 B.C.?

5. Why did the Demosthenes and criticize the Peace of Philocrates? What were the perceptions of Philip II among the other Greek states after 346 B.C.?

# The Third Sacred War
## Lecture 6—Transcript

In this lecture, I want to look at the Third Sacred War that officially raged from 355–346 B.C., and several associated conflicts, notably the clash between Philip II and Athens in northern Greece that raged at the same time, and also a war known as the Social War that pitted Athens against several dissident allies in 357–355 B.C. These wars in the 350s and early 340s B.C. proved to be really a turning point in Greek political history; and the Athenians, who at this point thought that they could somehow resurrect their confederacy in the Aegean, their naval league, in a new guise and essentially snatch the hegemony (the leadership) of the Greek world, saw the Third Sacred War as a means of pitting Sparta against Thebes, the two principal land powers. Officially the Athenians had sided with Sparta, and it was hoped that, in effect, a stalemate would result in mainland Greece.

That would allow the Athenians to pursue their interests overseas: to secure important islands such as the great island of Euboea, which had been in alliance with Thebes since the 360s; also positions in the Chalcidice; the great city of Amphipolis that had rebelled in 424 B.C. and on five occasions was recognized as Athenian territory, except the Amphipolitans did not want to come back under Athenian control. This city had been vital for Athenian timber and metal interests, particularly gold mines in that part of the Greek world. They also hoped to regain control of the Hellespontine regions—what we would today call the Dardanelles, the ancient Hellespont, and the Bosporus—and those were the key routes that led to the grain shipments from the Black Sea, and the Black Sea was one of the main areas that fed the Greek world.

The Athenians ended up being disappointed in this, and by 346 B.C. had to acknowledge—at least part of the Athenian population had to acknowledge, notably the leaders Aeschines and Eubulus—that Athens probably was no longer in a position to act as an imperial power in the wider Greek world. Ironically, it was Philip of Macedon who exploited the Third Sacred War to elevate himself to a position where he became the arbiter of Greek affairs. This was by no means inevitable, and it's doubtful that this was Philip's overall goal when he got engaged in these conflicts. You have to recall that in 359 B.C. when he came to the throne, he faced a crisis on his frontier; he spent years reorganizing that superb army that was eventually to win for him the Battle of Chaeronea and the mastery of Greece. The final conclusion from these struggles was by no means was inevitable, and the Athenians made some crucial poor decisions along the way; and Philip turned out to be, at least in his diplomacy, his mendacity, and his skill on the battlefield every much a Hellene, and I think the reason he was disliked so much by Demosthenes—the famous Athenian orator who came to see Philip of the suppressor of Greek liberties—is the fact that Philip was so successful and he outmaneuvered the Greeks in their own game.

It requires us to look at a couple of key points, and then we can move into this struggle of the Third Sacred War. When this war erupted in 355 B.C., the Athenians had been in alliance with the Spartans ever since the Battle of Leuctra. The Athenians had grown concerned about the rapid rise of Thebes under Epaminondas and Pelopidas; the Thebans had reorganized the Boeotian League as a democratic federal league and in some ways as a counter to Athens; and furthermore, they had signed up as allies areas that were traditionally thought to be Athenian.

This included the great island of Euboea, immediately to the east of the Greek mainland; it also included the vast plain of Thessaly to the north of Thermopylae, which was a federal league of four leading cities—Larissa, Pherae, Pharsalus, Lamia was another important city—and these cities had long been in association with the Athenians, especially the cities of Pherae and Larissa had long ties with Athens. Furthermore, the Thebans had intruded in Peloponnesus; they had humbled Spartan power; they controlled Megara and the key passes into Attica—that is, Athenian territory—and so to the Athenians, it was useful to team up with the Spartans to check Theban power.

In 362 B.C., at the Battle of Mantinea—where the Thebans defeated the Spartan army once again but Epaminondas was slain—in this particular battle, the Athenians were actually allied to the Spartans. The battle was apparently a variation of the Battle of Leuctra—it's difficult to reconstruct—and Xenophon, who wrote a history of this period, closes with the Battle of Mantinea. In fact, one of his own sons was serving in the Athenian cavalry and was killed in the action. In Xenophon's opinion, he concludes—or more accurately stops—his history with the following remarks:

> The result of this battle [Mantinea] was just the opposite of what everyone expected it would be. Nearly the whole of Greece had been engaged on one side or the other, and everyone imagined that, if a battle was fought, the winner would become the dominant power and the losers would be their subjects. But God so ordered things [the Greek word hotheos there is vague, it probably refers to Zeus] that both parties put up trophies, as for victory, and neither side tried to prevent the other from doing so; both sides gave back the dead under a truce, as though they had won, and both sides received their dead under a truce, as though they had lost. Both sides claimed the victory, but it cannot be said that with regard to the accession of new territory, or cities, or power either side was any better off after the battle than before it. In fact, there was even more uncertainty and confusion in Greece after the battle than there had been previously.

Let this, then, be the end of my narrative. Someone else, perhaps, will deal with what happened later. Xenophon had lived through much of the 4$^{th}$ century —he'd participated in the March of the 10,000; he'd seen the Corinthian War—and his expression is in some ways indicative of how many Athenians were beginning to come to see their situation in the Greek world as increasingly essentially hopeless in restoring that hegemony of the 5$^{th}$ century B.C. Furthermore, the Athenians had placed initially high hopes in an alliance in 378–377 B.C.—that is, in the Athenian calendar year of the archon that ran from midsummer to midsummer—when they had issued an invitation throughout the Aegean world to create a new naval league. We do have the document that records this new Athenian Empire or new Athenian league—and we really should call it a league; it never evolved into an empire the way the league did in the 5$^{th}$ century B.C.—and it starts with the usual narrative of all the officials who were there; and then the Athenians state the following, and this is probably in what we would call the later part of 378, the late summer of 378 B.C.:

To the good fortune of the Athenians and of the allies of the Athenians, in order that the Lacedaemonians [that is, the Spartans] may allow the Hellenes, free and autonomous, to live in peace holding in security the land that is their own. Let it be voted by the people [the demos, the Athenian assembly]. If anyone wishes of the Hellenes, or of the barbarians [that means the Persians] who are living on the mainland or of the islanders, as many as are [not] subject to the King [at that time, that's King Artaxerxes II, that's a reference to the King's Peace of 386 B.C. where the Ionian cities, the Greek cities of Asia, are under Persian rule], to be an ally of the Athenians and their allies, it shall be permitted to him to do so, remaining free and autonomous, living under whatever constitution he wants, neither receiving a garrison nor having a governor imposed on him, nor paying tribute. But he shall become an ally on the same terms as those on which the Chians and the Thebans and the other allies did. At the time, Athens had an alliance with Thebes in 378 B.C.; seven years later, they reputed it to ally with the Spartans.

The decree is significant: The Athenian Second Naval Confederation never embraced anything like the number of states of the Delian League of the 5th century B.C., and the provisions make very clear that the Athenians are quite restricted in what they can do. All of the allies remained free; they met in a league council known as the synedrion; the Athenians did not attend. The allies voted policy; the Athenian Assembly voted policy. The Athenians disavowed the collection of tribute; and the imposition of garrisons or democratic governments. Essentially this loose confederation was more of a burden than an advantage to the Athenians, because they found themselves often protecting weaker allies from their stronger neighbors; and, as we shall see, in 357 B.C., they had to battle a coalition of allies, and by the time this war was over in 355 B.C., the Athenians essentially had to acknowledge the independence of these dissident allies and that was essentially signaling the Athens's time had passed.

Back to the Third Sacred War and Philip of Macedon and the various Greek states: The Athenians went into this conflict with high hopes; it was Philip who came out of this conflict as the ultimate victor. The war itself is a rather odd war that boiled up in a border dispute between the Phocians and Thebes and the Boeotian League. Phocis is a small area immediately to the west of Boeotia, and it borders on the great sanctuary of Delphi, the Oracle of Apollo, the omphalos, the center of the world. Delphi, since the 6th century B.C., had been regarded as an international shrine. It was administered by an ancient league known as the Amphictyonic League, with 22 voting members. It was a federal league representing various peoples from central Greece. It was arranged by people rather than city-state; that is, by an ethnos, as the Greeks would say. It had very heavy representation from the various peoples of Thessaly in central Greece; the Athenians represented the Ionians, the Spartans represented the Dorians; essentially, the league was controlled by the Thessalian voters, the various states that made up the Thessalian League, north of Thermopylae and south of Mount Olympus. This was the great sprawling plain home to a number of powerful cities that were aristocratic republics; and Thessaly was able to field the only significant cavalry force in Greece. It also happened to be the southern neighbor of Macedon, and there were long contacts between the Macedonians and the Thessalians.

In 356 B.C., the Boeotians, headed by the Theban magistrates in the Boeotian League—the so-called Beotiarchs—pressed the Phocians on a number of matters, and fined a number of leading individuals ruinous sums of money. The Phocians responded under the command of their general, a man named Philomelus, by occupying the Delphic oracle, forcing the Pythia—that is, the woman who gave the oracle who went into a trance and actually died two weeks later from the uncertainties and the pressure of giving the reading of the gods will—end seized upon what the Pythia said as justification for the Phocians to borrow the treasuries of Delphi and arm a mercenary army.

They did this apparently in 356 B.C.; they claim that they were only borrowing the money—and Delphi was home to thousands of gifts over the centuries, it was veritable museum; every Greek city-state had its own treasury there, these were spoils it up for various victories—and as a result, Phocis instantly became military power. Thousands of mercenaries signed up, the Phocians used the treasuries to hire these men, and Philomelus turned out to be a very able general who pressed the Boeotians a great deal. The Phocians had alliances with Athens and Sparta, who backed the Phocians against the Boeotians; the various allies of Boeotia in the Peloponnesus—

Argos, Arcadia, Mycenae—attacked the Spartans; the Spartans fought their former allies in the Peloponnesus; there was a stalemate there. There was a stalemate between the Boeotians on one side supported by the Thessalian cities, and the Phocians on the other side with their mercenary army.

This war raged on down to 346 B.C., and it proved to be militarily a stalemate; no one could really get an advantage until very late in the war. The Athenians gave moral support and financial aid to their Phocians allies, but the Athenians eagerly seized upon this conflict as a means to reassert their control in northern Greece and in the Aegean. They had high hopes at this point. The war, which erupted officially in 355 B.C. when the Amphictyonic League declared the Phocians in impius; and the way the Phocians, by the way, were to be punished is the entire population was to be marched up to the cliffs of Delphi and thrown into the Gulf of Corinth, with Philomelus leading the crew.

The Athenians, on the other hand, thought that they could bargain with this new king of Macedon and gain back Amphipolis. They entered into some kind of dubious agreement within a year of Philip coming to the throne in 358 B.C., and Philip actually withdrew his garrison—there was a Macedonian garrison in Amphipolis, probably a mercenary garrison—and gave the Athenians, apparently, a free hand to take back this very important city that they had not controlled since the Peloponnesian War, since 424 B.C. when the city, which was an Athenian colony, had rebelled.

Unfortunately for the Athenians, they could not make their presence felt; they were immediately distracted by a rebellion of their allies—this is the so-called Social War to which I referred—the cities of Rhodes, Koss, Cnidus, and Byzantium broke away from the Athenian Confederation; they won several naval battles over the Athenians; they were backed by the Carian dynast Mausolus; and in 355 B.C., the Athenians had to admit that this war was a failure. The chief financial figure in Athens, Eubulus, and the panhellenist Socrates at that point urged the Athenians to be sensible and to get out of the empire business in the Aegean. They become the nucleus of a powerful peace party in Athens whose members eventually come to the conclusion that they really can't resist Philip and the only way to have any kind of hope of independence was to come to terms with Philip and sign a peace with Philip.

While the Athenians were engaged fighting these dissident allies—and this war ended up in some really nasty prosecutions as Athenian generals prosecuted each other, their recriminations of what went wrong in commanding Athenian forces—Philip II was free to seize Amphipolis in 357 B.C., take it back, gain control of the very important gold mines immediately to the west (those are the gold mines of Mount Pangaeum), and eventually he founded a city named Philippi, named after himself, which became a Macedonian colony east of the Strymon River and allowed Philip to exploit the gold and silver mines and issue a vast coinage in gold and silver that enabled him to buy his victories in the Greek world. This is money paid for military reforms, the colonies the roads, and also for the many expensive diplomatic gifts by which Philip bribed various politicians, backed pro-Macedonian factions in Greece, and much the alarm of the Athenians even bribed, apparently, a number of Athenian political figures although it was never quite proved in trial.

In any event, Philip found himself in a remarkable position: He was building up that new model army of his, he had gained control of Amphipolis, and he had very wisely signed an alliance with Olynthus and the league of the Chalcidian cities that had long been suspicious of Athens. This was a federal league of the Greek cities in northern Greece in the Chalcidice, a former Athenian possession in the 5th century B.C., and a possession that had been in alliance with Amphipolis against Athens. Olynthus and the lesser cities of this league were more than happy to sign up with the Macedonian king because their notion of Philip was essentially of the kings of the 5th century B.C.—the Macedonians were useful allies to keep the Athenians out of northern Greece—and they really didn't have much idea of what Philip was doing within his kingdom.

At the same time as Philip had this alliance with Olynthus and had gained control of Amphipolis, the Athenians declared war on him; but they couldn't do anything—they were too distracted with Social War—and Philip had this bad habit of attacking cities during the winter when the Athenian fleet couldn't sail. There are always remarks by Demosthenes the orator—who came to really detest Philip starting from 351 B.C. on—who said Philip is really unfair, he wages war with the Etesian winds; that is, the winds that blow in the autumn and winter and prevent Athenian ships from sailing north. Of course, the Athenians had their own way exploiting season wind; they were just angry at Philip that he was so successful.

In any event, Philip very quickly came to appreciate that to secure his interests, especially Amphipolis, against the Athenians and an Athenian counterattack that it would be useful to intervene in the Third Sacred War. What could be a better situation for "Phil?" By 355 B.C., most of the Thessalian cities—the one exception was Pherae, the city feared by all the other Thessalian cities—were lined up with Thebes and other states fighting on behalf of Apollo and Delphi. Philip could prove that his family was Greek, that he was pious, that he was loyal to Apollo, and that he upheld Panhellenic shrines like Delphi by entering the Third Sacred War on behalf of Delphi; and so, in effect, became an ally of the Thessalians and Thebans. The Thessalians didn't mind this too much, and Philip intervened several times in Thessaly, and on these occasions he always picked up a Thessalian wife—you know, Macedonian kings were polygamous anyway—and cemented good ties with the Thessalians; and the Thessalian aristocrats found rule by a Macedonian king pretty congenial. But the Thebans and the other Greek cities south of Thermopylae really found Philip more than a bit frightening; in fact, Thebes saw Philip as a rival for mainland Greece, and the alliance was always uncomfortable from the start.

Furthermore, the war dragged on longer than anyone thought. Philomelus proved an able general; he was defeated at the Battle of Neon in 354 B.C. and forced to essentially jump over the cliffs to escape capture. But he was succeeded by new commander known as Onomarchus, the Phocian general, who proved just as able; and Onomarchus actually beat back the Thebans, crossed Thermopylae north into Thessaly, and it looked like the war would widen and the Phocians would gain the upper hand. Philip intervened to prevent this; and in 353 B.C., his first Macedonian army entered Thessaly— the first time he entered at the head of a large Macedonian army—and he encountered Onomarchus and the Phocian army in a battle in Thessaly. As a result, Philip and the Macedonian army were apparently very badly mauled; certainly it was forced to be driven off the battlefield. There is very limited information on this battle, but the most significant thing about it is mentioned by Polyanus, and that is the marvelous fellow who tells all these military anecdotes. He tells us as follows:

> Onomarchos, drawing up his men in battle order against the Macedonians, kept a crescent-shaped mountain at his rear and, after concealing on the peaks on either side rocks and rock-throwers, led his force forward into the plain below. When the Macedonians came out to meet them throwing javelins, the Phocians feigned flight (and retreated) half-way up the mountain. As the Macedonians were pressing them hard with a spirited and rapid pursuit, the men from the peaks [these are the Phocians in concealment] shattered the Macedonian phalanx by throwing stones. Then Onomarchos gave the order to the Phocians to turn about and attack the enemy [these would be largely professional mercenary hoplites]. The Macedonians, attacked both by the soldiers in their rear and by those from above who were throwing stones, with great difficulty retired in flight. In this flight Philip, king of the Macedonians, is reported to have said, "I have not fled, but I have retired, as rams do, in order that I may make a more vigorous attack next time."

In the next year, in 352 B.C., Philip returned; and at the Battle of Crocus Plain, crushed the Phocian army and its mercenaries, Onomarchus committed suicide, and Philip now occupied Thessaly. He was elected *tagos*, an ancient term that means "commander of the Thessalian League," and he now added the best cavalry of Greece to his own army. He was also just north of Thermopylae, the strategic pass that enters into central Greece. At this point, all the Greek city-states become alarmed (Thebes, the Athenians); and it is at this point that the Demosthenes—who was a rather obscure orator who won his fame in civil suits—stepped forward and began to articulate the policy of those Athenians who wished to have confrontation with Philip, to end the Third Sacred War, and to unite the Greeks in a new coalition against Philip as the foreign invader. In Demosthenes's mind, this was sort of a recreation of that grand alliance in 480 B.C. that had eaten back the Persians.

Unfortunately for Demosthenes, he didn't have anything like the forces at his disposal either in Athens or among the other Greek city-states. By the time Demosthenes started issuing his orations against Philip—and these are known as Philippics or Olynthiacs. There are four of the orations known as the Philippics that Demosthenes delivers between 351 B.C. and 348 or 347 B.C. They are masterpieces of misrepresentation; he urges the Athenians on to action. Ever after, the term "Philippic" means a narration that completely blackens the reputation of your opponent. Cicero uses the term for his orations that he gives against Marc Antony in 44–43 B.C. What Demosthenes did was a very, very good hatchet job on Philip hoping to convince an Athenian Assembly that was now financially broke, with a league that was more of a burden than an assistance, and with a citizen body smaller and reluctant to take on the sacrifices of an imperial venture. He was also attempting to convince the Athenians to come to terms with Thebes over the Third Sacred War and form a common alliance against the invader. That was difficult, because the Thebans and Athenians never played well together, they had lots of outstanding territorial issues; but nonetheless this was Demosthenes's policy, and eventually it comes to fruition at 339–338 B.C. and ends up at the Battle of Chaeronea that, as we know, turns out to be a disaster from Athenian and Theban side.

Meanwhile, Philip was gaining territories in Thrace, in the regions to the east and to the north against the Illyrians, he had control of Thessaly and Amphipolis; and at the behest of the Athenians, Olynthus and the various cities of the Chalcidice provoked a dispute with Philip. This was a very ill-advised move on their part, and in large part Olynthus was convinced by Demosthenes and company—and there were a number of followers of Demosthenes—that Athens would provide military aid; and that the Macedonians really were more of a paper tiger. After all, what had they achieved? They defeated a mercenary army in Thessaly; there had been an embarrassing defeat earlier; Philip beat up a lot of barbarians, but he had never really fought a real Greek army, that is, Athenians, Spartans, or Thebans. The result was that the war was provoked; and in 349 B.C., after efforts at negotiation, Philip decided, "Okay, all bets are off," and he invaded the Chalcidice.

The Athenian forces arrived too late; they come under the command of a fellow named Chares, some 2,000 citizens plus mercenaries. What they didn't realize about Phillip's army is that Philip had, sometime in the 350s, created two important additions to his army: one was a siege train, with engines of war—these are catapults, billistae, storming towers, the latest techniques in siege warfare that he learned from Greek technicians who were then operating in Sicily in the interests of the tyrant of Syracuse, Dionysus I; Philip brought in all these engineers—and second, he also had created a logistical system so the Macedonian army could move light and quickly; we know much more about that system under Alexander. Within 18 months, the Chalcidice was overrun, the cities were taken, Olynthus was sacked, and the whole area was incorporated directly into the Macedonian kingdom.

This was a shock. By 47 B.C., "Phil" had the Chalcidice, he had captured some 2,000 Athenian prisoners, and even Demosthenes had to admit: It's time to talk terms. A series of embassies were exchanged in 347 B.C. and 346 B.C.; Demosthenes accompanies the first one, and he actually agreed with his political opponents. At this point there are two major figures that have emerged: One is Aeschines, regarded as an orator really second only to Demosthenes; and a fellow named Philocrates.

These men urged peace with Philip; and Philocrates eventually is the man who negotiates the final details. In 346 B.C., the Athenian Assembly is forced to conclude a peace with Philip. It is not a general peace; and the Athenians agreed to an alliance with Philip—they are an independent ally—and they recognize Philip's conquests (that means Amphipolis, the Chalcidice, and the Thessalian League). This is approved by the Athenian Assembly in 346 B.C. Later, Demosthenes tries to back out of it; but at the time of the ratification of this treaty, Demosthenes is on board because they really have no other option and they want those 2,000 prisoners back.

Furthermore, the Athenians back off on the Phocians, and they allow Philip to intervene decisively in ending the Third Sacred War. Onomarchus had been killed; there had been a succession of lesser leaders among the Phocians; and in 346 B.C., the Phocians negotiated a surrender to Philip, the Thessalians, and the Boeotians that represented the interests of Delphi. The Phocians were lucky that they were allowed to survive. The mercenaries who had fought for the Phocians were told to leave Greece; some of them found employment in Crete, others went to Sicily. The Phocians were fined; they would have to pay a fine of 60 talents a year and restore the treasures seized at Delphi. Philip was hailed as the pious defender of Apollo; he received the two votes that the

Phocians had had a the sacred council (the Amphictyony) that administered Delphi; and with those two votes of the various Thessalian members—that were now controlled by Philip who was the head of the Thessalian League—Philip controlled Delphi as well.

It was a masterpiece of diplomacy of Philip's part. He celebrated the games at Delphi—the Pythian Games—in 346 B.C., and withdrew to his kingdom because he had grander interests in the Balkans and perhaps a war against Persia. Philip had hoped that these peaces in 346 B.C.—first the Peace of Philocrates with Athens, and then the general settlement of the Third Sacred War—would free him up for greater imperial adventures in Asia. Unfortunately, he had not banked on the Athenians, particularly on Demosthenes, and the resentment that many Greek city-states now felt that their guardian, Philip, a king of Macedon, was now granting them their autonomy and freedom as a gift rather than recognizing it as a right. Despite the settlements of 346 B.C., the Greek cities and Philip were on a collision course.

# The Macedonian Conquest of Greece
## Lecture 7

> Current scholarship now think Philip ... may not have the title "Great" the way his son does but he may deserve it.

In 346 B.C., Philip intended to abide by the Peace of Philocrates, and to court the good will of the Athenians, for he wished an alliance to deploy the Athenian fleet in an invasion of the Persian Empire. The peace confirmed Philip's conquests of Amphipolis and the Chalcidice, and his control of the Thessalian league. Philip was more than willing to indulge the Greeks their liberties and their traditional autonomy, so long as they didn't pose a threat to Macedon. On the other hand, the Greeks had very mixed opinions about Philip.

Opinions in the Greek world differed depending on your city-state. Many of the lesser cities, especially in Peloponnesus, actually looked to Philip as a protector. On the other hand, Thebes, Sparta, and part of the Athenian population were very suspicious that Philip. The peace of 346 B.C. was a major concession on the part of the Athenians. Any arrangement with Philip in the long term would probably compromise the Athenians.

Panhellenists such as Isocrates convinced themselves that Philip would unite the Greeks in a national war against King Artaxerxes III of Persia. Sober Athenian politicians headed by Aeschines and Philocrates reckoned Athens lacked the money and manpower to oppose Philip, and so they urged accommodation. Demosthenes and his radical democrats intrigued to undermine the peace, and to forge an alliance with Thebes against Philip whom Demosthenes repeatedly denounced in his orations as a restless foe.

In his *Philippics*, Demosthenes denounced the king for waging war without formal war. In 343 B.C., Demosthenes masterminded an embassy proposing an amendment or epanorthosis that would have assigned Amphipolis to Athens. Philip politely rejected the proposal. In 340 B.C., Philip laid siege to Perinthus and Byzantium, and so threatened the Athenian lifeline in the Black Sea. When Philip seized the Athenian grain fleet. the Athenians declared war, and entered into alliance with Thebes. In a brilliant winter march in 339 B.C., Philip bypassed Thermopylae, entered central Greece, and fortified Elatea. Athenians, Corinthians, and Thebans united to oppose Philip's advance.

On August 2, 338 B.C., Philip decisively defeated the Greeks at Chaeronea. Philip dismantled the Boeotian League and imposed a garrison and oligarchy on Thebes, but offered Athens generous terms on the condition Demosthenes was exiled. Furthermore, Philip announced a panhellenic conference at Corinth, protesting that he had come to secure rather than destroy the freedom of the Greeks. ■

## Suggested Reading

Borza, *In the Shadow of Olympus.*

Cawkwell, *Philip of Macedon.*

Ellis, *Philip II and Macedonian Imperialism.*

Hammond and Griffith, *A History of Macedonia.*

Hansen, *The Athenian Democracy in the Age of Demosthenes.*

Roberts, *Accountability in Athenian Government.*

Sealey, *Demosthenes and His Time.*

Trittle, *Phocion the Good.*

Worthington, *Demosthenes: Statesman and Orator.*

———, *Philip II of Macedonia.*

1.  What were the aims of Philip II immediately after the Peace of Philocrates? Did King Artaxerxes III of Persia have cause to fear the ambitions of Philip II before 338 B.C.?

2.  Why did the Athenian assembly turn to Demosthenes, Hyperides, and their associates who advocated confrontation with Philip? Did the Athenians possess the resources and will to defeat Philip II? Why did a powerful Hellenic coalition, like one that opposed King Xerxes in 480 B.C., fail to rally around Athens?

3.  How did the sieges of Byzantium and Perinthus, the campaigns of 339–338 B.C., and the Battle of Chaeronea mark a major shift in warfare?

4.  Was the conquest of Greece by Philip II inevitable or did the Battle of Chaeronea unexpectedly change the course of history?

# The Macedonian Conquest of Greece
## Lecture 7—Transcript

In this lecture, I plan to deal with how Philip of Macedon ended up conquering Greece. That conquest was unusual in one way in that Philip did not attempt to incorporate the Greek city-states within his kingdom; and we'll have to reserve the actual arrangements to a separate lecture. But what I wish to cover today is the period from 346 B.C. down to 338 B.C., the Battle of Chaeronea.

In 346 B.C., Philip of Macedon could really congratulate himself on pulling off some stunning achievements. Given the fact that he had come to the throne in a crisis—his brother had been slain in a battle against the Illyrian king, Bardylis, and Macedon looked on the brink of disintegration—he had built Macedon up into the leading power of the Greek world in about 12 years or so. This included his famous army reforms—which I discussed in a separate lecture—the economic and social transformation of Macedon; and above all, his adroit diplomacy and very, very fine generalship that won him control of Thessaly, the Greek cities of the Chalcidice, and large sections of Illyria and Thrace, so that he had doubled the size of his kingdom by time he concluded a peace with Athens in 346 B.C.

In my opinion, and in the opinion of many scholars, Philip was probably content with what he had. He had no desire in 346 B.C. to become involved in running the various Greek cities south of Thermopylae; that is, the great Boeotian League and Thebes, Sparta and the various cities in the Peloponnesus, and above all Athens. Instead, he wanted treaties, particularly with Athens—he had a treaty, the so-called Peace of Philocrates—and in the event that Philip should expand his interests into Asia Minor to launch an expedition against the king of Persia, the Athenian fleet would be invaluable. He probably saw Thebes and Sparta more as rivals for control of mainland Greece; but again, in 346 B.C., Philip was content with what he had. He couldn't have been more content in the success of settling the Third Sacred War, in which he came out as the guardian of the great sanctuary of Delphi; and he had the controlling votes on the religious league—the Amphictyonic League—that ran the international Greek shrine.

The question is: How did this settlement fail? Between 346 B.C. and 338 B.C., Philip found himself at war with the various Greek city-states, primarily Athens and Thebes. In Athens, there was a very, very strongly anti-Macedonian party led by Demosthenes and Hyperides, who were regarded as two of the leading orators in Athens. He did have friends scattered throughout the Greek world; but in the end, Demosthenes was able to misrepresent Philip and to point to Philip as a threat to Greek freedoms that resulted in a coalition that went down in defeat Chaeronea in 338 B.C. To answer this question of why we ended up with a war, how we ended up on the road to Chaeronea, it's important to look at two points: First, what were Philip's ambitions in the years immediately after the Peace of Philocrates and the settlement of the Third Sacred War? Then the second point is exactly what was going on in Athens; because the Athenian political scene was extremely complicated, and really the Athenians had not been so divided politically for a very long time.

As for the first question: Philip in many ways was a really admirable king, and he has been the subject of a number of recent biographies over the last 30 years, which has reassessed his reign and has really put him in a new light. Until this last generation of scholars, Philip was usually seen as a suppressor of Greek liberties at least in the English-speaking world. Most British and American scholars were reared on the traditions of the Athenian democracy, they had all read the orations of Demosthenes, and for the longest time Demosthenes was taken at face value. Demosthenes was often regarded as a champion of Athenian liberty, of Athenian democracy, and in many ways Philip was the negation of that Athenian democratic ideal. German scholars always had a better appreciation of Philip, starting with the great scholar Droysen in the 19th century who saw Philip engaged in state building. German scholars loved to make comparisons between the Prussian monarchy and the creation of a national German state; and so they could see in Philip a figure that in many ways prefigured the Hohenstaufen Dynasty, and particularly Otto von Bismarck and his amazing diplomacy to create Germany.

In any event, Philip himself really gets high marks, and current scholarship now thinks of Philip as, "He may not have the title 'Great' the way his son does but he may deserve it." I often ask as a trick question to my students: Who knows who Constantius Chlorus, Æthelwulf, and Frederick William are? I usually get blank looks; and my response to that is: They are the respective fathers of Constantine the Great, Alfred the Great, and Frederick the Great. One of Philip's problems was to have a son named "the Great"; and unfortunately he does not hold that title, but one can almost set up a society to award it to him. By 346 B.C., he had done what no Macedonian king could ever have done, and that was to forge effective kingdom that was now the arbiter of Greek affairs.

In that regard, that gets us to that question of: What to Philip intend after 346 B.C.? He saw the destinies of his kingdom to the north and to the east. He spent a good deal of time in the immediate aftermath of the Peace of Philocrates waging campaigns along his northern and eastern frontiers. He scored a major success in the conquest of Thrace, which was completed by 342 B.C. Thrace is a huge area encompassing much of what is today Bulgaria, and these bellicose and warlike peoples were incorporated into the Macedonian state as a special province; the Greek term is estrategia, that is a generalship. This was a significant achievement; it changed the balance in the Balkans. In addition, he was already looking eastward into Asia Minor. I mentioned that many Panhellenists—such as Socrates of Athens as early as 380 B.C.—called for a national war against the Great King of Persia; the conquest of Asia Minor, today Asiatic Turkey, that would include the liberation of Greek cities on the western and southwestern shores; and also the conquest of regions such as Lydia, Caria, and Phrygia, long in contact with the Greek world. These Anatolian peoples had many cultural and economic ties. To Socrates and other Greeks it would be logical to set up Greek city-states or colonies in these regions; and this area has long been disaffected from the Great King of Persia. I lectured earlier how the governors in these regions had repeatedly rebelled from central authority.

Philip was apparently looking in that direction, and we have several indications of this. For one, the satrap of Hellespontine Phrygia—it's the region along the Sea of Marmara today, and the capital was at a town called Daskyleion—was very important, it guarded the straits; that is, the crossing at the Hellespont and the Bosporus, the various crossings from Europe to Asia. Artabazus was the satrap who was ruling in this district. He had come to control this area shortly after the Great Satrap Revolt in 360 B.C. He staged his own revolt in 358 B.C., and after about five years or so checked out and found a reception at Pella—that is, at the court of Philip—where he arrived his daughter Barsine; she'll reappear in the story later on. This Persian satrapal family, which was one of the leading families in Persia—it was linked to the royal family—spent some time in Pella, some would argue as much as 10 years, and Philip undoubtedly treated them with an eye to an alliance. Eventually Artabazus made his peace with King Artaxerxes III and returned to Persia, and we find him loyally serving Darius III against Alexander the Great.

There were other moves to contact local rulers in Asia Minor—the Hecatomnid rulers in Caria; petty princes, dynasts who ruled in various cities of western Asia, the Greeks would call these "tyrants"—and Artaxerxes III had good cause to be concerned that Philip's next move would be into Asia Minor. From Philips viewpoint, that would be logical: These regions were extremely wealthy and rich; they were linked to the Balkan regions of his kingdom; and furthermore, he could avoid dealing with Greek city-states in most of his regions, they were used to monarchy. Artaxerxes III therefore sent various missions, and contacts were made in the Greek world, usually through these people known as proxenoi; that is, "guest friends" to the Persian king. Artaxerxes had contacts in Argos, Thebes, and Athens, and his agents were constantly encouraging the Greeks to oppose the Macedonians; for anything that kept the Macedonian king tied up with affairs in Europe was to the advantage of the Great Ling of Persia. Anyway, Artaxerxes just simply wanted Greece to be a very docile mercenary market; in 343 B.C., he hired some 13,000 Greek mercies for the reconquest Egypt. So Philip mucking around in Greece and conquering this area would affect also Persian military power; it would deny the Great King access to the mercenaries.

Philip himself was content to be on generous terms with Athens. He saw Athens not only as a cultural and intellectual center; and there was something to this, because the Macedonian court was consciously attempting to be philhellene. Philip tried to inculcate these notions in his son Alexander—that is, to make him a Macedonian king who appreciated Greek civilization and Greek aesthetics—and Athens was clearly the cultural center of the Aegean world. But he also had another pragmatic region for this: that Athenian fleet. If there were to be an invasion of Asia Minor, Macedon essentially had no fleet; and the Macedonian kings never really wanted to launch a fleet because fleets have to be rowed by large numbers of sailors who turn out usually to be citizens, and then when you do this you get things like democracy and opposition to monarchy. Fleets were never really high on Philip's agenda; armies were something else, but the navy was something that the Macedonians would never excel in.

From 346 B.C. down to 343 B.C., in my estimation, Philip really did abide by the terms of these general peace proposals, and was more than willing to indulge the Greeks their liberties and their traditional autonomy, the freedom to pursue their own constitutions and live under their laws so long as they behave themselves and didn't pose a threat to Macedon. On the other hand, the Greeks had very mixed opinions about Philip. Opinions in the Greek world differed depending on your city-state. Many of the lesser cities, especially in Peloponnesus, actually looked to Philip as a protector. This is a point that's often neglected if one spends his time reading the orations of Demosthenes, and even his opponent Aeschines in Athens who tended to favor peace with Philip, because they concentrate on Athenian affairs and they see everything through Athenian eyes. But many of the lesser city-states saw Phillip as someone to substitute for either Thebes or Sparta. In the Peloponnesus, the city-state of Argos, the Arcadian League that had been created back in 370–369 B.C., and above all Mycenae, which had once been part of the Spartan state but had been liberated by the Thebans in 370–369 B.C., looked to Philip for support. There were other lesser states in central Greece that did the same, and they felt that an alliance with the Macedonian king would protect them from encroachment by the great states, Sparta, Thebes, or Athens. The Spartans had as their policy the recovery of Mycenae and the subjugation of that area back to Spartan rule; so obviously the Mycenaeans looked to Macedon.

On the other hand, Thebes apparently was very suspicious of Philip, so was Sparta—they both aspired to control central and mainland Greece—and the Athenians, too, or at least part of the Athenian population, listened to Demosthenes and Hyperides and the other radical Democrats who harped upon the fact that any peace with Philip, no matter how generous, was ultimately a deal with the devil; that Philip, no matter how Philhellene, no matter how accommodating he was, was ultimately in a superior position. The peace of 346 B.C. was a major concession on the part of the Athenians;

they recognized the loss of the Amphipolis, which Philip had taken back in 357 B.C., and the Athenians had spent nearly 80 years in an effort to recover this wayward and very important colony. Philip's advances in Thrace and the overthrow of the Thracian king Cersobleptes—which finally ended at 342 B.C. when Thrace was conquered—these moves by Philip threatened an ally of the Athenians; the Thracian king had long been linked to the Athenians, and these moves brought Philip dangerously close to the Hellespontine regions and the grain trade.

Philip, with his superior military position and with his many conquests, his moves to the east towards the Hellespontine regions meant that ultimately the Athenians enjoyed their economy and their freedom as a gift of the Macedonian king. In this regard, Demosthenes was correct: Any arrangement with Philip in the long term would probably compromise the Athenians. Demosthenes spent his entire career after 346 B.C. torpedoing that peace treaty and repeatedly attempting to forge a wider coalition of Greek city-states, notably Thebes—and as I mentioned, Thebes was a very, very hard sell to most Athenians—in a coalition to oppose the Macedonian king.

Maybe Demosthenes's overall perception was correct, but on the other hand, he really overlooked some very important tactical issues. These were points that were understood by Demosthenes's opponents. Demosthenes's opponents did not form a single political party as we understood it, they were critics; and in some instances they could persuade the Athenian Assembly to follow their resolutions, their policies. They included certain men—notably Socrates, now very advanced in years—who had championed Panhellenism; who had championed the idea that the Athenians and Spartans should wage this common war against the Persians in Asia Minor. But that was a policy back in 380 B.C., and by 346 B.C. Athens had traveled a very long way from those optimistic days.

Socrates himself made a major shift in policy in 355 B.C. when the Athenians ratified a peace with their wayward allies; he stood forth as a very important Athenian politician who argued that the days of empire were over, that Athens was now a cultural center, that her achievements in oratory and art would civilize the world, he harped upon the notion that "Hellene" was becoming increasingly a cultural term, and that the Athenians would lead the way in this redefinition of Hellene. He was supported by other members of the Athenian elite, notably a man named Eubulus who I had mentioned earlier; Eubulus took over control of the Theoric Fund, and this is the fund that was used to distribute money to the Athenian citizens; it was used to fund public projects; and it essentially represented money collected by taxes levied on the propertied classes. In contrast to Athens of the 5$^{th}$ century B.C., the Athenian democracy in the 4$^{th}$ century B.C. did not have an empire, they could not raise tribute (taxation) from their allies—that was written into the charter of 378 B.C. in the Second Athenian Confederacy: no tribute, phoros; the word was off-limits—and second, the Athenians no longer controlled the Aegean so they could levy various types of customs, duties, and taxes on trade, which is what they had shifted to in 412 B.C. Those revenues were just not available; essentially revenues had to come from taxes collected in Attica (the territory of Athens) as well as—and these would be import-export duties—direct taxation on the propertied classes.

Eubulus made it quite clear that the Athenians just didn't have the money. In 346 B.C., one of the reasons for concluding the peace with Philip was not only because you couldn't beat Philip militarily, but the Athenians just didn't have the money to wage the war. Eubulus was followed by a number of prominent Athenians, particularly members of the highest class, who saw war as ruinous to their property, as potentially playing into the hands of radical Democrats such as Demosthenes and Hyperides, who would had also called for who knows what next—more democratic reforms, redistribution of wealth; there were all sorts of bogus charges raised against Demosthenes along those lines—so the Athenian public was really very divided on these issues. Demosthenes struck some very, very powerful emotional chords in the Assembly. The Athenians resented that loss of Amphipolis; they still had a sense that they were the imperial city-state, even though that empire was now fast eluding them. On the other hand, Eubulus, Aeschines, and Philocrates—the man who negotiated the peace—pointed out some very pragmatic and hardheaded conclusions on this. They were also supported by some of Athens's leading generals: Phocion, who held the generalship 45 times in his career, was a conservative but very loyal follower of the Assembly. He repeatedly pointed out that the Athenians just didn't have the military power, although he was a very fine tactician, and he was present at Chaeronea even though he was against the idea of fighting Philip in 338 B.C.

The same could be said of the Athenian general Chares who eventually finds himself as one of the major commanders at Chaeronea.

Within the Athenian political elite—not only the orators but the generals—there was a lot of strong opinion against opposing Philip and living by the peace. It really took all of Demosthenes's efforts to depict Philip not only as a monster, as a tyrant, and as a foreign ruler comparable to king Xerxes of Persia back in 480 B.C.; and these images—that especially come out in the third and fourth Philippics, which are delivered in the late 340s B.C.—and associated orations with similar images paint Philip as the national danger to the Greek world. This is what helped move the Athenian Assembly along. He also vilified the reputation and the motives of his opponents. Aeschines and Philocrates were attacked; Demosthenes had excelled in forensic debate earlier in his career, especially in civil suits, and we have a number of cases. In fact, he successfully got his friends to prosecute Philocrates for corruption in signing the peace; Philocrates was banished, although the peace was ratified. He launched repeated attacks against his political foe Aeschines. By 343 B.C., Demosthenes was gaining the upper hand.

Philip was largely unconcerned about all these events; these were really rather petty events in Athens, day-to-day political wrangles, orations, and debates, that were pretty much beyond Philip's comprehension, at least in the details. Once the Athenians made a change in policy he understood that, but the day-to-day workings of the Athenian assembly and the Athenian government were not much of Phillips concern; in fact, the reason he had the peace was so that he didn't have to deal with this stuff. But by 343 B.C., Demosthenes had gained the ascendancy in the Assembly. He came up with an amendment or rectification of the treaty in 346 B.C., and this was an amendment that came up when Philip had sent a mission into Athens headed by a fellow named Python of Byzantium, a Greek diplomat in Philip's employ, to settle some minor issues. What Demosthenes did in the Assembly is essentially sidestep that whole issue and raise the point that there were problems in the original peace, and he proposed something known in Greek as the epanorthosis (the amendment). What it did was it amended one point in the Peace of Philocrates in which the language was changed from hekaterous ekhein ha ekhousin to hekaterous ekhein ta heauton; it sounds pretty close. The first phrase, the original phrase, meant, "each signatory holds what he has"—that means

Philip at the time had Amphipolis, that's Philip's—to change the language to "each signatory holds what is of his own"; that is, what belongs to him. That means the Athenians could raise the issue of Amphipolis and they had five previous treaties that indicated that it was Athenian property.

This thing was sent up to Philip; it arrived at Pella; the Athenian mission was essentially thrown out of the capital. Philip angry; he was probably enraged. He believed that the Athenians at this point were just impossible; and I think by the summer of 343 B.C. Philip's attitude is "all bets are off." If the Athenians want war he'll be glad to give it to them. At this point, Philip starts making moves in northern Greece that the Athenians rightly see as dangerous to their interests. That includes a war against the Thracian king and the eventual conquest of Thrace. In 340 B.C., Philip laid siege to cities on the European side of the Sea of Marmara. This included the cities of Byzantium and the city of Perinthus, both crucial cities on the grain route. The cities at this point were independent; the Athenians sent aid to the cities in the form of mercenaries commanded by Chares; even the Persian governors in the area supported these cities. The siege of these cities—which were record-breaking because Philips showcased some of his first siege engines including artillery—actually failed. Philip didn't have a fleet to blockade these cities effectively—not a large enough fleet—but nonetheless they're seen as moves by Philip essentially to cut that grain route and put Athens in his power.

In Philip's case, these moves were brought on by the attitude of the Athenian Assembly. Philip also gave money and supported governments—usually oligarchies; that is, ruled by the propertied classes—in Euboea, the great island that was a Federal League and ally of Athens; among city-states in the Peloponnesus, notably the strategic cities of Megara, Argos, and Mycenae. Demosthenes, in his later orations, points to these, and he calls Philip polypragmosyne; that is, constantly in motion, constantly doing things to undermine Athenian interests. There really isn't an English word for it; you'd have to use a German word like beschäftigkeit or something like that. He also calls Philip's moves polemos apolemos, "a war that is an undeclared war." Under those circumstances, the Athenians and Philip of Macedon were drifting ever-increasingly on a collision course.

In the complicated fighting that went on in the Hellespontine region in 340–339 B.C., Philip was able to seize one of the Athenian grain shipments. Some 240 ships were seized by the Macedonians; it was embarrassing; it got Chares in a lot of trouble back at home, he was lucky he wasn't prosecuted; and this meant that wheat was not coming in from the Black Sea and many Athenian citizens would go hungry. That event was it; that was the event that gave Demosthenes the opportunity to convince the Assembly to declare war on Philip. We actually have an inscription that records what happened, and it gives us all the various names of who was in charge of Athens at the time:

> Well now, as to the fact that it was in the time of Theophrastos, who held the archonship after Nikomachos, that the stelae [that is, the stones with the inscribed peace of Philocrates] were destroyed, it is manifestly sufficient to quote Philochorus, who writes as follows in the course of his sixth book: "When the People had heard the letter, after Demosthenes had urged them to war and had himself proposed the decree, they voted to destroy the stele that had been set up to record the peace and alliance with Philip, and to man a fleet and to put themselves on a wartime standing."

The inscription with the treaty was destroyed—we're told this in this literary account that is paraphrasing the inscription; it records the substance of the inscription—and this was a very dramatic act because treaties represented oaths sworn to the gods, and the destruction of that stelae meant with the Athenians: it's war. Demosthenes immediately approached the Thebans, and began to conclude an alliance with the Thebans, with Corinth, other cities in the Peloponnesus; approaches were launched to Sparta. The Spartans said, "We'd be glad to come but we have two provisions: First, we're in charge of the alliance; and second, give us back Mycenae." The Spartans kept resonating with these appeals through the whole 4th and 3rd centuries B.C.; it's really marvelous, the Spartans were still living in the 6th century B.C. in some ways, and never quite got over the Battle of Leuctra. They are essentially conveniently annoyed.

In early 339 B.C., Athens and Thebes were at war with Philip. The question is: How is this war to be waged? Fortunately for Philip, through a coincidence of events there was yet another sacrilege committed to Delphi, this time by their immediate neighbors known as the Locrians of Amphissa who were a small state near Delphi. They plowed up some sacred land, and "Phil," who controlled the Amphictyonic League, had himself voted as the commander of all forces to crush the Locrians, which would take about all of 10 minutes by the Macedonian army. In a whirlwind campaign, the Macedonian army marched back from the Hellespont, crossed Thermopylae, absolutely beat up the Locrians in the winter of 339–338 B.C., and appeared in central Greece. Phillips seized the city of Elatea in Phocis and fortified it; the Phocians all turned out in force hailing Philip and later got their indemnity renegotiated down and some of their towns restored; and the Thebans and Athenians were taken by surprise.

Demosthenes really stepped forth at his finest hour in terms of oratory; he encouraged the Athenian Assembly to march out with the other allies and oppose the invader. In the spring of 338 B.C., Philip outmaneuvered the Allied army, entered the region of Boeotia, and at the town of Chaeronea, at the battle I had discussed earlier—one of the pivotal battles in Greek history—probably on August 2, 338 B.C., the Macedonian army crushes the alliance of the Athenians, the Corinthians, and Thebans in a grand battle in which literally the Greek citizen forces were wiped out. Demosthenes himself fled the field, he threw away his shield and ran; 2,000 Athenians were captured; the Sacred Band was wiped out; the Thebans took very, very heavy losses; and by the evening of August 2, 338 B.C., Philip was now master of Greece. One could call him a reluctant conqueror in some ways, but there's no doubt he held the fate of the Greek cities in his hands.

What he would do next was actually a surprise to the Greek city-states; because once again, ever the pragmatist, Philip came up with a very generous settlement that allowed him to harness the energies of the Greek city-states and avoid the onus of direct rule.

# The League of Corinth
## Lecture 8

**The Hellenic League, founded in the year after the Battle of Chaeronea, represented Philip's solution to running the Greek world. It really is an ingenious arrangement—and one of the reasons why Philip should get high remarks in his own rank.**

In 337 B.C., Philip II preside over a Panhellenic conference at Corinth attended by plenipotentiary representatives from the city-states of Greece except Sparta. There, Philip announced a general peace (*koine eirene*) and alliance of the Greeks in a war of national vengeance to punish the Persians for the destruction of the temples of Athens in 480 B.C.

In its provisions, the alliance Philip outwardly respected the freedom and autonomy of the member states. While the Thessalian cities were enrolled in the league, the Macedonians were not, for they were not Hellenes. In avowed aims, Philip embraced the language of the Panhellenists. War was declared to liberate the Greek cities of Asia Minor and Cyprus. Foremost, Philip was only the supreme general of the league of free Greek cities. A federal council, or *synedrion*, administered the finances and relations among the member states. Yet, Philip fashioned the league to avoid the odium of ruling the Greek cities as a foreign conqueror.

In many cities, Philip backed conservative rule by the propertied classes headed by pro-Macedonian leaders. Macedonian garrisons held strategic points at Ambracia, Lamia, Thermopylae, Chalcis, and the Acrocorinth. The Athenians retained their ancestral democracy, but they were compelled to dissolve their naval alliance and to put their fleet at the disposal of Philip.

In 336 B.C., **Parmenio**, Philip's leading general, and 10,000 men secured the crossings at the Hellepont in preparation for an invasion of Asia Minor. Philip, however, never crossed to Asia. He was struck down by an assassin's dagger in October 336 B.C., a victim of the lurid dynastic intrigues at the Macedonian court. The Greeks rejoiced at the death of the barbarian tyrant, but they failed to appreciate that Philip had left not only a powerful Macedonian state, but a son and heir, Alexander, the greatest military genius of all time. ∎

## Name to Know

**Parmenio** (c. 400–330 B.C.): Macedonian noble and most trusted general of Philip II; loyal to Alexander the Great, commanded the left wing at the Battles of Granicus, Issus, and Gaugamela.

## Suggested Reading

Borza, *In the Shadow of Olympus*.

Cawkwell, *Philip of Macedon*.

Ellis, *Philip II and Macedonian Imperialism*.

Hammond and Griffith, *A History of Macedonia*.

Larsen, *Representative Government in Greek and Roman History*.

Worthington, *Philip II of Macedonia*.

## Questions to Consider

1. Why did Philip II avoid conquest and annexation of the Greek city-states south of Thermoplyae in contrast to his annexation of the Chalcidice in 348–347 B.C.? What convinced Philip II of the wisdom of opting for indirect rule through a federal league?

2. How did the leading states view a Macedonian overlord? Why did the Spartans refuse to join the League of Corinth?

3. How did the lesser city-states of Greece view the League of Corinth, and alliances with Philip II?

**4.** How was Philip II such a master in drawing upon Greek political and legal precedents to fashion his federal league? Why would Alexander the Great, later Macedonian kings, and even Roman conquerors never be able to match Philip II in handling their Greek allies?

# The League of Corinth
## Lecture 8—Transcript

In this lecture, I am going to discuss Philip of Macedon's settlement of the Greek world after the battle of Chaeronea, and above all, his creation of an outfit known as the League of Corinth, or probably more correctly known as the Hellenic League. This was founded in the year after the battle of Chaeronea in 337 B.C., and it represented Philip's solution to running the Greek world. It really is an ingenious arrangement, and one of the reasons why Philip should get high marks—perhaps even the title "Great"—in his own right.

There are a couple of important points to stress about this, because Philip lays the foundations of the relationship between Macedonian kings and Greek city-states that persist down to 197 B.C. when the Romans, called in by the Greek city-states, crushed the Macedonian army at the Battle of Cynoscephalae and then come up with a new set of arrangements. The relationship between the Macedonian kings and Greek city-states goes back to this arrangement in 337 B.C., and in time—though not in Philip's own lifetime—Philip's arrangements were really seen as the model against which Greek cities would measure the philhellenism, the generosity, and the seriousness of the Macedonian overlord. Was this king really committed to the liberties of Greek city-states, or was it just a way of controlling them indirectly?

Let's look at the events immediately after the battle of Chaeronea. Late on the afternoon of August 2, 338 B.C., it was clear that the Greek armies had been crushed; the carnage must've been remarkable because this was a battle of annihilation. Philip had large numbers of prisoners in his hands; we know of at least 3,000 Thebans captured and 2,000 Athenians. Philip literally could have done anything, and already he had made major advances in siege warfare, his son Alexander would make more; many of the Greek cities probably worried that Philip's army would show up, lay siege to their city, and storm into the city (that is, capture them by assault). Philip did none of this. He very, very cleverly divided and conquered the Greek city-states, a principle the Romans later used, and terms were offered to the various belligerents who had been on the Hellenic side at Chaeronea.

Athens was in an absolute turmoil; Demosthenes and the other survivors came rushing into the city, explained what happened; the city was in, literally, hysteria. The senior general Phocion kept his head and urged caution, moderation; Demosthenes and some of the radicals wanted to hold out until the end, but this was just impossible. Philip essentially took the initiative. He sent his son Alexander, then age 18, along with his senior General Antipater—Antipater acted as essentially the regent for Macedon when Philip was out of campaign, and Antipater and Alexander developed a very, very close relationship because Antipater in some ways was a surrogate father to Alex. In a way, that was more than one would imagine because Antipater didn't get along with Alex's mom Olympias, nor did Philip get along with his wife Olympias, but more of that later—but in any event, Antipater and Alexander were sent to Athens with a small escort. They carried the ashes of the Athenian dead that were returned to the Athenians at no cost; usually the dead would have the ransomed or at very least a recognition that they had been surrendered under a treaty to recognize that Philip had won the battle. The Athenians were not forced to do this.

Philip gave generous terms of the Athenians. They did have to dissolve their naval confederacy—that is, this alliance they put together back in 378–377 B.C.—but at that time, the League was largely more of a burden than an assistance; there weren't all that many allies left. There were cleruchies. A cleruchy is an unusual Greek colony; it is a colony of Athenian citizens who retain their citizenship at Athens and vote in Athens. Most Greek colonies were established as separate cities; that is, you left Corinth to establish Syracuse, you now became a citizen of Syracuse even though you were originally a Corinthian. There were a number of important cleruchies in the Aegean, notably on the island of Samos, three northern Aegean islands that had long been Athenian territory, vital for the grain route; Athens was allowed to keep these.

The Athenians were probably surprised. There were no indemnities (that is, no fines); there was no restriction on the Athenian navy, far from it, Philip wanted an alliance they could use that navy; and the democracy was not changed. Demosthenes and Chares, the commander at Chaeronea, had to check out of Athens for a brief time, but there were no reprisals, exiles, confiscation of property; Philip did not impose a Macedonian garrison, and, in fact, no Macedonian army entered Athenian territory at all. It was an astonishingly generous settlement, and Philip could argue very easily, "Well Athens, as Isocrates and the Panhellenists have all been saying, is the center of Greek culture; it should be respected." On the other hand, as I mentioned, Philip was ever the pragmatist and he realized that the majority of the Athenian ruling classes at this point knew that Demosthenes's policy was bankrupt and they were willing to accept almost any settlement that at least preserved the outward symbols of autonomy and freedom.

In the rest of Greece, Philip was just as pragmatic. He humbled Thebes. He saw the Thebans as a possible rival and rightly so. The Theban government was changed. Thebes at the time of the Battle of Chaeronea was at the head of a democratic federal league—this is the league that had been reorganized in 378 B.C. by Pelopidas—that federal league was broken up. All of the cities of Boeotia, the other 10 cities, were declared free. Cities that had long been obnoxious to the Thebans—such as little Plataea, a long ally of Athens, and that city had essentially been abolished—were reestablished. Certain border areas that were in dispute with the Athenians were handed over to the Athenians, notably Oropus. And Thebes's own government was changed from a democracy to an oligarchy: That is, a rule by some 300 properties families; a garrison was imposed on the citadel (that's known as the Cadmea in Thebes) a Macedonian force was stationed there; and Thebes was never again going to challenge the Macedonians in central Greece. On the other hand, the lesser Boeotian cities were generously treated.

Likewise through the rest of Greece, Philip did not garrison many strong points. He garrisoned the citadel of Corinth (the Acrocorinth); the Cadmea at Thebes; the city of Chalcis on the island of Euboea which is a strategic crossing between Euboea and mainland Greece. We're not sure he had forces in or near Thermopylae, but essentially he controlled a few strong points necessary for the movement of Macedonian forces through Greece. Other than that, he kept a very low profile. He supported governments that were friendly to him; he rewrote the constitutions of only those states he absolutely had to do so; many of the states in the Peloponnesus were allowed to continue under their constitutions, some of them democratic, some oligarchic.

He went out of his way to punish the Spartans. The Spartans hadn't been at the Battle of Chaeronea; and at the time, the Spartan kings were finding themselves really in desperate financial situation. What Spartan kings did in the 4th century B.C. was take the Spartan army, along with a bunch of mercenaries, out on loan and would fight for pharaohs in Egypt or Greek colonies in southern Italy. King Archidamus III of Sparta was busy fighting in Italy on behalf of the city of Taros, a former Spartan of colony; he was trying to collect money so Sparta could mount a recovery in the Peloponnesus, and it goes to show how bad Spartan financial situation was. What he did in the Peloponnesus was to give border areas to his friends—Argos got Cynuria; the Messenians got certain ports; the Arcadians got various mountain districts—and that is they now were committed to Philip because these areas had been given to them by the Macedonians and they would back Philip against the Spartans in any case. This proved to be a very, very judicious policy, and it really explains why most of the Peloponnesian states did not rally to Sparta under their king, Agis III, who attempted to mount a rebellion in Greece while Alexander the Great was out conquering Asia; it just never came off.

The Phocians themselves did pretty well. For one, they were allowed to reestablish their cities—their cities had essentially been abolished because of the sacrilege of the Third Sacred War—their indemnity was scaled back, they reduced it from 60 to 10 talents a year; they did very, very well.

Overall, Philip, by the end of the year 338 B.C., had pretty much ordered the Greek governments the way he wanted them and he could conveniently ignore the Spartans. He then issued an invitation that fall to a general conference to be held at the city of Corinth. The choice of the city of Corinth was no accident. Corinth was the seat of the meeting—probably held in the spring of 480 B.C.—where Sparta, Athens, and the other Greek city-states had gotten together to form the alliance that had opposed Kings Xerxes of Persia and had led to the defeat of the Persian army in Europe and the emergence of Athens as a great naval power in the 5th century B.C. Philip summoned all the states of Greece—they could all send representatives with the full powers to negotiate—and he would reveal to them what he had in mind. Once again, the Spartans sent their delegation and made their usual demands; that is, Sparta should be the head of whatever they're creating, and by the way, give us back Messenia, and then the Spartans went home with nothing as usual.

Meanwhile, the other states were in a more agreeable situation or mood; and at that conference Philip revealed what he had in mind which was an alliance. The Greek terms that come down to us are clear: It's a symmachia; it is a full offensive and defensive alliance. We have two fragments of the oaths that were sworn by the various members of this Hellenic League, or as moderns like to call it, the League of Corinth. We also have a notice about the league written by Justin, who is a Roman writer who wrote essentially the Readers Digest of Greek history—he has a Latin summary, Epitome, of an earlier work by Pompeius Trogus which is in turn based on an account from Philip's day—and he tells us some information about this league as well; and finally we have an inscription in probably 303 or 302 B.C. in which a version of this league was re-founded by Antigonus and Demetrius, a father and son, they are two of the successors of Alexander. From this incomplete information we can get some idea of what the organization was in the League of Corinth.

Furthermore, this League of Corinth as created by Philip was also resting on three important precedents in Greek diplomatic and political history. Let's first talk about what we know from the sources of this league: It was a federal league; all the Greek city-states who were enrolled in this league—and that included most of the Greek homeland; the city-states that were not involved included the cities of Crete, the Greeks of Asia that were under the rule of the Great King, and the distant colonies in Sicily and southern Italy—otherwise, all the states, with the exception of Sparta, were in. They had a federal council, a synedrion; and the synedrion was a term that was used for a number of these federal leagues, and this represented the governing council of the various member states. A synedrion could be either organized federally—that is, proportionally by population—or it could be organized as each state gets one vote. In the Second Athenian Confederacy it apparently was the latter, every state had a vote. But we gather in the League of Corinth based on the notices that this was done as a proportional representation as we would understand it in the United States; that is, accounting for population.

Justin goes out of his way in his Epitome to mention that the league could raise 15,000 cavalry and 200,000 infantry. This is essentially a census list of the total manpower of Greece—it's probably rather generous to say the least—and no force like this was ever raised. But some type of census was undertaken—or each city-state was forced to take a census—and the Greek cities would be very good about it because it represented their population and therefore the number of representatives that would sit on the council. Athens would of course be well-represented; little states such as Phocis and Locris actually shared representatives, we know that. This was a federal league proportional based on population.

The council, the synedrion, had the powers to determine—and the term was syntaxis, "contribution," not tribute—which contributions the members would provide. This could be done in the form of military forces—in the case of the Athenians, they would provide a fleet—or money; in many instances from the start many of the city-states furnished money to the common cause, and in some instances when they did furnish soldiers they hired mercenaries rather than sending their citizen soldiers. The Thessalian League was enrolled; the Thessalian cities were members of this Hellenic League. Macedon was not, which is a telling point and indicative of the fact that Philip understood that the Macedonians were not regarded as Greeks, and anyway they were his subjects and there's no need for them to be represented in a federal league.

The other important provision that come to the sources is Philip was elected for life as supreme commander of the forces; the term used in Greek was apparently strategos autokrator, "supreme commander, no colleagues." This was at variance with Greek political policy: All Greek city-states had multiple commanders, multiple magistrates; they were fearful of monarchy in any guise. Philip, therefore, directed all league forces, and in effect represented Macedon in the capacity of commander-in-chief of the league forces. From the start, Philip had a very powerful say on that federal council; the Thessalians and many of the lesser cities obviously would go along with what Philip wanted. When Alexander the Great went to Asia, Antipater took over the place of Philip, and Antipater represented Alexander's interests while Alexander was conquering the Persian Empire; and he, too, could count on the support of the majority of the members on the council. Therefore, the lesser Greek city-states willingly went into this federal council as a means of maintaining the Macedonian overlordship, but they also saw it as protection against the powers of Athens, Sparta, and Thebes, the great cities that for so long had attempted to construct great hegemonies but in doing so would suppress the liberties and the autonomy of the lesser states. There's a good reason to believe among the lesser city-states that, at least under Philip II, the league was popular, or least acceptable; certainly not what was expected as a result of the victory at Chaeronea. Philip could essentially have done anything he wanted in the spring of 337 B.C.

Finally, what was the whole purpose of this outfit? This is where Philip was really marvelous. The purpose of the Hellenic League was to avenge the impiety of the Great King of Persia, which translates as follows: In 480 B.C., King Xerxes of Persia had burned the Acropolis of Athens, all the great temples, and had sacked the city. This was proclaimed as a national humiliation—and I think the Athenians sort of liked that: Athens was damaged by the Persians and therefore all of Greece must avenge it; people such as Aeschines could get along with it, Demosthenes, of course, would never buy anything—but that the burning of the temples by Xerxes was the height of Persian arrogance and impiety, and that a war would be waged by all the Greeks, a Panhellenic war, an all-Greek war, under the command of Philip to avenge this insult. One wonders what the king of Persia made of this in 337 B.C.—that would have been Artaxerxes IV, the young son of Artaxerxes III; and later he was to be replaced by Darius III—I think the Great King had no illusions about what this meant, it was pretext for Philip to mobilize the military forces of the Greek world in combination with his royal Macedonian army and all those marvelous, bellicose, crazy Balkan people he had conquered to invade Asia Minor and take over the Western satrapies of the Persian Empire. But it was couched in this Panhellenic language.

That was very important; and that is one of the reasons why give Philip such high marks. Philip was a diplomatic and political genius. He, in many ways, preferred that method rather than fighting on the battlefield. To be sure, he was a very, very fine commander, although there is a remark attributed to Philip that he owed a great deal to his best commander Parmenio who will appear in the Asian expedition as the second in command to Alexander, and Parmenio is of the generation of Philip. The remark is that Philip once said that yes, the Athenians have many generals—and they did, as did other Greek city-states—and I have only one, one good one: Parmenio, a great general.

In any event, Philip himself did prefer diplomacy; and there are a couple reasons for that. One was those years he spent in Thebes, somewhere between 368 and 366 or 365 B.C., when he was an adolescent. At the time, he was only the third son of the king of Macedon, he was not destined to become king of Macedon—the death of his two older brothers put him on the throne in 359 B.C.—and in Thebes, he may not have seen the Theban army in military action, but he learned a great deal on how politics were conducted and a democracy. He saw the Theban assembly; the assembly of the Boeotian League; he had a very good understanding of Theban power; and Philip learned about the importance of those two crucial words: autonomia, eleutheria; that is, autonomy and freedom. Autonomy, the right to live under one's ancestral constitution and laws—all Greek city-states aspired to this—and eleutheria (freedom), meaning the right to conduct one's foreign policy, one's destiny, without interference by an outside power. That was always trampled upon by the great hegemon, Sparta or Athens, in one way or another; and so Philip was acutely aware of these Greek political sensibilities and that's why he crafted the League of Corinth the way he did. That's why he did a minimum of garrisoning points in the Greek world—that is, only the three or four strategic points he absolutely must control had a Macedonian garrison—and that garrison was not the governing body even of Thebes; that is, the Thebans ran their government, there just happened to be a Macedonian garrison on the Cadmea in the event there's an uprising or the Macedonians have to move in.

In this regard, Philip's background—that time he spent in Thebes—was a very formative and important time. It was probably between, roughly, around the ages of 13 and 16. When we turn to Alexander the Great soon, at that time in Alexander's life, Macedon was a great power; it was expanding; Alex was studying with Aristotle and his friends at Mieza; Alexander was reared as a great prince to succeed to brilliant political heritage. He had a very different view of Greek city-states, whereas the father understood these matters. He also learned how to bribe and intimidate Greek politicians, and in terms of mendacity, he was far better than any Greek and in that regard he was Greek as any Greek politician and won the admiration of some and the jealousy of all.

Philip put together this league, and he really was following three Greek political principles that he understood. These were notions that had been circulated among Greek intellectuals, particularly in Athens but in other city-states as well; and we can break them down to the question of Panhellenism, what is known as the common peace (the koine eirene); and then the federal leagues. Philip drew on all three of these to craft this League of Corinth, and this made this League of Corinth palatable in many ways. When Philip achieved the position he did in the Greek world, Isocrates, now in his 80s, wrote letters to Philip and encouraged Philip to undertake that crusade or that Panhellenic war—"crusade" is a real loaded term and doesn't really apply to the Greek world—that he had proclaimed back in 380 B.C. He also urged upon Philip to colonize Asia Minor; to export the excess population. This goes back to a point that was made very, very strongly back in 380 B.C. in his so-called Panegyricus when Isocrates essentially redefined Greek identity, and he said in that oration as follows:

> Athens has so far outrun the rest of mankind in thought and speech [meaning in the powers of oratory and reasoned government] that her disciples are the masters of the rest, and it is due to her work that the word "Greek" [actually "Hellene" is the word he's using] is not so much a term of birth as of a mentality, and is applied to a common culture rather than a common descent.

Isocrates and his followers liked to see in the League of Corinth the fulfillment of that notion; "We are going to create a Panhellenic league; we are going to conquer regions of the Persian Empire; we will send out colonies; and yes, even the native peoples—Lydians, Carians, Phrygians, Phoenicians—they could, if they adopted the city-state institutions and the culture of Athens, become part of that wider Hellenic world. Philip was not unaware of these notions; and perhaps only a small number of Athenians really genuinely believed in them, but that whole Panhellenic dimension to the League of Corinth was extremely important, and the stressing of the avenging of the temple burning by Xerxes. Even Alexander the Great—whose interest in these Panhellenic appeals was not really very strong—when he finally occupies the Persian ritual capital at Persepolis has to order the destruction of that palace probably in the spring of 330 B.C., although at that point Alexander really liked the job Lord of Asia and was really reluctant to torch such a neat palace, but he had to do so in fulfillment of these Panhellenic ideals that go back to Philip's original organization of the league. That gained Philip support, at least in certain circles of Athens. Some of that support carried over in Alexander's time and explains some of the reactions of Athenians later on during Alexander's campaigns in Asia. There was a powerful clique that really didn't want to confront Alexander, although Demosthenes was more than willing to embarrass Alexander and raise a war.

The second point I mention: Philip also drew on notions of what were known as the koine eirene, and this has been the subject of some very important scholarly study; there are several important works on it. This was a concept that evolved in the 4th century B.C. It was an extension of the types of treaties that had been voted in earlier Greek history. Treaties were always religious acts; they were oaths. Oaths were taken, they seriously intended to abide by them—there is a scholarship that argues that the Greeks were rather cynical about it; it's realpolitik—but the passage I read earlier on a based on the inscription that is reported in a literary source that the Athenians went out of their way to destroy the Peace of Philocrates was an indication that Philip had violated the oaths and that the gods would bring retribution on Philip and his entire house.

The koine eirene was a proclamation within a treaty, ending a war, which called for a cessation of all hostilities. Many times treaties were just between two states; sometimes that state controlled the allies and the allies had no choice; but you would get into very, very complicated situations as in 421 B.C. where Athens and Sparta agreed to a treaty—the so-called Peace of Nicias; but various members of the Peloponnesian League refused to sign it, some of them cut their own deals with Athens—no more of this. A koine eirene meant a complete cessation of hostilities. It also had another important provision to it, and that was the recognition that all belligerents and neutrals at the time that the treaty was proclaimed, their governments were legitimate and outstanding issues would be settled by arbitration. This often took the form of calling in the priests of Delphi or of Olympia, or some type of third party, to arbitrate border disputes and other issues, release of prisoners and the like.

The first such treaty was proclaimed in 386 B.C.; that is the so-called Peace of Antalcidas, the King's Peace. King Artaxerxes II at the time was actually a signatory of that treaty, and Sparta used that treaty as a way to impose her hegemony in mainland Greece, but the principle had been established. That is, that treaty was the basis for recognizing governments and arbitrating political issues. There were several others issued after the Peace of Antalcidas, there was one in 374 B.C.; and we have every reason to believe that in 337 B.C., Philip proclaimed a general peace, a koine eirene, a cessation of all hostilities—that's practical; he wants to use the Greek military forces to assist him in his conquest of Persia—but above all the cessation of hostilities brought with it the recognition of all governments as legitimate. That was a very, very important concession to the Greeks, and one that Philip abided by. This later becomes one of the main problems between Alexander the Great and the Greeks, particularly in the last year or so of Alexander's life where Alexander was now conqueror of the world, Lord of Asia, and abiding by these terms was becoming increasingly inconvenient.

The third element was the federal leagues that were quite common in the Greek world. There was an effort by some scholars argue that if the Macedonians had not entered Greece and the Spartans had not mucked up stuff in the early 4th century B.C.—both premises, I think, are really dubious—that somehow Greece would have evolved to a United States of Greece; that is, a wider federal league. That the league in Boeotia, the Arcadian League, the League of the Chalcidice, offered a way out of reconciling the intense autonomy and freedom of the individual city-state with a wider organization to provide protection. Unfortunately for that argument, when you look at all the federal leagues, they are regional in nature and very much ethnic; that is, Boeotians will band together, Chalcidians will band together, Arcadians, they had the same language, dialect, and cults. But all these federal leagues ever did was produce regional states that attempted to compete with the bigger city-states, Athens and Sparta, or in the case of Thebes was a way for Thebes to control Boeotia.

Nonetheless, the principle of federalism—the representation of all the states in a common council to protect local autonomy and provide wider defense—was held, was understood, by Philip and applied in the organization of the League of Corinth; and therefore the League of Corinth in many, many ways conformed to Greek political and diplomatic notions. It had Athenian elements of Panhellenism; it was federally organized; there was an effective koine eirene; it was a brilliant solution. It is really a testimony to Philip's genius that he came up with this solution. Alexander, as we shall see, was temperamentally not as understanding and inclined to run the Greek city-states as just an ordinary commander. But later Macedonian overlords had to take Philip as their model rather than Alexander because of that very, very intense loyalty that every Greek citizen had to his particular city-state.

Even the Roman conquerors, the great Roman magistrates of the Roman Republic, realized the value of this league. In 196 B.C., Titus Quinctius Flamininus proclaimed a version of Philip's league as an exit strategy for the Romans to leave Greece and let it run itself on its own. It didn't work very well because the Romans didn't have anything like Philips acumen in dealing with the Greeks; nonetheless, Philip's league still stood as a model. As the most distant echo of it, I close with the fact that the most depraved and delightful of all early Roman emperors, Nero, in a fit of philhellenism actually proclaimed his own version of the Greek league which essentially meant, "I will tax you too much, and vote me first place in all musical contests." That is the last record we have of this notion of a Hellenic League going back to Philip.

# Alexander, Heir Apparent
## Lecture 9

From the start, Alexander was devoted to the heroes of Greece, the heroes of his ancestors, what motivated his career was ... a *pothos*, a longing, a yearning, a desire to emulate his ancestors and to exceed them.

Alexander the Great, the son of Philip II and **Olympias**, was born in 356 B.C., and later accounts report portends of his future greatness. Both parents were brilliant, passionate, and ambitious whose tempestuous marriage divided the court at Pella into scheming factions. Yet, Philip loved his son, and trained Alexander to succeed to the Macedonian throne. Philip sought out the finest tutors, most notably the Greek philosopher, **Aristotle**.

For three years at Mieza, Aristotle instructed Alexander and his companions–Hephaestion, Leonnatus, Lysimachus, and Ptolemy–destined to be generals and kings. From Aristotle, Alexander learned his Homer and Hellenic aesthetics, but he remained a Macedonian king who never accepted the distinction of Greeks and barbarians.

Plutarch reports how Philip took pride in his son's accomplishments such as Alexander's taming of the stead Bucephalus, and predicted his son's greatness. Yet, Alexander had ambivalent feeling towards his father, and later in life he denied his paternity in favor of descent from Zeus. Olympias clashed with her husband Philip. Alexander was devoted to his mother who schemed against Philip, for she rightly preferred her son over her husband as king. In 337 Philip divorced and exiled Olympias. Relations between Alexander and Philip deteriorated after Philip married **Cleopatra Eurydice**, niece of Attalus, one of the Macedonian generals.

At the ceremony of reconciliation of father and son in Aegeae, Philip was struck down by an assassin, **Pausanias**, reportedly for a private grievance. Olympias returned to Pella to dispose of her rival queen. Alexander, age 21, ascended the throne, determined to succeed to his father's legacy, and to perform the heroic deeds of a new Achilles. ■

**Aristotle** (386–322 B.C.): Philosopher and scientist. He tutored Alexander the Great in 343–341 B.C., and thereafter retained a friendship with his brilliant student.

**Cleopatra Eurydice** (d. 336 B.C.): Niece of Attalus, married Philip II in 337 B.C. linking Philip to the powerful Macedonian house.

**Olympias** (c. 378–316 B.C.): Married to Philip II and mother of Alexander the Great. She alienated most Macedonians by her violent temper, erratic political intrigues, and barbaric ways.

**Pausanias** (c. 64–120 A.D.): Geographer and local historian; wrote a Description of Greece in 10 books with a wealth of information about local shrines, cults, and traditions of the Greek world.

## Suggested Reading

Andronikos, *Vergina: The Royal Tombs.*

Bosworth, *Alexander and the East.*

Carney, *Olympias, Mother of Alexander the Great.*

Cawkwell, *Philip of Macedon.*

Hammond and Griffith, *A History of Macedonia.*

Macurdy, *Hellenistic Queens.*

Pomeroy, *Women in Hellenistic Egypt.*

Worthington, *Philip II of Macedonia.*

Yalouris, Rhomiopoulou, and Andronikos, *The Search for Alexander.*

1. How did Philip II and Olympias influence Alexander the Great? How did Alexander view his parents, and his future role as King of Macedon?

2. In what ways was Alexander a Greek in language and culture? How was his a Macedonian king? In what ways was Alexander even more menacing to the Greeks than Philip II?

3. How did heroic ideals motivate Alexander? How did he view his role as a king and commander in 336 B.C.? How did Alexander see himself as the new Achilles?

4. Was there a plot to assassinate Philip II or did Pausanias act as the lone assassin? How did Philip's sudden death put the Macedonian kingdom in jeopardy?

# Alexander, Heir Apparent
## Lecture 9—Transcript

In this lecture, I plan to bring onto the stage Alexander the Great himself as the heir apparent of Philip II and his principal queen Olympias. This lecture requires us to look at the parents of Alexander; the type of life that existed at the court of Pella, which in some ways was very Hellenic and in other ways it was very traditionally Macedonian; and then we'll also deal with the whole ambiguous relationship that Alexander apparently had with his father, his devotion to his mother, and how both parents really shaped and motivated Alexander. Both of them inculcated Alexander with a sense of destiny, with a sense of position as the King of Macedon. Finally, we'll conclude with the very lurid politics that put Alexander the Great on the throne, and is still the subject of controversy whether Alexander was somehow involved in the death of his father.

In the last lecture, I had concluded with Philip of Macedon at the height of his power. In the summer of 337 B.C., Philip had very good reasons to be congratulating himself: He had brought the Greek cities under his control, and he was beginning to look east towards an expedition against Persia. Early in the next year, in 336 B.C., Macedonian forces actually crossed over into Asia Minor—they crossed the Hellespont under the command of Parmenio—and began to prepare a bridgehead for the Macedonian invasion. Philip had every intention of leading this expedition, and his son Alexander—at the time who was probably about 20 years of age, maybe 21 years of age; we're still a little uncertain exactly when Alexander's birthday was because it was subject to a lot of legend—was to accompany him; and what happened is Philip never lead that expedition. He was cut down by an assassin man, a man named Pausanias of Orestis, who killed Philip reputedly for a personal grievance; and Alexander suddenly found himself in charge of the Macedonian kingdom, the Hellenic alliance, and heir to the expedition against Persia.

This was an unexpected turn of events; and it was to the credit of Philip that the kingdom of Macedon did not fragment, that Philip's death did not lead to the disorder typical of previous Macedonian kings in which the position was very personal. Philip had built the types of institutions—a committed army, court, administrators—that would ensure the continuity of the kingdom. But his greatest gift was his son, Alexander, his heir; and Philip always regarded Alexander as really his only true heir, even though Philip had seven wives and a number of different children and more different extracurricular activities than one would care to enumerate. Nonetheless, his son proved to be one of the greatest conquerors of all time, and arguably the greatest general of all time.

Let us take a look at Alexander and how he was prepared for this position that he assumed that either age 20 or 21. He very much was a product of both of his parents. Philip II of Macedon and Olympias were both clearly brilliant individuals. They were also extremely passionate, they both could be a bit erratic and vindictive, and one could even argue that each was genius and at the same time a bit crazy. Philip himself had never expected to get to the throne; he was the third son of King Amyntas III who died in 369 B.C., and he was preceded by his two older brothers. When Philip came to the throne at around age 24 or 25, he was in effect the backup heir. That had a profound influence on Philip in terms of surviving the very, very rough court politics at Pella; he had that time in Thebes as a political hostage; and so when Philip came to the throne he was very well aware of the need to secure his dynasty, and he conducted a number of different marriages in his career. These marriages were often political in nature; and as I've mentioned in passing, the Macedonian kings, the Argead family, did practice polygamy. This was a state policy; this was typical of Macedonian kings; it persisted into the Hellenistic age. Members of the nobility, we suspect, may have done the same if it afforded them advantages. This type of marriage arrangement was not what was practiced by Greeks, especially Greek aristocratic families where the marriage was between a man and woman of a great family; they were equals; the lower classes apparently were monogamous. This polygamy characterized the Macedonian kings as kings, at least in the eyes of the Greeks.

As I said, the marriages were dynastic; and when he came to the throne, Philip quickly concluded several marriages. One was to a leading aristocratic woman of Macedon, it cemented relations with the great families of Western Macedon, her name was Phila; another one was an Illyrian princess, Audata, who was actually a relative of Bardylis who was the political opponent of Philip, the Illyrian king who had killed his brother. In the course of his interventions in Thessaly he acquired two different Thessalian wives, both of them from leading aristocratic families. By the first of these, Philinna, he had a son called Arrhidaeus, the later Philip Arrhidaeus, a half-brother of Alexander the Great; by the second Thessalian wife he had a daughter named Thessalonice, which means essentially "victory of Thessaly." There was another Getic princess—that is, a woman from Thrace—her name is rendered in Greek as Medea; we're not sure exactly what her name was in Illyrian or Getic. But without a doubt, the principal wife—and these five wives I've mentioned were all political marriages; there were some children from them—was a woman named Olympias.

Philip and Olympias met probably in 357 B.C. at the Great Mysteries held on the island of Samothrace in the northern Aegean. These were ancient mysteries dedicated to the Greek gods; we know that Olympias herself was a devotee of Dionysus, the god of wine and enthusiasm. According to Plutarch and some of the anecdotes he reports, she was really good at getting involved in these Bacchic dances, she had a really wild nature, and she kept tame snakes that tended to frighten the spectators; and that was just part of the cult. She was the daughter of King Neoptolemus of Epirus. Epirus is essentially northwest Greece; the Epirotes were a Greek people who had never coalesced into city-states and were looked upon by their Greek cousins as really a bit retarded politically, they looked like something out of Homer. But Neoptolemus—and it's the same name of the son of Achilles to avenge his father Achilles in the later accounts after the Iliad—absolutely was Greek by lineage, there was no doubt; Olympias was a direct descendent of Achilles, and she never let Philip forget it and she always reminded her son Alexander.

She was clearly regarded as a queen of great bearing. She was a Greek speaker; she was of Greek ancestry; she was not a Thessalian or Macedonian aristocrat; she was not a barbarian princess; she was the real queen, and her two children—Alexander, born in 356 B.C., and about a year later his sister Cleopatra—both of them were clearly the principal line of the Argead house, and Philip never had any doubt that Alexander was his true heir. Arrhidaeus, the only other legitimate son of Philip, had been born about a year earlier, and he turns out to apparently be some kind of halfwit. The story put out is that Olympias actually fed Arrhidaeus poisoned mushrooms so he never developed mentally; we don't think that story is true, but it ought to be, and certainly Olympias would like us to believe it. She always protected the interests of her son against any potential rival. There were other potential heirs to the Macedonian throne, but not among the children of Philip; these were other collateral lines we'll get to.

Olympias and Philip, when they met, it was a tempestuous love match by all accounts. The two of them were taken with each other; they were married in less than a year. It was an important political alliance, but it also—at least in its initial stage—was a love match, and then they fell out of love and became quite vindictive to each other. The only comparable marriage I can come up with—and at this point Philip was in his late 20s and Olympias was probably towards her mid-20s—would probably be Henry II and Eleanor of Aquitaine; it really was the marriage of the 4th century B.C. The relationship between Philip and Olympias cooled very early on. Philip was no novice to various sensual exploits, but Olympias keeping pet snakes in the bed caused Philips order to cool according to Plutarch. There were other reasons why they clashed: Olympias didn't tolerate well Philip's extracurricular activities—and that's not the political marriages, but all sorts of other activities that Philip conducted outside the marriage—there was the all-night drinking parties with the nobility; but above all, Olympias understood that her position at court would improve when her son would come to the throne in his own right. As in many Mediterranean societies—and in this regard, the Macedonians were very Mediterranean—a Queen Mother always had a far greater power over her son that she did over her husband, particularly if that husband was such a dramatic and able figure with very great ambitions of his own and with other wives and other potential heirs. From the start, Olympias became increasingly disenchanted with her husband; she became, in time, disdainful and even vindictive in the number of ways; and there were repeated clashes—ugly clashes—that Alexander must've experienced early in his life up until he was 13 when he was reared at court.

Nonetheless, Olympias was very, very important in forming Alexander for several reasons. She certainly was, up until age 12 or 13, in charge of Alexander's education; she picked the tutors, and this was a traditional role that Macedonian queens performed. We know of the earliest tutor, a fellow named Leonidas—the same name as the famous Spartan king who fell at Thermopylae—he was a taskmaster in many ways and imposed a very, very strict diet and exercise regimen on Alexander, and also constantly lectured Alexander about being frugal. There's an incident reported in Plutarch that this tutor really chided Alexander for putting too much incense on the altar, which was a burnt offering to the gods. He reminded Alexander that he really didn't have the money to do this; Macedon was a relatively small and poor kingdom. Later in life when Alexander conquered the world and got all of his incense captured from the Persians, he sent a huge consignment back to that tutor to remind him, "Now I can do it; I've done my job, I've conquered the world; here, have some incense on me." It's a marvelous anecdote that is typical of the types of stories that were associated with Alexander. Leonidas was, however, Olympias's choice.

She had a profound influence on Alexander also because Philip was so often campaigning. He was a restless king; he was always fighting the northern borders engaged in diplomacy with the Greeks; and Alexander grew up devoted to his mother. There is no doubt from the sources that she was his confidant in many ways; he apparently wrote repeated letters to her in Macedon. He had no illusions about her ambitions politically, but he was devoted to her, and he really paid attention to the various stories that Olympias put out later on. Apparently, according to some sources in Plutarch, Alexander was told by Olympias, "By the way, dear, it wasn't Philip who impregnated me; it was that serpent who was really Zeus who came to me." Then there are other stories that it was the ex-Pharaoh of Egypt and everything. But somehow in these disputes between Olympias and Philip as Alexander was growing up, this notion that Alexander had some kind of divine parentage, he was linked to Zeus, came out in the really complicated mind games played between Olympias and Philip over who would control that son.

Nonetheless, Philip himself was an absolutely devoted father and really gave the best education he could to his son. By age 13, as Alexander was coming of age, he took him out of the charge of Olympias and entrusted him to a man who was recommended to him for various contacts in the Greek world, a fellow named Aristotle, who turns out to be the great philosopher. Aristotle spent three years with Alexander at a Macedonian retreat known as Mieza (it's essentially a summer retreat from the court at Pella) where Alexander and a group of boyhood friends, many of them coming from the leading families of the Macedon—they were the sons very often of the great noble families of Western Macedon or other important families, these included men such as Ptolemy, the future king of Egypt; Hephaestion, the closest of Alexander's friends; Leonnatus, who saves Alexander's life in India; and all of these men later became bodyguards to Alexander, they ended up becoming major generals, and some of them became kings after Alexander—they were all reared together and trained by Aristotle, and it must of been a remarkably powerful intellectual experience; a really heady experience to grow up with such extraordinary people as your playmates and being taught by a man who turned out to be the greatest successor to Plato's philosophical system and one of the great thinkers in the Western tradition.

Furthermore, there are anecdotes that are told about Alexander with two notions in mind: One was to stress the devotion of the father to son; others were to show the precocious nature of Alexander which Philip recognized, and despite the sort of ambivalent feelings Alexander might've had, Philip never had a doubt that his son was extraordinary and would succeed to him. I take two of those anecdotes out of Plutarch, and really Plutarch's Life of Alexander is a marvelous reservoir of different types of stories that came down through different traditions. I started this course stressing the fact that Plutarch as a biographer was interested in the character and personality of Alexander rather than the great deeds, and we really owe it to him that Alexander, and to some extent Philip and Olympias, come alive as individuals because of that biography.

One of the most impressive anecdotes that comes down to us is the anecdote associated with Alexander taming the horse Bucephalus. This is a favorite theme in Western art and literature. Alexander was an adolescent at the time; Philip had paid enormous sum for this charger, this force Bucephalus that had distinct markings, and no one could break the horse, the horse unrideable. On the other hand, Alexander, observing the efforts of various trainers to ride that horse, understood that the horse was essentially skittish and afraid of its own shadow. He then offered himself as the man to break the horse. Everyone was concerned; he was, after all, crown prince, he was really the only son to follow Philip, the halfwit didn't count. Nonetheless,

Philip allowed it to be done; Alexander turned the horse away from the sun and positioned the horse so he could not see his shadow. He mounted the horse, immediately leapt on it—which is quite a feat because they didn't have stirrups in the ancient world—and broke the horse immediately and rode him. Bucephalus becomes the charger of Alexander and his battles in Asia, and when the horse dies in India shortly after the Battle of Hydaspes, he builds the city in honor of the horse, Bucephala. Philip was overjoyed; it showed his son's brilliance as well as his courage and his resourcefulness; and Philip's comment apparently after this was, "My son, when you grow up you will have to find greater kingdoms because Macedon will not hold you." Philip already saw in his son that genius that would lead him to conquer the Persian Empire and, in effect, the ancient world.

There are several other stories, I think, that are telling, and it's worth bringing in: There is a story, associated apparently when Alexander was about the same age—somewhere between 12 and 15—that reports came in of one of Philip's great victories. Alexander's response to the news was, "If Philip [and he referred to him as "Philip," not "my father"] continues to win these victories, there will be nothing left for me." This certainly shows the sort of attitude that Olympias would approve of. There is a series of incidents and anecdotes that come down to us that lead us to suspect that from age 15 on, when Alexander was taken out of the charge of Aristotle and introduced in effect into public life, that Alexander was always very, very uneasy that he might be replaced as the crown prince, and undoubtedly Olympias fed these notions all the time.

Alexander was such a remarkable figure that later generations—or maybe within even Alexander's own generation—created all sorts of omens and portents that Alexander was destined to greatness. The favorite one I always like to talk about is either on July 20 or July 21, 356 B.C., the year of Alexander's birth, a fellow named Herostratus—who's essentially the first pyromaniac known in history—burned down the temple of Artemis at Ephesus, the great Artemisium, one of the Seven Wonders of the ancient world. When he was questioned by the city fathers, "Why did you do it," he said, "Because it's there and I like to see things burn." I think we can judge the personal motive there. On the other hand, the story was put out that the reason why the fire took place is because Artemis was away in Pella making sure that Alexander would be born. Alexander liked that kind of story; it's the sort of story Olympias might have approved of. There are other stories. At the time of the birth, Philip gained three important messages: One was the birth of his son, the most important; a victory by his general, Parmenio; and his horse took first place in the Olympic Games. These stories are all associated with the birth; they're augmented and elaborated by later accounts.

At age 15, when Alexander was coming of age, there are again two other incidents that are reported that show his precociousness. One was a series of Persian envoys who arrived, and the suspicion was these fellows were negotiating with Philip at this point—somewhere around 341–342 B.C.—because they're afraid that Philip had designs on the Persian Empire and he had received Persian exiles at court. Philip was not available, only Alexander with his regent Antipater—the senior general that essentially took Philip's place while Philip was on campaign—and according to the accounts, and one wonders what the official report was back at Suza, I would always reconstruct it this way: These Persian envoys came into the court of Pella and were met by this 14- or 15-year-old boy. The immediate reaction to him was, "Where's King Philip?" He said, "My father isn't here, but let me ask you some questions." They were absolutely amazed at Alexander's knowledge of the size of the Persian Empire, the roads and everything; little did they know that five years later he would be overrunning their empire. It's always a marvelous story prefiguring the greatness that was to come.

The other side of that aspect of Alexander inquiring with the Persian envoys is shortly afterwards, on his own, probably at age 15, he commanded a Macedonian army, defeated a Balkan tribe known as the Maedi, and founded a city named Alexandropolis ("City of Alexander"); that's the sort of things kings should do. By the time Alexander is fighting at the Battle of Chaeronea at age 15, he had been groomed for this position of king of Macedon; and whether these anecdotes are elaborated, augmented, true, or invented, they all point to a remarkable side of this young prince. He was without a doubt precocious to his own generation and to later generations as well.

This gets us into the question of what inspired and motivated Alexander the Great. He saw himself as the descendent of Heracles on his father's side—that is, the Roman Hercules—and Achilles on his mother's side. Both were great heroes, perhaps the greatest figures recognized in the Greek world; in the case of Heracles, he eventually was elevated to join the gods at his death, he was an apotheosis (a point we'll come back to). Unlike his father Philip, he did not have much exposure to Greek political notions. Despite the education of Aristotle, he never accepted Aristotle's distinction of Hellenes versus barbarians, as we shall see when Alexander's in Asia and when it is politically opportune and appropriate he will marry Persian or at least Iranian women of high rank as his queens because that's what Macedonian kings do; they have to marry the aristocracy of noble defeated foes, something no Greek would ever consider. He saw his Persian subjects—once he had conquered Persia—especially the aristocrats as worthy members at court, people that he must pay attention to, ennoble, and make use of. Again, he had not bought the Greek political notions that Greeks are unique because they live in a polis and are distinct from barbarians.

In other ways, he was completely a Greek aristocrat: He carried his own version of Homer around, annotated (he had personal reasons for that, it was annotated by Aristotle); he saw himself as a Greek in his language, he spoke Attic Greek usually, he did know Macedonian; in his aesthetics, in his choice of literature, he was thoroughly a Greek aristocrat, he undoubtedly knew his Homer well, he had read widely; and above all, he encouraged his depiction by various artists, notably the artist Lysippus. Lysippus apparently really captured the portrait of Alexander very well; there are some who would argue that the great mosaic in the archaeological museum at Naples found in Pompeii is based on an original painting that goes back Lysippus. It depicts Alexander—who was not particularly tall in height and had light brownish hair and a ruddy complexion but was powerfully built, absolutely heroic and brave—and if anyone has ever seen that mosaic, it's really a stunning piece, and it is probably our best representation of what Alexander looked like; we do have statue heads, coin types, and other things, but that seems to go back to an original.

From the start, therefore, Alexander was devoted to the heroes of Greece, the heroes of his ancestors, and what really motivated him in his career to carry out the great conquests was not a Panhellenic war, not even imperialism to expand the Macedonian monarchy or the types of motives that would be assigned in a modern nation-state, it's what Arrian and Plutarch speak of repeatedly: a pothos, a longing, a yearning, a desire to emulate his ancestors and to exceed them. Alexander, throughout his career, was constantly attempting to approach Achilles and Heracles; later on, in Central Asia, he took Dionysus as another example (there's a reason for that we'll get to); but as one goes through the expedition there are certain instances where Alex was directly imitating Homer, or at least Achilles. For instance at Ilium—that is the site of ancient Troy—he picked up what apparently is a tourist item, which is the shield of Athena that he carried through Asia; he propitiated the spirits of King Priam and the Trojan royal family because they had been killed, they had been defeated, by his ancestor Neoptolemus, the son of Achilles. When he captured the city of Gaza, the Persian governor-general there, a fellow named Batis, the body was strapped to a chariot and dragged around the city in imitation of Achilles's treatment of the body of Hector in the Iliad; so we have some of these direct imitations. But it went much deeper than that: It was the driving force behind all of Alexander's actions; it was also the driving force that led Alexander to conclude by his lifetime that by his great and glorious deeds he would enter the company of the gods, and that, of course, would run him into trouble with both his Macedonians and then, above all, with his Greek allies.

This young prince, who by age 18 was clearly marked as the heir apparent to Philip of Macedon, had ambivalent feelings towards his father, and this is brought out by two incidents that fed into the assassination of Philip and eventually the succession of Alexander. At one point, as Philip was preparing for his expedition to Persia, there was an arrangement with one of the Carian dynasts—a fellow named Pixadorus, a brother of Mausolus—and Philip offered Arrhidaeus to a daughter of Pixadorus as a political marriage. Alexander's friends heard of this and reported it to Alex. Alex immediately took this as a slight—what is his father doing; he's marrying his half-brother off, the halfwit—Alexander was not yet married, was Philip going to put him aside? Alexander at his own initiative sent invitation to the Carian dynasts and offered himself as the groom to this Carian princess. Philip was enraged; he took Alexander aside and said, "Look, this is a minor small-town dynast, marrying Arrhidaeus is just a political move. This doesn't count; I'm saving you for greater things. By the way, some of your friends are going to be exiled because they gave you bad advice." Alexander was fuming over this, because he took it as a slight; and it goes to show how sensitive he was about it.

In 337 B.C. (our best guess), Philip had finally had it with Olympias. He was getting ready for his expedition in Asia; he settled all the affairs in Greece; and he repudiated Olympias. We don't know if there was a formal divorce, but Olympias went home to Epirus and she was at the court of her brother, a fellow also known as Alexander, Alexander of Epirus. Alexander the Great was very upset about this; and furthermore, Philip took a seventh and last wife, and this wife was named Cleopatra, sometimes Cleopatra Eurydice, she was a high noble Macedonian lady. Her uncle was Attalus, one of the leading generals a Macedonian army who was a protégé and friend of Parmenio, and the marriage clearly was an intention to set up an alternate line to the royal house. Philip was practical—he was about 47 at the time, Cleopatra was in her mid-20s—they would have children; there would be alternate heirs in the event that Alex and Phil got killed in Asia.

Alexander was upset by the whole thing, and at the marriage celebrations where there was the usual heavy drinking, Attalus got up and toasted Philip and said, "To the health of the king and his wife, and to their legitimate children." Alexander, at the other end of the table—who was spoiling for a fight all day—got up and said, "Then, sir, I believe you regard me as a bastard." Philip was enraged that Alexander had challenged Attalus; he got up, he called for his spear—he was quite drunk—and he stumbled, because Philip had suffered a very severe wound in one of his legs and he was a bit lame, he fell on the floor, and Alexander, in contempt, said, "Here, Macedonians, is the man who will lead you to Asia, yet he cannot get from one end of the table to the next." Alexander's friends did him a great service and got him out of the hall and he went into exile for awhile, and it took some months before Alexander was reconciled.

There was a big reconciliation at Aegae—Vergina, where the great tombs have been found—and this occurred apparently late summer or early autumn of 336 B.C. Philip was marching to the theater with Alex on one side and Alexander of Epirus of the other—that is, Olympias's brother—and a man came through the crowd, Pausanias of Orestis, put a dagger in Phil, and ran. He was cut down; no questions were asked. There have been numerous accounts and a lot more speculation on what motivated this assassin. Some have attributed it to Olympias, other to the Persian, some would say Demosthenes; but many suspect—some scholars suspect—that Alexander had a hand in it to get rid of his father. An author such as Tarn would say, "No, that is not the way Alexander acted"; modern scholars who have a diabolical Alexander said, "Of course he did, this is typical, this is what goes on." The case is really nolo contendere, and I doubt that Alexander really had anything in it involved in this conspiracy. Pausanias of Orestis was apparently a lone assassin. He had suffered a humiliation at the hands of Attalus; actually Attalus was angry—that is, the uncle of Philip's last wife—and actually turned Pausanias, the assassin, over to the stable boys who had their way with him. Philip would not restore Pausanias's honor—and this is the sort of stuff that went on at Pella all the time—and Pausanias decided to go at him with the dagger.

In any event, it was unexpected; Alexander suddenly found himself as king; Olympias was delighted; Cleopatra Eurydice, of course, disappeared with her children; and there were the executions of a few individuals who were possible heirs to Phil but no grand reprisals. In fact, the event came very unexpectedly and put Alexander in some ways in jeopardy. The Greeks cheered as soon as the news came back of Philip's death: The monster is dead. Demosthenes held sacrifices to Zeus for their sense of freedom. Little did they know that Philip left not only a great kingdom but an even greater heir; and Alexander, within 18 months, would secure that legacy and be marching off to Asia.

# Securing the Inheritance, 336–335 B.C.
## Lecture 10

> Alexander waged a remarkable set of campaigns and pursued some very fancy diplomacy to bring the Balkan regions, as well as the Greek city-states, under his control. ... an extraordinary achievement by the young king—20 or perhaps 21 years of age.

With the assassination of Philip II in 336 B.C., Alexander faced possible civil war in Macedon and disturbances on the northern frontiers among Thracians, Paeonians, and Illyrians. Between 336 and 335 B.C., Alexander waged a remarkabel set of campaigns and pursued some very fancy fiplomacy to bring the Balkan regions as well as the Greek city-states under his control.

In Athens, Demosthenes called for a rising against the hated Macedonian overlord in the name of "freedom of the Greeks." Parmenio urged caution, and so spoke for Philip's veteran officers, but Alexander, age 20, had confidence in his destiny, and in the Macedonian army. At Pella, Alexander ordered the execution of his cousin Amyntas, a possible rival, and members of the family of Attalus.

In 336 B.C., Alexander awed the Thessalians into electing him *tagos* of their league, and then entered central Greece to be elected general of the League of Corinth. In spring of the next year 335 B.C., Alexander conducted two campaigns in a single season to chastise Thracians and Illyrians—an ambitious strategy never attempted by Philip.

In these Balkan campaigns Alexander demonstrated a genius in swift strategic movement and logistics as well as mastery in small wars, sieges, and guerrilla operations. Thebes and Athens rebelled on rumors of Alexander's death in Illyria. Alexander descended upon Thebes and savagely sacked the city, enslaving 30,000 survivors. The Athenians, once again, exiled Demosthenes and his associates, and offered their navy for the impending invasion of Asia.

In less than two years, Alexander secured his political inheritance, and the cooperation of the resentful Greeks in the Panhellenic war. His success was a testimony to his own audacious genius, and to the institutions forged by his father Philip II. ∎

## Suggested Reading

Bosworth, *Conquest and Empire.*

Engels, *Alexander the Great and the Logistics of the Macedonian Army.*

Fuller, *The Generalship of Alexander the Great.*

Heckel, *The Conquest of Alexander the Great.*

―――, *The Marshals of Alexander's Empire.*

Parke, *Greek Mercenary Soldiers From the Earliest Times to the Battle of Ipsus.*

## Questions to Consider

1. Why did the Macedonian kingdom not lapse into political anarchy after the murder of Philip II? Why was Alexander correct in his determination to assert his rule in the Balkans and Greece?

2. How did Alexander view the subject peoples and lands in the Balkans?

3. In his campaigns in 335 B.C. how much did Alexander owe to his veteran officers and men, and how much to his own genius? What do these campaigns reveal about Alexander as a great commander?

4. Why did the Greeks fail to shake off Macedonian rule during 336–335 B.C.? What were the rivalries among Athens, Thebes, and Sparta? How did the lesser Greek states view Alexander?

**5.** What do the anecdotes reported by Plutarch reveal about Alexander's attitudes to the Greeks? In what ways was Alexander a Hellene? And in what ways was he a Macedonian king, and so a barbarian to the Greeks?

# Securing the Inheritance, 336–335 B.C.
## Lecture 10—Transcript

In this lecture, I plan to deal with how Alexander the Great secured the political legacy left by his father, Philip of Macedon. Between 336 and 335 B.C., Alexander waged a remarkable set of campaigns and pursued some very fancy diplomacy to bring the Balkan regions, as well as the Greek city-states, under his control. This was an extraordinary achievement by the young king; at the time of his father's death he was either 20 or perhaps 21 years of age, and the sudden death of Philip ordinarily, at least in previous Macedonian history, should have signaled civil wars, challenges from various pretenders, there were several men who could have challenged Alexander for the throne of Macedon, and certainly was a potential signal to the Greek city-states to repudiate the League of Corinth, not to elect Alexander as the new commander-in-chief (strategos autokrator) and essentially to return to their independence before the settlements of Philip back in 337 B.C. The fact that this did not happen—that the kingdom did not fragment, that Alexander managed to secure the kingdom quickly as well as bring the Balkan peoples under control, and to have himself elected commander of the Hellenic League is a testimony to not only Philip's work—Philip had created this new kingdom with its institutions—but also the precocious genius of Alexander himself.

In 336 B.C., soon after his father's assassination, Alexander really did confront a crisis; and it's difficult for us to appreciate how much the Macedonian monarchy was still very largely personal. The army would follow a king who had the charisma and the ability to win victories that proved the favor of the gods, and Alexander had to do this in order to make his rule stick with the Macedonians. This included the nobility, who formed the Companion cavalry; the elite hypaspists—that is, the guard of the king—as well as the various *taxeis*, or regiments of the phalanx, that represented the various regions of the greater Macedonian kingdom. Furthermore, Alexander had to make his rule stick with the various subject peoples in the Balkans, to the north different Illyrian tribes, to the east the various Thracians; his mother could return from exile in Epirus and there was no danger there because his uncle Alexander of Epirus was an ally and he knew he could count on the Epiro king. That was about the only ally that was secured to him.

To the south, he had to collect all of the titles and positions that Philip had gathered in running the Greek league, notably he had to be elected head of the Thessalian League; he had to make his will known to the Greek city-states said that the synedrion would elect him commander of the Greek forces. This was a tall order, and Antipater—who was, in effect, Alexander's senior adviser at the time—advised caution; that Alexander secure the kingdom, perhaps beat up some Thracians, but take it slowly, because there would be no way that this young king could succeed to the splendid heritage of his father that had taken over 20 years for Philip to build. Alexander did not take this advice. He, from the start, knew that destiny was on his side, that he had the ability to win victories; and a remarkable aspect about Alexander's generalship is we don't see in his career—and we have a pretty good account of his campaigns from Arrian and the other sources—we don't see an Alexander an evolution in generalship the way we do with some commanders; I think of someone like Frederick the Great of Prussia, whose first victory was actually won by his generals because Fritz was driven off the battlefield by his opponents. Alexander from the start seemed to be able to wage sieges, small wars—that is, guerrilla operations—set piece battles, hard marching campaigns; to be sure, he had inherited a superb army from his father, but he achieved victories and deeds with that army that I don't think Philip ever had in his wildest dreams. He had the extreme confidence in his ability to master the battlefield, to impose his will on the battlefield, by understanding the terrain and the intentions of his opponents and then countering it. He really was truly an exceptional commander, and at age 20–21 he already had these abilities.

There were some executions; to us it would seem very nasty, but this was probably typical politics at the Macedonian court. Two brothers were arrested; they were members of the Lyncestian house—that is, one of the royal families of western Macedon—their names were Attalus and Amyntas; they were very well-known; they were kept in custody until 330 B.C. Attalus, the uncle of Philip's last wife, of course was suspect; he was recalled from Asia, and later implicated in a plot and executed. Finally, there was Alexander's first cousin, named Amyntas—again, a very common name in Macedon—he had been married to one of the daughters of Philip by the Illyrian princess and he was arrested on grounds of complicity and executed. The two executions, both of them were on treason, but one of them was a potential heir, the other was the uncle of the rival queen, Cleopatra—she was done away with apparently by Olympias—but that was it, there was no major purge; and those historians who attempt to see Alexander as murdering his father and then clearing Macedon of all these people have really overstated the case. Many of the generals who would serve with Alexander in the first four years of the Asian expedition were his father's generals, above all Parmenio who proved to be the second-in-command, an able and very loyal second-in-command in the Asian expedition. Alexander, just as his father, was quite pragmatic: His job was to inspire his nobles and get the best out of them; and those people arrested and executed were either actually involved in the plot or clearly were much too close to the throne that they would be potential threats.

That left Alexander two areas to bring under control; there was no question that the Macedonians acclaimed him king immediately. The first is the Balkan regions. These were areas that had been brought into the greater Macedonian kingdom during Philip's reign. These people were non-Greek, non-Macedonians; they were reputed to be excellent warlike races; they loved the Thracians. Thracians were marvelous light infantries, they were very, very tall by Greek standards, they probably stood 5'10" with flaming red hair and would scare anyone off the battlefield. There were also mountain peoples such as the Agrianians, excellent javelin men; they became one of Alexander's favorite units in Asia. They were light-arm skirmishing forces; they were everywhere with Alexander. There were Illyrian and Thracian horsemen. The military potential of these regions was important: 25 percent of the army taken to Asia came from these Balkan peoples. Furthermore, there was a distant frontier, the lower Danube, which was known to Alexander. His thoughts were to push the frontier to the Danube, to secure that northern and northwestern frontier from barbarian peoples, because he planned to depart from Asia and it was necessary to impress these peoples with the majesty of the Macedonian king, the son of Philip II.

Then there was the matter of the Greeks, and I think the best way to handle this problem is to first look at the Balkan peoples and then look at the Greeks in this two-year period. In the winter of 336–335 B.C., Alexander received reports that the tribes in the Balkans were restive; there were a danger of major rebellions in Thrace and among the Illyrians. The Thracians occupied the region between the Rhodope Mountains today—which would be known as the Haemus Mountains to the ancients—that's the great mountain range that essentially bisects Bulgaria today east-west and the North Aegean shore. The Illyrians were the regions to the west and the northwest of upper Macedon. Both of these peoples had cause to make common alliance—they had traditionally raided Macedonian borders whenever method a Macedonian king had died—and none of the various princes or rulers among these tribal peoples were really rather eager to accept Alexander as their lord; they had been beaten into submission by Philip, and this was now the signal to become independent.

Early in 335 B.C., Alexander decided to target the Thracians first—it was easier to get to them, the military highways were there—and he, however, planned not only to chastise the Thracians, but as soon as he had done that to turn around and defeat the Illyrians. This is very ambitious. In looking at his father's career, Philip had never waged a campaign against Thracians and Illyrians in the same season, they were always separate campaigns; Alexander does them both in a single year, in the year 335. The army marched along the various military highways to the city of Philippopolis, which is the Macedonian colony in Thrace, and then pressed north; and the speed of this advance essentially stunned many of the Thracian tribes into submission. One king, named Syrmos of the Triballians, which is a sub-branch of the Thracian peoples—and he dwelled in the mountain zones and the northern slopes of the Rhodope or Haemus Mountains stretching to the Danube—refused submission, and he occupied the passes of the the Haemus range; and probably at the modern pass of the Shipka Pass, he prepared to oppose Alexander.

What he did is what's typical in this type of mountain warfare: The various Triballians had assembled and they loaded up these carts with huge amounts of boulders, and they were going to roll these carts down on the Macedonian army and then attack; it sound like something out of the northwest frontier from India and Lord Roberts's march from Kandahar to Kabul. Alexander saw this immediately; he ordered his infantry to form up in what is known as a testudo—that is a tortoise formation; it comes from a Roman word—where they lock their shields, and they advanced and positioned themselves so as the carts came down apparently they rolled and bounced off this wall of shields and harmlessly fell into the pass, and Alexander immediately attacked with his light-armed infantry and archers and drove off King Syrmos and his Triballians. They took refuge in fortresses in the Danube; Alexander crossed into the Triballian homeland and began to torch the area. Various tribes, again, came and submitted to Alexander; it was a matter of time before he would secure all the submissions because he was attacking at the time when the grain was harvested.

He did, however, confront a threat from across the Danube, and this was from various nomadic peoples known as Getae, distant relatives of the later Dacians; and they rode up along the northern shores of the Danube and made demonstrations, jeering at Alexander's army and challenging him to cross and take them over. Alexander decided to make an example of them—he didn't really need to do so—but what he did was he took a strike force of some 4,000 men including infantry and cavalry; they stuffed their tents and various leather containers with straw and crossed the Danube by swimming across on these improvised sort of vests almost, leather vests filled with air and straw, and took up a position in a wheat field. The next day, when the Getic cavalry came riding down to the river bank and insulted the Macedonian army, they were greeted by artillery fire on the far bank by the Macedonian army that prepared to cross, and on signal Alexander's army popped up out of this wheat field and attacked the Getae in the rear. He probably was outnumbered, but Alexander understood that audacity, stealth, and surprise could win victories. The Getae were essentially chased off; they were chastised. The impression apparently had its effect; that is, the northern frontier was never again threatened by these people during Alexander's reign or even far after Alexander's death. The defeat of these nomadic peoples who were potential allies to the Thracians essentially demoralized the remaining Thracians, King Syrmos himself of the Triballians surrendered shortly afterwards, and Thrace was secured probably in a matter of a couple months. It was an extraordinary campaign of marching, and largely stealth and surprise with very little fighting. Nonetheless, the impression had been made, and Alexander was free to move against the Illyrians.

The Illyrian tribes had concentrated to the west of Macedon at a town called Pelion—we're not quite sure of its location—and Alexander approached this town at rapid speed, forced march, with an army of about 25,000 men. From what we gain from the descriptions, Pelion was in a plain that was ringed by mountains, and Alexander's army came in and drove the main Illyrian force into this fortress. It was commanded, actually, by a grandson of King Bardylis—who was the old opponent of his father, Philip of Macedon—and his name was Cleitus; and there was a relief force of Illyrians coming under another prince called Glaucias. It looked as if Alexander had mistimed his advance, because he drove Cleitus and the main Illyrian force into the fortress and put it under siege. Then the relieving Illyrian forces, or the reinforcements, arrived under Glaucias and they seized the heights, and particularly the crucial pass that led east to Macedon that was the line of supply for Alexander. It looked as if Alexander's army was trapped; it would be difficult to take the fortress. The Illyrians occupying the high points could cut off supplies; and the Illyrians were really quite self-satisfied about this.

Alexander again used a remarkable ruse to get his army out of this predicament; and what he did was he set up a parade in which the Macedonian army performed all sorts of complicated maneuvers marching around in front of the city of Pelion. The Illyrians, both on the walls and the mountains, were absolutely dazed by this; they came down stunned, looking at what was going on—the Macedonian army could do things that these Illyrians couldn't even begin to do—and what he did over the course of several hours was he turned these Illyrians from opponents into spectators. They came down from the mountain apparently to get a good look at this parade and all this armor, the cavalry, and the bodyguard, and they performed different maneuvers in this way and that way; and then he position his forces in such a way that he ordered them to charge. They came barreling at these Illyrians who at first were looking at, "What's happening? They're actually coming at us." They scattered and ran away, and Alexander took his army out of the pass, regrouped and returned several days later and clobbered these guys and defeated them; and the Illyrians submitted. It was a brilliant ruse; it's typical of this type of stealth and audacity that characterizes Alexander. It's these types of tactics—the surprise of the nomadic cavalry on the banks of the Danube; the clever ruse to take the city of Pelion, or at least to get yourself out of a predicament—that will appear again when Alexander is fighting in Central Asia and in India where he has to fight these types of wars of pacification. As I said, he already shows at age 20–21—well, at this point he would be 21 years of age—an extraordinary ability to turn any situation into his advantage.

In disappearing in these regions of Elyria and Thrace, it took them out of the limelight of the Greek world. No sooner had he finished chastising the Illyrians at Pelion, probably sometime in August of 335 B.C., he received news that the city of Thebes had rebelled and that the Greek city-states were moving to put together another general coalition—thank you, Demosthenes—to oppose the Macedonian overlordship. So with the Balkans secure, let's turn to the Greeks next. That requires us to back up a bit chronologically. The revolt that broke out at Thebes in August, 335 B.C., was fed by a rumor that Alexander had been killed fighting the Illyrians. The rebellion of the Thebans was by no means to be unexpected, because at the very start—when Philip was killed sometime in late summer or fall of 336 B.C.—the Greeks had not wanted to accept Alexander as their commander-in-chief. Let's pick up the story of the Greeks and what had happened there.

The news received by the various Greek city-states that Philip was dead caused celebration, at least among the great city-states; as I said, many lesser cities probably saw Philip as their protector. In Athens, for instance, Demosthenes—who had just lost one of his daughters to a premature death—held sacrifices to Zeus and to liberty, threw his house open to an enormous party, celebrated that the monster was dead, and really took no note of Alexander. He saw this as the beginning of eleutheria (freedom) and autonomia (autonomy). Again, there were also dissidents in Thebes. The Spartans no doubt were eager to challenge the Macedonian allies in the Peloponnesus. Above all, the Thessalians, who were vital for their cavalry forces, refused to elect Alexander as the head of their league; and if Alexander could not be elected tagos, or commander of the Thessalian League, which Philip had held since 352 B.C., he really couldn't command any of the Greeks. Alexander, therefore, in the autumn of 336 B.C.—that is, about six months before he waged his Balkan campaigns against the Illyrians and Thracians—moved south to assert himself in the Greek world.

The Thessalians had occupied the key passes near Mount Olympus—and there are three of them—that allowed access from Macedon into Thessaly. Alexander circumvented those blockading forces by sending out his engineers and cutting steps in a track—which is still visible today apparently, and can be traced in some parts—around Mount Olympus. He sent a force at night around the Thessalian forces in the passes, and in the next morning when the Macedonians appeared in the rear, the Thessalians reconsidered their options and decided that maybe it was a good idea to elect Alexander the commander of their league. Without actually any fighting, the Thessalians were immediately brought in line; and this was important: The Thessalian cavalry was almost as good as Macedonian, they were the best cavalry in Greece, they fought as heavy cavalry comparable to the Macedonians as lancers, and it was important to have this force with them. They always served on the left wing of the Macedonian army and they were really very essential for those types of battles of encirclement.

Alexander pressed south through the pass of Thermopylae; he moved so quickly they he took most of the Greeks by surprise. Demosthenes was embarrassed; he decided it might be a good idea to check out of Athens for a while. The Thebans had been talking of rebellion, but as soon as Alexander appeared, that was it; no one would move against the Macedonian army, the memories of Chaeronea were too vivid. Alexander then made his way to Corinth and visited the city of Corinth, probably for the only time of his life as far as we know. At Corinth, he summoned the synedrion—that is, the great federal council—and they unanimously elected him the commander-in-chief of the Hellenic League; that is, strategos autokrator, the position that his father had held. In the late autumn of 336 B.C., Alexander had put himself at the head of all these Greek city-states and announced his intention to carry out the Asian expedition of his father. This is extraordinary; Antipater, Parmenio, all the senior commanders back in Pella would have told Alexander not to attempt this. Nonetheless, legally Alexander was now heir to the political legacy that Philip had built up in Greece.

There are a couple of anecdotes that are very telling about Alexander at this time; they come from Plutarch. One of them is that while Alexander was in the city of Corinth, he happened upon Diogenes—who is a Cynic philosopher, and the Cynic philosophers were those who essentially renounced worldly goods and sought to find fulfillment in oneself—and Diogenes, there were a lot of anecdotes associated with him, he's the man who was remembered for walking around with the oil lamps seeking an honest man. Actually, attempting to do that in Corinth was really quite hopeless; Corinth as the major port town of the Greek world was notorious for its decadence as you would expect, and in St. Paul, if I remember, there's a verb called korinthizomai that means "to behave like a Corinthian"—that is, to be depraved—so you can understand what that city was like. In any event, Alexander wanted to meet this famous philosopher; he goes to Diogenes and Diogenes is living in some slum area of Corinth—in the stories he's living in a barrel or some type of makeshift residence—and he presents himself, "I am Alexander, the son of Philip [not quite yet Great] and what can I do for you as the head of the Greek league." Diogenes was totally unimpressed and said, "Well, young man, could you move a little to the right because you're blocking the sun? I want to sun myself." Alexander obliges him, and Diogenes is quite self-satisfied; and Alexander makes the remark, "If I were not Alexander, I would be Diogenes," which is the greatest compliment Alexander could give to this philosopher who would renounce the world.

The other anecdote was apparently a visit to Delphi, and it would be at this time; and that would be important because he, given his position as head of the Thessalian League, he controlled the religious council that governed Delphi, which was without a doubt the most important shrine in the Greek world. He gets the Pythia to sit on her stool to give an oracle; he wanted her to tell him something about his success, and she's really very reluctant to do this. Eventually Alexander's ready to pull her off her seat and she says, "You are invincible (aniketos)," and Alexander took that as a portent, "I will conquer the Asian world."

Most of the Greeks would have had opportunity, at least the major Greek political figures, to see this young king in 336 B.C.; they would see him again in the next year. They must have already seen the difference between the young king and the father. Philip acted quite differently towards his Greek allies, he was much more sensitive to their notions of autonomy and freedom; Alexander was full of confidence, he was just stunning in how fast he moved that army, but there was clearly a difference. This was a crown prince who did not understand the politics and dynamics of running Greek city-states; and over the course of the next 10 or 11 years, the tensions between Alexander and Greek allies would mount, and in the end, it would be the Greek allies who would be the most difficult subjects of

Alexander to run and would ultimately, I think in some ways, do in the unity of the Macedonian Empire in the Wars of the Successors. For the moment, Alexander returned to Macedon for the winter of 336–335 B.C., and then took off to defeat the Balkan peoples.

I mentioned by going on campaign against Illyrians and Thracians, this was a very audacious move; and the impression Alexander had made among the Greeks the previous autumn was quickly lost. Rumors circulated that Alexander had been killed fighting the Illyrians; witnesses who were produced who gave wonderful stories on what had happened to the young king; and there's a lot of speculation of who was behind this. In any event, Alexander, who had just finished defeating the Illyrians at Pelion, received news that Thebes had rebelled. The Macedonian garrison on the Cadmea was under siege; that the Athenians were moving to form an alliance; that the Spartans might mobilize an army in the Peloponnesus to take back their old allies; all of this information came to him. At an unbelievably record march—and it's still difficult to understand the distances involved because it's hard to figure out the precise distances of where was Pelion located— but within a period of 10 days, he marched his army from somewhere in a rather remote place in Illyria to the suburbs of Thebes. The advance was so stunning that initially the Thebans couldn't believe it was Alexander, the son of Philip.

Alexander promptly put the city under siege; the Thebans fought as best they could; but the Macedonian army was able to break into the city very rapidly. There was a sortie by the Theban army—that is, an attack from the city on the Macedonian armies—and the Macedonian phalangites, the men of the phalanx, drove it back; particularly the battalion or the regiment, if you will, of Perdiccas, later to distinguish himself in Asia. They pursued the Thebans into the city and actually burst into the city. Many of the lesser Greek city-states—the Thespians, Plataeans, the Phocians—actually turned out to join the Macedonians in the sack of the city. Alexander spared no one. The city was brutally sacked; it was apparently leveled to the ground. The only building not damaged was the house of the poet Pindar; after all, Alexander was brought up on Greek literature, and you really shouldn't destroy those sorts of things. Otherwise, the city: He made an example of it. 30,000 units were captured; they were enslaved; they were sold off immediately; and the city was essentially left desolate.

Later in life, when Alexander was in Central Asia, he regretted this (or he claimed to have regretted it). He did promote certain Theban mercenary officers, he allowed the city to be rebuilt, and he also attributed one of his rash actions—that is, essentially the manslaughter, the killing in a drunken rage of Cleitus, one of his commanders in 328 B.C.—to the ire of Dionysus who is the protective god of Thebes, and Alexander had offended Dionysus because in the sack the temples have been destroyed. It was also put out that the synedrion had voted the destruction—we're not sure how that would of been done, one argument is that those Greek city-states that were sending contingents in fighting at Thebes cooperated with Alexander's Macedonians and then they essentially held an impromptu meeting and voted the punishment of Thebes—but whatever the legal niceties, it had its effect: After the stack of Thebes, most Greek city-states realized that if they dared cross this king, there would be consequences. The message was well-learned; there would be an attempt by the Spartans to raise a rebellion against Alexander when he's in Asia, but on the whole the lesson was well learned.

It also was a lesson, however, that never really reconciled the Greeks to Alexander. To them, the sack of Thebes was an active Macedonian barbarism; there were various stories circulated on how unpopular Alexander was while he was in Asia. One of the most favorite stories that would be told is that in the army of the Great King there were more Greeks fighting than in the army of Alexander who represented the Panhellenic cause and that is because many Greek soldiers—mercenaries, officers, including generals from Athens—took service in the Persian army, and after all the Macedonians aren't Greeks, and so they don't count; and he has all these Balkan peoples, and the number of Greeks, really, in Alexander's army was rather small for especially a Panhellenic army. But it underscores the fact that Alexander had gained the acceptance by the Greeks; whether he had won their loyalty was another story, and we will see as the story unfolds that the Greeks do seize the opportunity to rebel after Alexander's death.

Nonetheless, in the summer of 335 B.C., Alexander had secured his inheritance. He had control of the Balkan regions, the kingdom of Macedon, all of the Greek league, and he was now prepared to invade the Persian Empire and never was there a more audacious act in history.

# The Invasion of Asia
## Lecture 11

It looked like sheer folly that Alexander would pit this army of 50,000 against the mighty forces of Darius the III. ... Many of the Greeks hoped that Alexander would be swallowed up in the depths of Asia. Unknown to them, Alexander had already shattered those hopes when he defeated the First Persian Army on the banks of the Granicus.

In May 334 B.C., Alexander invaded Asia Minor with a strong army, who's core was comprised veteran Macedonians devoted to their king. Alexander possessed talented senior commanders of Philip, notably his second in command Parmenio and his son Philotas; Antigonus Monophthalmos, and Antipater. Alexander's boyhood friends also proved superb commanders: Hephaestion, Craterus, Leonnatus, Ptolemy, and Lysimachus.

This Macedonian army was unmatched until the legions of Julius Caesar. The hetairoi and Thessalians, totaling 3,600, were the heavy cavalry decisive in shock action. The infantry included six regiments of the Macedonian phalanx and the elite hypaspists who represented half the national levy. The remaining units consisted of professional specialists, notably archers, slingers, and the Agrianian javelin men as well as hoplites provided by the Greek cities.

Alexander stood against the arrayed ancient Near East's mightiest empire whose Great King could mobilize huge armies of Iranian cavalry and Greek mercenary hoplites, and an imperial fleet. Alexander's expedition looked like sheer folly. Many Greeks shared Demosthenes' hopes that Alexander's army would be swallowed up in the depths of Asia. Yet, Alexander's genius defied contemporary expectations.

Alexander pursued a strategy to overthrow. He aimed to smash Persian field armies in decisive battles, and then to capture the ports of the eastern Mediterranean so that Darius' subject fleets would defect. The Achaemenid court, surprised by Alexander's invasion, was strategically at a disadvantage.

Furthermore, a lurid palace revolution had put on the throne **Darius III** Codomannus, who faced rivals and, while personally brave, could not compare to Alexander in generalship. Therefore, when Alexander crossed the Hellespont, Darius III was preoccupied at Susa so that the satraps of Asia Minor alone took the field against the youthful Macedonian invader. ∎

## Name to Know

**Darius III** (b. c. 380 B.C.; r. 336–330 B.C.): Codomonus, king of Persia. In 330 B.C., Darius fled east when Alexander surprised the Persian court at Ecbatana. Darius was deposed and enchained on orders of Bessus, satrap of Bactria. Darius was murdered near Hecatompylus in Parthyae when Alexander descended upon Bessus's camp.

## Suggested Reading

Bosworth, *Conquest and Empire.*

Engels, *Alexander the Great and the Logistics of the Macedonian Army.*

Heckel, *The Conquest of Alexander the Great.*

———, *The Marshals of Alexander's Empire.*

Mørkholm, *Early Hellenistic Coiange from the Accession of Alexander to the Peace of Apamea.*

Parke, *Greek Mercenary Soldiers From the Earliest Times to the Battle of Ipsus.*

1.  How important were the senior officers such as Parmenio? What were the strengths of the Macedonian officer corps?

2.  In tactics, discipline, and morale, how did the Macedonian army compare to Persian forces in 334 B.C.? Why was Alexander so confident in his ability to win decisive battles?

3.  How important were logistics and money for Alexander the Great and Darius III? Why would Darius III and his satraps inevitably accept decisive battle rather than wage a war of attrition?

4.  How did Alexander's strategy negate many of the strategic advantages of Darius III? Why was a naval war in the Aegean Sea not likely to be decisive?

# The Invasion of Asia
## Lecture 11—Transcript

In this lecture, I plan to introduce the Macedonian expedition into Asia. Asia to the Greeks essentially denoted everything stretching from the Aegean to the Hindu Kush or Indus Valley; they had very little knowledge of the entire continent as we understand it today, and so for Alexander, crossing into Asia in 334 B.C., he was essentially conquering the known world—or most of the civilized known world—for his generation.

This invasion has been seen from a number of different perspectives; one wonders what exactly Philip had in mind, because he obviously planned this invasion and Alexander fell heir to it. The best description that we have from antiquity is from the historian Polybius writing in the 2$^{nd}$ century B.C., and he wrote a work dealing with the rise of Roman power; but he couldn't help but comment on the war in Asia as conducted by the Greeks and Alexander the Great because he created the world he knew.

In Polybius's opinion, Alexander's crossing over to Asia was the beginning of a war that was essentially inevitable since the March of the 10,000 by Xenophon, which we talked about a number of lectures earlier. Polybius's perspective is as follows:

> The nature of these factors is clearly enough indicated from the examples quoted above [he's talking about methods of history]. The true causes and the origins of the war against Persia are easy enough for anyone to recognize. The first of these was the retreat of the Greeks under Xenophon from the Upper Satrapies, a march during which although they traversed the whole of Asia and were constantly passing through hostile territory, none of the barbarians dared to stand in their way [this was the retreat of 401–399 B.C., the so-called Anabasis that I said was essentially a guidebook for how Alexander could conquer the Persian Empire]. The second was the invasion of Asia carried out by the Spartan King Agesilaus [Agesilaus II who invaded Asia Minor and penetrated deep into the Persian Empire], during which he encountered no opposition worth mentioning in any of his campaigns, and was only compelled

to return without achieving his aims because of the outbreak of troubles in Greece [for which you read Corinthian War; thank you, Persian diplomats]. These events convinced Philip of the cowardice and indolence of the Persians compared with his own military efficiency and that of the Macedonians; they also opened his eyes to the size and the magnificence of the prizes to be gained from such a war. Accordingly, no sooner had he obtained the avowed support of the rest of the Greeks for his enterprise than he found a suitable pretext in his ardent desire to avenge the injuries which the Persians had previously inflicted on Greece [that was the burning of the city of Athens and its shrines, and the formation of the League of Corinth]. Thereafter he lost no time in deciding to go to war, and put in hand all possible preparations for this purpose. We must therefore consider the first set of factors I have mentioned as the cause of the war [that is, Xenophon] ... the second as its pretext, and Alexander's crossing into Asia as its beginning.

In Polybius's view, the war was inevitable going back to Greek clashes with Xenophon and Agesilaus; that this was the true cause (the itea); that Philip created pretexts to avenge the temples of Athens; and that Alexander carried out the actual war itself and that was the beginning (the archae). In this way, Polybius is reasoning in a wide historical perspective very much along the lines of other Greek historians, notably Thucydides. However, there is a bit of rationalization in all of this, and I contend as we go through the following lectures that we may well question Polybius's interpretation; it stands behind many views that somehow Alexander represented a Panhellenic enterprise, and it also raises questions of what Philip would have done as opposed to his son Alexander. In my opinion, when Alexander crossed to Asia in 334 B.C., he didn't have in mind any of these causes and pretexts as Polybius understood and many later generations, but for him, it was a great heroic event; a reenactment of the greatest of all expeditions, the war against Troy in which his ancestors Achilles and Neoptolemus excelled, and as I stressed before, Alexander really took to heart these Homeric images. These images probably meant much more to him, and in time, to his Macedonian army and even his Greek allies and mercenaries, than the musings of Polybius about a grand historical set of causes.

In any event, in May, 344 B.C., when Alexander invaded Asia, he took with him a superb army. Much of what we know about the Macedonian army comes from the account of Arrian, as well as other information, especially from Curtius Rufus, one of Alexander's historians, and reports in scattered sources as well as archaeological evidence. The army is difficult to estimate in size. There were already some 10,000 men in Asia commanded by Parmenio who had secured a bridgehead; that is, the strategic crossing across the Hellespont between the cities of Sestos and Abydos—that's where the ferry goes today—and essentially it's the same point where Xerxes had built the bridge of ships back in 480 B.C. to invade Europe. The army crossed over with no particular difficulty; there were 160 triremes and other high-deck ships including quinqueremes—these were new, state-of-the-art, heavier ships—they were furnished by the Athenians and other Greek allies; primarily it was an Athenian navy although commanded by a Macedonian admiral, a man named Nicanor.

In any event, what apparently assembled in the Troad—the region around Troy where Alexander visited the various tourist attractions as well as the so-called tomb of Achilles and carried out various rites to both his own ancestors (Achilles) as well as Priam and the Trojans so they would not go against him—he had in his army a Macedonian core that was superb. There were six regiments, maybe battalions—you could translate either way—of the phalanx, these were infantrymen armed with a great pike, the sarissa; they were the core of the Macedonian army. Each was a *taxeis* (regiment or battalion) commanded by a taxiarch; the men who commanded these regiments, the taxiarchs, were superb officers, and in the six regiments that crossed over to Asia, several of those taxiarchs distinguished themselves and rose to high command. In fact, fighting in the phalanx was one of the key ways of distinguishing yourself, getting the attention of the king, and eventually rising to command cavalry or independent columns; we'll talk about that in a moment. So you had this wonderful core of Macedonian infantry. There were also at this point 3,000 *hypaspists*—these were the equivalent of grenadiers—they took a position between the phalanx and the cavalry; they stood on the right flank. Within the        was a guard known as the agema, the personal guard of the king; and then, of course, there were the Companion cavalry, armed with a thrusting spear and body armor. They were organized into ilai or squadrons; and there were some 2,000 men—

somewhere between 8 and 10 squadrons; the size of these squadrons is debated—and this was the core of the army: the Companions, the hypaspists, and the phalanx.

However, Alexander also brought along with him many other important military units. These included various Greek forces: Some 7,000 Greek hoplites served under the terms of the treaty arrangements of the League of Corinth; many were likely mercenaries. All of them were under veteran commanders, either Greek veteran mercenary commanders or, in some instances, Macedonian commanders. There were also various Balkan contingents, and these people served out of an alliance to Alexander as King of Macedon and their overlord. One of the crack units was the Agrianians, the javelin men, who were used to screen cavalry and infantry formations; they were used for all sorts of guerrilla operations; to seize advance points. They were one of Alexander's favorite units, and they came from the highlands of Macedon—they were actually just beyond the Macedonian frontier—and these people were probably more or less Illyrian in descent. There was also Thracian infantry and cavalry.

Above all, Alexander had two advantages that he inherited from his father, but I believe he also innovated on: One was the siege train and engineering corps that followed him. The expedition was virtually an expedition of exploration, particularly after 330 B.C. when the army crossed the Tigris and really moved into regions that no Greek had ever seen before; and that is Iran, Central Asia, and India. Up until that point, they more or less were moving in areas that were either part of the Mediterranean world or at least within Greek knowledge such as Babylonia; the Greeks had been to Babylonia, which would today be middle Iraq. But once they invaded Persia, this was a whole new ballgame. In the ranks of Alexander was a superb engineering and medical corps created by Philip, but in my opinion greatly innovated by Alexander. These included men who could reckon distances and calculate supplies, the bematists, the men who actually did foot counting; they actually measured out the regions that Alexander traveled. There was also an engineering corps that would become essential at the sieges. These were men who could construct towers—that is, towers that you would move up against walls—battering rams, various defensive sheds to protect the engines of war, artillery, catapults, and ballistae. There is an argument to be made that Alexander's engineers improved the artillery significantly, because in the three great sieges—and we will discuss several of them—at Halicarnassus and Tyre in particular, Alexander's artillery could batter down masonry walls, whereas apparently Philip, back in 340 B.C., couldn't do it at Byzantium and Perinthus; so we suspect there was an improvement in the artillery as a result of Alexander's encouragement and just the fact that these engineers got much better at doing their job under both Phil and Alex.

The logistical system was superb. There has been a groundbreaking work written by Donald Engels on Alexander the Great and the Logistics of Macedonian Army, and it really is a marvelous read and study. Engels has demonstrated that Alexander—and really we know very little information about this—had inherited and, again, improved from his father the logistical system. The army that crossed into Asia in 334 B.C., numbering some 50,000 men perhaps, would require about 125 tons of grain and 100,000 gallons of water per day just to move around. That meant that supplies had to be secured from the area in which you were moving; that the Macedonian army could not stay in one region more than a couple of days—you have to think of this army as essentially a moving city; 50,000 combatants alone represents the size of a very impressive Greek city, that's a huge force—and furthermore there were the draft animals and warhorses. Warhorses are enormously expensive and have to be replaced; they can only be marched so many days; they must rest; you have to find fodder.

All of these details were worked out. Alexander's army achieved record speeds in both marching and pursuit; and the reason is that Philip and Alexander both discarded carts. There were no wheeled vehicles in the army. Persian armies, for instance—as most Near Eastern armies—had enormous wagon trains and a cattle drive to go along with it. Darius's army was lucky if it could move at six, seven, or eight miles a day; the army would stretch out for miles; there were enormous number of carts and wagons. The Macedonian infantry and cavalry even carried their own arms and equipment; they used pack animals but whenever possible men carried the burden rather than animals. Engels has worked out that three men could carry the pack of an animal, and actually their water and food requirements are less. There were occasions where the Macedonian army used pack animals—we know, for instance, to the visit at Siwah, they used camels when they were in

Egypt, one of the earliest references to camels in Egypt—but on the whole, the supply system was superbly worked out, and as a result, the Macedonian army could achieve record speeds—forced marches of 20–25 miles a day, which they could sustain for several days running—repeatedly in fighting in Central Asia, the rebellious person satraps were always taken by surprise how quickly Alexander could turn about and come to their territory because they rebelled thinking that Alexander was just too far away, and there are repeated references to this. The pursuit of Darius across central Iran is absolutely stunning; no ancient army would ever again achieve those kinds of record speeds. Within the army of Alexander was a superb number of veterans; men who had common service; who had an unbroken record a victory under Philip; who were trained and in superb condition; with logistics that really we wish we knew more, because it really was one of the most remarkable logistical systems until the time of Napoleon.

In addition to this army, Alexander had superb officers. This raises the question of exactly how much of this incredible achievement—overthrowing the Persian Empire within 10 years—was the result of Alexander's inspired generalship, or the collective achievement of the various Macedonian officers. There is a large body of scholarship that tends to favor the second explanation; and I should be honest in that I tend to favor the first explanation. I do not believe an army as large and as removed and far from its homeland as the Macedonian army was could have functioned by committee; there had to be a single commander for whom these soldiers would fight, and at the same time for whom these officers would give their lives and their honor in his service.

The officers were overwhelmingly Macedonian nobility. Even Greek mercenary and Greek allied contingents were usually commanded by Macedonian officers. There are two major studies—the most recent one in English that was released by Waldemar Heckel on the marshals of Alexander—that provide the collective biographies of all these officers that served with Alexander. If one goes through these and plots various careers, you can see there's a certain logic in the way the whole officer system operated. First, it would be deceptive to call these men professional officers as we understand it, or even as the French or Swedish armies would understand it in the early Modern Age; you think of the armies of Gustavus

Adolphus or Louis XIV. They were first and foremost nobles. They were men who came from the extended Macedon of Philip: that included many officers from those great western districts like Lyncestris, Orestis, Elimea; regions that were home to proud, warlike nobles. Furthermore, they had gained estates, honor, and money in the service of Philip and they would continue to gain that under Alexander. They had a sense of service and loyalty to the Argead house, the Argead family, the royal House of Macedon, and that was one of the most important bonds between Alexander and his officers.

Those officers represented two generations of men: One was those men who had essentially fought with Philip and represented Philip's generation. Many of them were senior to Alexander; someone like Parmenio, who acted as second-in-command for the first four years of the expedition, was essentially Philip's age. Others, such as Philotas, the son of Parmenio, was anywhere from 10–20 years older than Alex. Another one would be a fellow named Cleitus the Black, by which the Greek means "a man who has black hair"; there's a fellow called Cleitus the White meaning "blonde hair," these were designations on the hair color apparently of these Macedonian officers. They all represented men who really seen their service under Phil.

There were, then, men of Alexander's generation: These included some very close boyhood friends; they would be men who would be enrolled in what was known as the Bodyguard—there was an honorary bodyguard of seven; Somatophylakes is what they would be called in Greek—and some of them had been trained with Alexander under the tutorship of Aristotle. These included men that, some of them, became kings later: Ptolemy and Lysimachus; Leonnatus who carried the banner of Alexander and actually saved Alexander's life at the city of the Malli in India in 325 B.C.; his closest friend Hephaestion who was almost the alter ego of Alexander, though a rather abrasive figure, he wasn't popular among many others; so you had this group of boyhood friends who had trained with Alexander and were devoted to him. There was also a wider generation of nobility, and these included very important men who commanded the regiments of the phalanx: men such as Craterus, Coenus, Polyperchon, and Meleager; all of them were of Alexander's generation and they were promoted and rewarded based on merit. Craterus eventually rose to second-in-command of the army, and he had started out as an infantry commander and showed enormous initiative at the Battle of Gaugamela.

All of these officers emulated Alexander, who always led the decisive charge, wherever it was; and Alexander, by the time of his death, could show wounds from almost every major battle and siege: He was wounded at the siege of Gaza; he was nearly killed at the Battle of the Granicus; he was almost killed in storming the city of the Malli in India. In terms of bravery, no one had any doubt or question about it, and Macedonian officers were expected to perform the same way. Arrian is extremely careful in recording these names—he's getting this information from Ptolemy, one of Alexander's friends who eventually became king of Egypt after Alexander's death—and this sort of information would have been known throughout the ranks of the Macedonian army (what officer led the battle, how they distinguished themselves) and it is indicative of the importance of these officers that the infantry regiments were named not after the regions in which they were recruited—they were all regionally recruited—but after their officer: They speak of Perdiccas's Regiment, Craterus's Regiment; the identity of the regiment was very much tied to those officers.

That raises some remarkable points about Alexander, and I think a measure of his greatness and why I come down on the side that Alexander probably should really get the credit for all of these victories; not even probably, I'm pretty definitive on this. For one, just think of who these men were: For 10 years, he took essentially the nobility of Macedon on campaign representing two generations. They were all proud and ambitious men; every one of them wished to distinguish themselves in the eyes of his king, and they were motivated by many of the same heroic traditions of Alexander. Just keeping these guys focused on a common objective was an enormously difficult task; and Alexander had to constantly use and get the best out of the men he had available, because he could only use those Macedonian officers in any kind of serious capacity. Very seldom would he entrust positions to Greeks; and later on when Iranian forces were recruited, they were ultimately put, again, under Macedonian command.

Second, think of the talent that followed Alexander after his death in 323 B.C: Some of those men, including the senior man, Antigonus the One-Eyed,

Monophthalmus, who was of Philip's generation and put in charge of Asia Minor; Antipater, who stayed as regent of Greece; Parmenio, the second-in-command—those represented the older generation—all of them fine generals in their own rank. Within the younger ranks, the secretary of Alexander, Eumenes of Cardia, who handled the military payroll and kept the daybook; generals such as Craterus; Leonnatus, a friend of his; even Ptolemy, who was very cautious as a general; all of these men were men of very high ability. In the case of Craterus, everyone thinks that he's almost Alexander in quality and ability, the same was true of Antigonus and Eumenes; it's extraordinary the types of men who served Alexander, and that is an index of Alexander's own greatness. He was never in awe of these men; he surrounded himself with the best of the nobility; he promoted based on merit. There will be several instances where he is defied by his officers—and there are two ugly incidents we must discuss, especially after 330 B.C. when Alexander crosses into Iran and begins to court the Iranian nobility—but the officers on the whole stood by him, and even though his policies of accommodating the Persians at court was unpopular, many of them went along with it because, in the end, Alexander adopted certain amount of Persian dress and ceremony to win over the Iranian ruling class rather than just to exalt his own greatness and megalomania, as some would argue. Arrian makes note of that; so does Plutarch; and I think they're correct in that regard. Alexander's generalship could easily be just tested by the people around him; and that is a measure of greatness for anyone. There are always two forms of greatness: One is to be truly great—and I think that's the case of Alex—and the other is to surround yourself with intellectual pygmies so you look great, and more of us have done that than we care to admit.

Finally, in the course of the campaigning in Asia, Alexander reformed this army. He inherited the army from Philip in 334 B.C.—the army looked very much as Philip would have commanded it; it was expanded with Balkan and Greek forces—but when the army crossed over the Tigris in 330 B.C., Alexander had to remount his cavalry (many of the horses had died); he reorganized the cavalry from squadrons into what are known as hipparchos, units of 1,000 men, and into those units he recruited Iranian cavalry who fought side-by-side with the Macedonians. He made greater use of Greek mercenaries: Well over 50,000 Greek mercenaries were hired in the course of the last six years of the expedition; they were often used as garrison forces; they were used for subordinate columns. He incorporated allies from the steppes; he mounted the so-called horse archers of the Dahae, these are a Scythian people; in India, he learned how to use war elephants and incorporated the armies of various allied rajas.

So the army, in many ways, transformed itself into an ever more imperial army in the course of the campaigning in Asia, and this was Alexander's doing. He had to reorganize the army; invent new tactics; modify the command structure; the wars in Central Asia and India required many more independent commands, men like Craterus and Ptolemy got to command their own forces, so did Hephaestion; and so all of this is part of Alexander's effort to keep that war effort going and carry out essentially the conquest of the world. This, again, is part of the genius of Alexander; he didn't just mindlessly apply the tactics of his father, and that army by no means was static. It's constantly changing, innovating on tactics, improving, officers were being promoted, and men were being summoned to call to account for defeats; Alexander was very conscious of those who succeeded and those who did not.

In the whole course of the expedition, Alexander himself was never defeated; and only at one point, in 329 B.C., on the Polytimetus River in Central Asia, was a column—largely Greek mercenaries, but some Macedonians under collective command—encircled and destroyed by insurgent Bactrians and Sogdians led by Spitamenes; that's the only significant defeat through the entire expedition, and that was, again, a subordinate column.

It is extraordinary that he had this army and that he has so little money to pay it. He essentially was broke when he crossed over into Asia Minor. We're told he had 70 talents; he was mortgaged to the hilt. At Miletus, he will demobilize the fleet because he can't pay for it. I always say that Alexander had to conquer the world not only for his own destiny to be the new Achilles, and also to meet mom's expectations—because Olympias kept telling Alexander he was, after all, the descendent of Achilles—but the second reason was to pay off his creditors. Fortunately, the Persian King Darius III lost the war more quickly than he could spend out his huge reserves, and in the course of conquering the Persian Empire—down to the first essentially four-and-a-half years of the war—Alexander is reported to have seized well over 230,000 talents (gold and silver bullion); enormous sums of money, which was then coined as Macedonian regal calling and quickly solved all of his money problems.

Despite all these advantages—the veteran soldiers, the officers, the amazing logistical system, the engineering corps of the Macedonian army—this was essentially unknown by Darius III. Persian perceptions of the Macedonian army, one would love to have what they were; but Darius had very, very little information on it. Macedon was regarded as, "Yeah, we once controlled that area as a funny part of a satrapy, what is it?" When Alexander invaded in 334 B.C., Darius III was taken strategically by surprise. Philip had been assassinated two years earlier; Darius and his satraps—his governors of Asia Minor—did not expect an invasion; Parmenio's advance force had essentially been driven back to the Hellespont, it was only holding a few towns; and to a large extent, Darius had major problems that involved the Egyptians and what to do on the northern frontier, and Macedon was a pretty remote concern. Furthermore, the Persian Empire was impressive.

Arrian and other authors in antiquity state that Darius III was responsible for the destruction of the Persian Empire, and in the two great battles in which Darius fought Alexander—the Battle of Issus and the Battle of Gaugamela—Darius fled the battlefield early in the battle. But that's because Alexander was about to capture him, and if he captured Darius the war was over; this was not done as simply an act of cowardice. It is clear that Darius was a generous and able king; that the Persian nobility stood by him; and when he was really ignominiously deposed by his satrap Bessus and then murdered, many of the Persian aristocracy at that point went over to Alexander because they hated what Bessus had done to their king, they blamed that satrap for Darius's death. Furthermore, many Greek mercenaries—in 334 B.C., there may have been as many as 50,000–60,000 Greeks in Persian service—held on with Darius despite his defeats, even after his arrest and deposition. Some of them actually went over to Alexander, deserting; they would not serve Bessus, their loyalty was to Darius III, and Alexander appreciated that among those Greek mercenaries who had long service under the king. Darius III, for all of his difficulties and his drawbacks, was clearly regarded as a serious and noble king to serve.

Furthermore, he had an impressive empire. It is difficult to give population estimates, but at the time that Alexander invaded Asia Minor, the Persian Empire could have numbered between 40 and 45 million residents. Huge cavalry armies could be assembled, and there's no doubt in the great battles at Issus and Gaugamela that Alexander was greatly outnumbered; by how much is anyone's guess, the sources tend to exaggerate the Persian numbers. These could be armies of 20,000 Greek mercenaries, 30,000 Iranian cavalry, and 100,000 additional combatants summoned from the empire; they were huge armies. In fact, Persian field armies were the largest armies in the Western tradition, probably until the Napoleonic Wars. The Persians themselves had a superb logistical system to feed and supply these forces, and they had their own engineering corps as well. Furthermore, they had enormous amounts of money, and they also had fleets. The Great King of Persia could launch great fleets from his subject peoples in Cyprus: the Greeks of Cyprus, the Phoenicians, the Egyptians, and other people dwelling on the shores of eastern Mediterranean.

So it looked like sheer folly that Alexander would pit this army of 50,000 against the mighty forces of Darius the III. Almost everyone concluded that this expedition was a foolhardy venture, and Demosthenes and many of the Greeks probably hoped that Alexander would be swallowed up in the depths of Asia and, of course, their freedom would then be regained. Unknown to them, early in spring of 334 B.C., Alexander had already shattered those hopes when he defeated the First Persian Army on the banks of the Granicus.

# The Battle of the Granicus

## Lecture 12

> The victory was stunning. Probably the cavalry battle lasted at most a matter of minutes, and within less than an hour the Greek mercenary army forces had been destroyed, either killed or captured, and Alexander was master of the battlefield.

In late May 334 B.C., Alexander won a decisive victory over the Persian satraps on the banks of River Granicus in northwestern Asia Minor. Arriving on the field late in the afternoon, Alexander drew the Macedonian army, numbering perhaps 50,000 men, out of line of march into line of battle. By successive cavalry attacks, he put to flight the Persian cavalry that held the higher eastern river bank, and surrounded and annihilated the Greek mercenary hoplites who were drawn up behind the main Persian line. The victory delivered Asia Minor to Alexander.

The Ionian Greeks welcomed the Macedonian king as their liberator, and Alexander confirmed the autonomy and freedom of Greek cities of Asia. Sardes, the satrapal capital and treasury surrendered. The Macedonians encountered resistance at Miletus and Halicarnassus, naval bases held by Greek mercenaries under the orders from Memnon of Rhodes but otherwise, Alexander marched virtually unopposed across western Anatolia.

In 334-333 B.C., the Macedonian army wintered at Gordion, the former Phrygian capital on the Anatolian plateau. In spring 333 B.C., Alexander invested the senior general **Antigonus Monophthalmos** ("the One-eyed") with the pacifying of eastern Asia Minor, while the Macedonian army marched southeast. The victory on the Grancius shocked the Persian court. Great King Darius III dispatched to the Aegean a fleet, commanded by the veteran mercenary officer **Memnon of Rhodes**, to raise rebellions in Greece. Darius himself summoned a great host, and so, for the first time, the Great King took the field against a Western invader. ∎

## Names to Know

**Antigonus Monophthalmos** (b. c. 382; r. 306–301 B.C.): "The One-eyed." A senior general of Alexander the Great, he was entrusted with the strategic satrapy of Phrygia in 333–323 B.C.

**Memnon of Rhodes:** Appointed Persian commander in the West by Darius III, he directed the defense of Halicarnassus, and commanded the Persian fleet in the Aegean in 334–333 B.C.

## Suggested Reading

Bosworth, *Conquest and Empire.*

Engels, *Alexander the Great and the Logistics of the Macedonian Army.*

Fuller, *The Generalship of Alexander the Great.*

Harl, "Alexander's Cavalry Battle on the Granicus."

Heckel, *The Conquests of Alexander the Great.*

## Questions to Consider

1. What accounts for the differences between the narratives of the Battle of the Granicus and siege of Halicarnassus reported by Arrian and Plutarch, and those reported by Diodorus Siculus? What do these differences reveal about the contemporary sources perceptions of Alexander?

2. In May 334 B.C., what were Alexander's strategic aims, and why was a decisive battle so urgently needed?

3. Why did Alexander's victory on the Granicus lead to the rapid collapse of Persian rule in Asia Minor? How did the members of the League of Corinth view the stunning successes of Alexander in 334 B.C.?

# The Battle of the Granicus
## Lecture 12—Transcript

In this lecture, I plan to discuss the Battle of the Granicus, fought in May, 334 B.C. This is the first of the four great battles of Alexander the Great, and in some ways it is the most controversial.

We have two different descriptions of the battle, one by Arrian—and Plutarch's anecdotes are consistent with Arrian's account—the other is by Diodorus Siculus; and I prefer the Arrian/Plutarch account for a number of reasons based on not only the sources but my own survey of the topography of the battlefield, I've been on the battlefield several times.

The battle is significant in a number of ways: It essentially delivered Asia Minor west of the Taurus Mountains to Alexander, and allowed Alexander to pursue a strategy of neutralizing the Persian imperial fleet by capturing the various ports along the Aegean and Mediterranean shore, which were the homes to the majority of the sailors in the Persian navy, and so essentially they went home and stopped serving the Great King. It also forced the Great King to take the field himself because Alexander defeated a group of satraps—that is, the governors of the provinces of Asia Minor—and so this battle was decisive. It shattered the Persian army, and for the first time, the Persians had a look at what the Macedonian army could do.

When the situation dawned in May, 334 B.C.—that is, Alexander was now in Asia with a large army—the satraps quickly assembled their forces. We're not sure who was in overall command of this army; the battle was fought in the satrapy known as Hellespontine Phrygia along the shores of the Sea of Marmora today, which the ancients would call the Propontis; and it's fought along the banks of a small river known as the Granicus (today, known as the Biga Çayı) and actually its tributary, the Koca Çayı, and we'll get to that in a moment.

Furthermore, there were satraps, and not only satraps but other high-ranking Persian officials, and a Greek mercenary commander by the name of Memnon of Rhodes. Memnon of Rhodes was not just a hired help; Memnon had married a woman named Barsine—who had been actually the wife of his older brother; she was the widow of his brother Mentor—and therefore he was married into one of the most illustrious houses in the Persian Empire. Barsine's father was the satrap Artabazus, who was one of the senior men in the Persian Empire; and when he came over to Alexander the Great in 330 B.C., that's essentially a signal for all the other Persian nobles to follow. Memnon was regarded as essentially one of the club, one of the ruling members of Persian Asia Minor.

Memnon urged, at a conference held at Zella—which is less than a day's march away from the Granicus—that the satraps, whose army was very well-represented with heavy cavalry and Greek mercenary infantry, should not engage Alexander directly but should pursue a war of attrition. He urged that the field be burned; that the cities of Ionia—that is, the Greek cities of western Asia Minor—be garrisoned; and that within a very short time Alexander would run into supply difficulties and the army would either disband or there would be an opportunity to destroy the army after it had been weakened.

The satraps rejected this advice—they were not about to torch their fields—and there are certain reasons for this: One, it was their fields, it would be their incomes; but second, they could not carry out such a strategy really plausibly as governors of the Great King and simply say, "This young Macedonian king showed up, we don't know who he was, and we decided to burn down half of Asia Minor because we really didn't want to fight him." That was just not possible; they were there to fight a major battle, they had no idea of the qualities of the Macedonian army—they thought it was just another weird version of Greeks—and they had as many Greek heavy infantry as Alexander did.

With good reason, they decided to fight; and they established a battle line on the Granicus, which some scholars have claimed is flawed. I don't think it was really a flawed battle line—it's very similar to the way Darius would deploy his army at Issus a year later—it was just that the plan was obvious; it was typical way of the Persians fighting. In any of these situations, once Alexander came on the battlefield and observed the disposition of the enemy forces, he had a remarkable sense of terrain and geography; could think very three-dimensionally in his mind; he could see where the weaknesses were in the enemy line; he could divine their plan immediately and then come up with a counter to it. This was the danger of fighting Alexander: No matter what plan you came up with, if you put your men on the battlefield, Alexander would look at it and could see the weaknesses, could understand what you are attempting to achieve, and come up with a counter immediately. Napoleon had the same quality; and in this way, Granicus in some ways is comparable to the way Napoleon could read the terrain at Austerlitz, one of his greatest victories (the Battle of the Three Kings, as it was called).

In any event, as I said, we have two accounts of the battle, two different versions of it; and the Diodorus account is believed by some scholars, but the majority goes with the account of Arrian and Plutarch, and that is the account that I prefer to follow. That's based not only, as I said, on the sources but my own experience of walking that battlefield. It was sometime late in May, 334 B.C., and Alexander had a large army of about 50,000 men.

The Persian army was, we think, about comparable size, maybe a bit smaller. The Persians drew up their battle line along the Granicus River. From north to south, the battle line ran probably well over two miles. The northern or right flank of the Persian army was protected by marshes; in that part of the world, especially in the spring, you really can't operate cavalry in marshes, if you walk out there in armor you just sink to your knees in no time. Their left wing was anchored on the confluence of the Biga Çayı today and the Koca Çayı; that is, the Granicus and its tributary. To get around the Persian left flank, you essentially had to cross two rivers; and the riverbanks there are quite high, and it would be difficult to move forces and maintain discipline and really to elude Persian detection.

The main forces of the Persians were thus drawn up on the riverbank on the east bank, and that bank is significantly higher than the west bank; that is, the bank that would be occupied by the Macedonians. Furthermore, the river is relatively small; it flows essentially at this time of the year in the middle of the riverbed. It's very sandy riverbed with a lot of smooth stones, and very quickly, any men fighting in this wide riverbed would find themselves in very slippery conditions. The Persian satraps and Arsites, who was the satrap of that region and was probably in overall command, and with the agreement, I suspect, of Memnon decided that they would draw up the Persian cavalry—

and these were largely Persian colonists settled in Asia Minor as well as Anatolian levies who were armed similarly to the Persian forces—they drew up their forces behind the riverbank, high up. The position was ideal for defense; the Persians have often been criticized for doing this, but Persian cavalry was not shock cavalry the way the Macedonians were.

Persians were armed with missile weapons, and the idea was that when the Macedonian army advanced and went into the riverbed, the Persians would break up those formations by throwing javelins and shooting arrows into them, and the likelihood was the Macedonian attack would just falter and the Macedonians would fall back. But in the event that they did get over that riverbank, the Persians had deployed their cavalry in such a way that they could move to the wings of their Greek mercenary infantry who were drawn up behind them on the high ground. Then, what you would have would be a powerful center of Greek heavy infantry armed with the hoplite thrusting spear and flanked by superb Persian cavalry, and they would simply move and drive the Macedonian army back into the Granicus River.

The plan was by no means flawed; it was a logical plan for the Persians to adopt. The problem was when Alexander appeared on the battlefield, he knew exactly what those Persians were attempting to do. Late in the afternoon, Alexander's army came across the open plain—called by Justin the Plain of Adrasteis—and that plain had essentially no obstacles to it. To the right of Alexander's army—that would be to the south—was high ground where Alexander could easily get up and survey the Persian positions. You have to remember, those Persian soldiers and Greek mercenaries had been standing there all day; undoubtedly they hadn't had a particularly good army day, they were put in position early in the day and were waiting.

The Macedonian army arrived and Alexander conducted an extremely difficult move—it reminds you of the kind of awe and audacity that he displayed at the city of Pelion against the Illyrians—he moved his army out of line of march, into line of battle, so that they actually deployed in front of the Persian army out of bow shot. Parmenio, who saw the Persian positions according to Arrian, said, "Look, why bother attacking now? It's late in the day; let's wait for the Persians to withdraw, and then we probably can cross the river either unopposed, because the Persians are not there, or at least come up with a more conventional battle." Throughout Arrian's account, Parmenio acts as a foil; we're not sure if he always said this, but in any event, Parmenio is used by Arrian as a way to represent the more cautious and older generation of officers. Some scholars believe that this has been deliberately done to magnify Alexander and diminish the achievement of Parmenio. Parmenio always was second-in-command and he always commanded the left wing, the left half, of the Macedonian army. His loyalty was unquestioned, and he clearly was a very, very able tactician.

Nonetheless, Alexander rejected this advice; and if we accept this tradition, he saw immediately that the Persians had put themselves in a flawed position. Riverbanks are not straight lines, and riverbanks always have exposed positions. Alexander saw two points: One was that the problem with Persian cavalry was to get it to commit into hand-to-hand combat, into close order combat, where the Companion cavalry could really make headway given their superior discipline—they fought in tight units—and their lances. The idea was to lure at least part of that Persian cavalry off the high ground into the riverbed. Once in that riverbed, the Companion cavalry could confine Persian movement and essentially mow them down with their lances, and push the Persians up and off the riverbank and flank the army. That meant if you could break the enemy position at one point and get your Macedonian cavalry up there the rest of the Macedonian army could probably cross with very little opposition, because the Persians would essentially quit the field.

To do this, he adopted a rather unusual variation of the battle of encirclement. In classic Macedonian battles, the Companion cavalry occupied a position close to the infantry. Alexander assembled his six regiments of the phalanx 8 deep rather than 16 because it was a long battlefront; the hypaspists took their position on the right next to the phalanx regiments; but instead of the Companion cavalry, Alexander deployed various light cavalry—notably the prodromoi, the scouts, Thracian units—and then the Companion cavalry was on the far right. The Thessalian and Greek mercenary cavalry was on the left commanded by Parmenio. In front of Alexander's Companions on the far right of the Macedonian line were light infantry and the Agrianian, the javelin men.

What Alexander did was order attack in two ways: Those various light cavalry formations between the Companions and the hypaspists were ordered in first, and they hit a point along the riverbank where there was an angle. According to the account of Arrian, the Macedonian army moved up in perfect discipline, everyone stopped and took their breath, and then Amyntas, in command of the prodromoi, led these squadrons down into the riverbed and the rest of the Macedonian army followed at a slower pace. The immediate reaction of the Persians was to throw those javelins at them; the initial attack got broken up—that's were probably most losses were suffered—and as the Macedonian and Thracian light horse fell back into the riverbed, the Persians were drawn off the riverbank to pursue and into the riverbed. Meantime, the Companion cavalry had swung around on the right flank, descended into the river, and then came barreling down the river as if it were a bowling alley and smashed those Persian forces that were right in the riverbed.

The impact was audacious and decisive. The Persians, who could not stand up to the heavily armed Macedonians, immediately attempted to regain the riverbank; many of them fled in panic. There was some desperate fighting at this point. As Alexander's Companions came over the riverbank, Alexander led the charge himself. He unhorsed one of the Persian commanders, a man named Mithridates—apparently a son-in-law of the king, Darius III—and he broke his lance in the process.

A fellow named Rheosaces, one of the Persian commanders, actually delivered a blow on Alexander's helmet that was deflected and partially damaged; and that may be the helmet entombed at Vergina. Alexander was given a spear by Demoratus of Corinth, one of the Companions; he unhorsed this fellow; and in the process of killing the second Persian commander, another one called Spithridates came up to get Alexander with his scimitar, and Cleitus the Black—that is, the senior officer of Philip's generation—absolutely saved Alexander by severing the arm of his fellow Spithridates, who fell from his horse. Later on, Cleitus reminded Alexander of that fact.

The result of that combat was several of the Persian commanders were killed in quick succession in a matter of moments; the Macedonians pushed the Persian forces out of the riverbed onto the riverbank; and the Persian left essentially fled the field. The other Persian cavalry forces, seeing this, too quit the field. The rest of the Macedonian army that had advanced to the riverbank and descended came up and popped up on the east bank of the river; and all of a sudden the entire Macedonian army was on the east side of the Granicus and Greek mercenary infantry were standing on this hilltop very alone. In fact, most of them were really quite puzzled because they didn't expect to do any serious fighting that day.

Immediately, the Greeks offered a deal that they would go into the Alexander's service or at least surrender on terms. Alexander refused to accept those terms; he ordered the Greek mercenaries to be surrounded and then liquidated the force. We're told there were 20,000—that might be too high—but we do know that there were 2,000 survivors; they were all taking captive and sent back to Macedon to work in the quarries. Alexander was making a point: You do not serve the Great King of Persia if you are a Greek. The result was that the message got out. Many of the mercenaries long in Persian service would fight on, but the idea was to prevent new men from signing up with the Great King of Persia from the Greek world.

The victory was stunning. Probably the cavalry battle lasted at most a matter of minutes, and within less than an hour the Greek mercenary army forces had been destroyed, either killed or captured, and Alexander was master of the battlefield; the Persian cavalry had scattered. The Persians lost at least nine satraps and senior commanders; Arsites, who had commanded the forces, committed suicide later. Memnon of Rhodes survived the battle, and later went on to command the Persian fleet in the Aegean; he was a most dangerous opponent. The victory was important for several reasons: For the first time, the Persians saw what the Macedonian army could do; and in the next encounter, Darius III, who would command the Persian army, would be a lot more careful in dealing with the Macedonians.

The second point is that it essentially killed the Persian leadership in Asia Minor and disorganized the western satrapies in what is today Asiatic Turkey; that is, the region west of the Taurus Mountains. Therefore, there was very little coordinated resistance to Alexander for the rest of the year. In 334 B.C., it was essentially a march—a long indirect march—going down the western shore of Turkey, liberating the Greek cities of Ionia, moving in the tough regions of Caria, through the coastal cities of Pamphylia on the southwestern shores of Asia Minor, and across the rugged Pisidian highlands to the city of Gordion that is on the plateau of Asia Minor and was really one of the major Persian centers. It was the old Phrygian capital; it was home to King Midas, the legendary king of the Phrygians. In effect, Alexander had won most of the regions that we think Philip of Macedon might have aimed for within a year; certainly it was these areas that the Panhellenists such as Isocrates targeted as the region to conquer. However, this was not going to satisfy Alexander; and in the next year he would cross the Taurus Mountains and move into what the Greeks would call Upper Asia; that is, the more distant areas farther from the Mediterranean shore.

The victory at the Granicus solved Alexander's financial and logistical problems immediately. As Alexander's army moved south from the Troad and followed the traditional routes to the western cities of Asia Minor— these are the cities that were settled largely by Ionian peoples related to the Athenians in the Greek Dark Age in the 10th through the 8th centuries B.C.; these cities had been liberated in the great war of 480–479 B.C., they had been returned to Persian rule under the King's Peace of 386 B.C.—these cities now welcomed Alexander as their conqueror; and I suspect about the only Greek cities that really liked Alexander were those cities of Ionia in Asia Minor and Cyprus that had been under Persian rule.

As far as we can tell, these cities were not enrolled in the League of Corinth or the Hellenic League, but they undoubtedly had specific treaty relationships with Alexander. In many instances, Alexander had to halt the usual reprisals in Greek city-states; he instituted democracies; the oligarchies or strong men were thrown out. At the city of Ephesus, in which the great Temple of Artemis had been burnt down in 356 B.C. more or less at the time of Alex's birth, Alexander actually contributed money for the reconstruction of the shrine. He was greeted at the city of Priene with great pomp and actually slept in a house there, and the residence later on became a major tourist attraction ("Alexander slept here"; I'm sure almost every city in Asia Minor had such a place, most of them probably phony by the Roman Age but who's to tell, the Romans will believe anything when they're on tour).

His only resistance was encountered by two cities: the city of Miletus and the city of Halicarnassus. Those two cities were major ports on the southwestern shore of Asia Minor, and the city of Ephesus—which many of us have visited as tourists—only became a great port in the Hellenistic and Roman Age; actually, the city as you see it is the city rebuilt by Lysimachus, one of Alexander's generals, and Ephesus as not a particularly important port. The mere real ports were Miletus and the island of Samos, and in the 4th century B.C., Halicarnassus, which had been built up as a major port by the Carian dynasts because they made it their capital. It is today the modern city of Bodrum, which is essentially the center of the Turkish Riviera where all the gambling establishments and yachts go. (I have to keep my students away from this place; it's much too dangerous for them, but a delight to visit for those of us who know how to handle these things.) In any case, he had to capture Miletus and Halicarnassus, which were heavily fortified.

His fleet moved into position, and in antiquity Miletus was on the southern shores of a huge bay that is now silted up into a great alluvial plain, so when you visit Miletus you have to position it on the shore. The city was quickly blockaded by the allied Greek fleet; the Persian fleet showed up too late to do anything. Most of the population was favorable to Alexander. The small Persian garrison, largely Greek mercenaries, withdrew to the citadel; Alexander's forces entered the city; and with his artillery, battering rams, and towers they quickly breached the citadel and captured the city.

The navy blockaded the port—the Greeks in Alexander's service—and essentially the city fell with very little fighting. Miletus was then, again, liberated and enrolled as an ally. The Persian fleet could do very little, and eventually had to retire from the general vicinity of Miletus to Samos—it ran into supply problems, and a number of ships went home for the winter—and Alexander decided at that point to disband his fleet. First, he was in the hock, he didn't know how to pay for these guys; second, most of them were Athenians he really didn't want the Athenians to fight the Persian fleet, which were Greeks from Cyprus and Phoenicia—and you never know who's going to be on what side when that happens—and so he was glad to get rid of the largely Athenian fleet.

That meant when he moved against the next major port, Halicarnassus, he did not have a fleet to blockade it, and the Persians could supply the garrison. That siege lasted for almost 12 months. Again, the general population of Halicarnassus was Greek; they would welcome Alexander. Alexander's forces, his engineers, made a breach in the walls on the north side of the city, broke into the city; there was hard fighting.

One of the anecdotes is one of the assaults was carried out because two men of Perdiccas's infantry battalion got drunk and dared each other so they attacked the breach and the Macedonian army had to follow; but once they got into the city, again, the Greek mercenaries, on Memnon's orders—that is, Memnon of Rhodes—retired to the port, where there were two fortified positions in the harbor, and essentially maintained their position there for almost 12 months. Alexander realized it wasn't worth besieging these cities, and he detached Ptolemy, son of Lagos—that is, the future king of Egypt—to keep the city blockaded, and eventually the garrison was forced to surrender; it surrendered shortly before the Battle of Issus in the next year. It was hoped by Memnon that Alexander would be distracted and attempt to capture the city, and Alexander was not going to deal with a secondary objective. He had more important things to do.

First, the Greek cities and other coastal cities—particularly within the region of Lycia and the Greek and native cities on the shores of Pamphylia—most of them came over to Alexander's side and contributed; that is, provided money and provisions (the Greek word is syntaxis). In the areas that were not Greek, notably the first major region Lydia, which is immediately to the east of the Greek cities of Ionia—the Lydians were an ancient people of Asia Minor long in association with the Greeks; their city was Sardis—Alexander freed the Lydians so they could live under their own laws and appointed a Macedonian satrap, a man named Asander, and essentially announced by doing that that the conquest of the Persian Empire outside of the Greek cities would be Macedonian, not Panhellenic; that is, as the satrapies fell to Alexander, Macedonians would be appointed to govern these regions and to command the military forces, the local populations would live under their own laws and customs as they had done under the Persians, and this was essentially Alexander's realm and had nothing to do with the Panhellenic League. The same was true in Caria, another people long in association with the Greeks. The Hecatomnid Queen Ada was invested with power at her capital at Alinda, she adopted Alexander as her son and heir, and when she died in I think it was 326 B.C., Alexander essentially inherited Caria. Of course, there was a garrison there.

When Alexander crossed onto the great plateau in the region known as Phrygia, which spans much of the inner half of the Asiatic Peninsula of Turkey today—great grasslands and range; a very, very fertile region for both winter wheat and barley as well as stock-raising; goats and sheep and cattle would be in great supply—at Gordion, Alexander very ostentatiously, again, indicated to the Phrygians that they, too, would live under their own laws. The man that he put in charge of central Asia Minor, Greater Phrygia— that is, Phrygia the interior as opposed to Hellespontine Phrygia; Phrygia the shore—was Antigonus the One-Eyed, Monophthalmus, a general who was regarded as almost as good as Parmenio, who had commanded the various mercenary forces in the expedition; and Antigonus essentially controlled Asia Minor and the vital lines of communication between the expedition and the kingdom of Macedon that was run by Antipater who stayed back at Pella with part of the Macedonian levy and supervised the Greek League.

It was a very intelligent use of senior men from Philip's generation: He had Antipater in Macedon; he had Antigonus in Asia Minor; eventually Parmenio was to take over Iran, but that didn't last long, and we'll get to it. The advantage of Antipater in Macedon was Antipater didn't like Olympias and Olympias didn't like Antipater, so they kind of neutralized each other. Alexander—most of these are fictitious—but we have all these letters from antiquity that purport to be letters of Alexander, but they are fun to read; and I get the suspicion reading these things that Alexander had to do an awful lot of letter writing back to mom and Antipater to try to assuage the bruised feelings of both and hope that the two would more or less cooperate in running Macedon in his absence.

In any event, the conquests were spectacular. Alexander spent the winter of 334–333 B.C. in great comfort at Gordion. His commanders Coenus and Meleager led all the younger men back to Macedon—the newlywed men so they could spend time with their wives; they brought reinforcements from Macedon in the spring—and essentially Alexander had no threat. The war would resume in the spring with a Persian offensive in the Aegean, a naval offensive, and the Great King taking the field; but Alexander had Asia Minor more or less in hand.

At Gordion, he could not help himself from solving an oracle. At the city of Gordion, which was the capital of the Phrygians, the Greeks claimed there was a legend—and this is more likely a Greek legend than a Phrygian legend—but there was a sacred chariot or cart of some sort in which King Midas, the legendary king of the Phrygians (and I suspect there were a lot of kings of the Phrygians named Midas, it was a dynastic name and Greeks get very confused to who they are, and this is the Midas of the golden touch; and unfortunately his ignominious fate in the United States is I think he's the logo for a muffler or something for a car, you can't believe anything more ignominious).

But in any event, King Midas had this cart and that's how he was received by the Phrygians; it was a royal cart. There was a legend around, an oracle about, that this cart had an extremely complicated knot that held the harness to the cart. That knot, known as the Gordion knot, if it could be loosened— and the Greek word is luo, which is very vague; you can do it in any of a number of ways—the man who did that would be the Lord of Asia; and at the time, "Asia" meant essentially western Asia Minor, it didn't really have the continental sense.

Alexander, being what he was, solved it. We have two reports: One was he pulled the pin out and the harness dropped; the one that Arrian and Plutarch like is that he whipped out his sword and cut it with one blow, cut the Gordion knot, still used as an idiom today of how to solve a very complicated and intricate problem. The Macedonians cheered him on; the Phrygian's probably were really quite boiled by the whole thing.

Nonetheless, it was one of a number of instances in which Alexander felt compelled to solve oracles or to fulfill prophecies, and these contributed increasingly to his own self image where he came to regard himself as somehow a son of Zeus in the sense of Heracles; that is, his great deeds would allow him to mingle with the gods and join them at Mount Olympus on his death. For the Macedonian army in the winter of 334–333 B.C., it was one of a number of instances of their king encouraging them, giving them a good winter quarters, and also attending upon the wounded and rewarding the brave. Alexander made sure that his men were in their best condition, because next spring his army was going to march east and face the Great King himself.

# Timeline

1250–1150 B.C. ............... Collapse of Mycenaean (Bronze Age) Civilization in Greece

1100–800 B.C. ................. The Greek Dark Age: Dorian invasions of Thessaly, Boeotia, and Peloponnesus; Ionian Movements to islands and Asia Minor

750–700 B.C. .................... Homer: composition of *Iliad* and *Odyssey*

736–716 B.C. .................... First Messenian War

725–700 B.C. .................... Origins of the *polis* (city-state)
........................................... Introduction of Hoplite Warfare

........................................... Hesiod: composition of *Theogony* and *Works and Days*

........................................... Beginnings of Greek colonial expansion

676 B.C. ........................... Constitutional Reform in Sparta: birth of Lycurgan Order

668–657 B.C. ................... Second Messenian War: Sparta supreme in Peloponnesus

594 B.C. ........................... Reforms of Solon at Athens

ca. 560 B.C. ...................... Organization of Peloponnesian League under Sparta

559 B.C. ........................... Accession of Cyrus the Great of Persia (559–530 B.C.)

550 B.C. ........................... Cyrus conquers Media

547–546 B.C. ................... Cyrus conquers Lydia; submission of Ionian cities

546–510 B.C. ................... Peisistratid tyranny in Athens

539 B.C. ........................... Cyrus captures Babylon

530 B.C. ........................... Accession of Cambyses King of Persia (530–522 B.C.)

525–522 B.C. ................... Cambyses's conquest of Egypt

522–521 B.C. ................... Great Revolt in Persian Empire

........................................... Accession of Darius I (521–486 B.C.)

........................................... Reorganization of the Persian Empire into satrapies

| | |
|---|---|
| 508/7 B.C. | Clesithenic Revolution: birth of the democracy in Athens |
| 490 B.C. | Battle of Marathon: defeat of first Persian invasion |
| 480 B.C. | Xerxes's invasion of Greece |
| | Battles of Thermopylae and Salamis |
| 479 B.C. | Battle of Plataea: end of second Persian invasion |
| 477 B.C. | Organization of the Delian League: origins of the Athenian Empire |
| 462/1 B.C. | Triumph of the radical democracy at Athens |
| | Leadership of Pericles (461–429 B.C.) |
| | Golden Age of Athens |
| 461–446 B.C. | "First" Peloponnesian War |
| 431–404 B.C. | The Peloponnesian War |
| 412 B.C. | Treaty of Miletus: Persians promise aid to Sparta in return for Ionian Greek cities of Asia Minor |
| 408 B.C. | Cyrus the Younger appointed lord (*karanos*) of Asia Minor |
| 405 B.C. | Rebellion of Egypt from Persian Empire |
| 404 B.C. | Surrender of Athens to Spartan navarch Lysander |
| | End of the Athenian Empire and Spartan Hegemony (404–371 B.C.) |
| 401 | Battle of Cunaxa: death of Cyrus the Younger |
| | Anabasis or the March of the Ten Thousand (401–399 B.C.) |
| | King Artaxerxes II (405–358 B.C.) declares war on Sparta |
| | Spartans send army under Thibron into Asia Minor (401–399 B.C.) |
| 399 B.C. | Accession of King Agesilaus II of Sparta (399–360 B.C.) |
| | Dercyllidas commands Spartan forces in Asia Minor (399–397 B.C.) |
| 396–395 B.C. | King Agesilaus II campaigns in Asia Minor |

Timeline

395–386 B.C. .................... The Corinthian War

394 B.C. ........................... Battle of Cnidus: Athenian Conon defeats
Peloponnesian fleet

387/6 B.C. ........................ Peace of Antalcidas ("King's Peace"): Ionian
cities returned to Persia

........................................ Sparta hegemon of mainland Greece

........................................ Athens free to pursue naval policy in Aegean Sea

386–376 B.C. .................... Revolt of King Evagoras of Cyprus from Persia

382 B.C. ........................... Spartan seizure of Thebes and Dissolution of
Boeotian League

........................................ Spartan suppression of the Chalicidian League
(382–379 B.C.)

380 B.C. ........................... Isocrates writes his *Panegyricus*, calling for
Greek unity

378 B.C. ........................... Democratic Rising in Thebes under Pelopidas

........................................ Expulsion of Spartan garrison and reorganization
of Boeotian League

........................................ Alliance of Athens and Thebes

377 B.C. ........................... Athens organizes the Second Naval Confederacy

371 B.C. ........................... Battle of Leuctra: defeat of Spartan army by
Thebans under Epaminondas

........................................ Theban Hegemony (371–362 B.C.)

370 B.C. ........................... Outbreak of Satraps's revolts (370–360 B.C.)

........................................ Theban invasion of the Peloponnesus
(370–369 B.C.)

........................................ Rebellion of Messenians and creation of Messene

........................................ Arcadian League and Argos ally with Thebes

362 B.C. ........................... Battle of Mantinea; death of Epaminondas

359 B.C. ........................... Death of Perdiccas III of Macedon in battle
against the Bardylis and the Illyrians

........................................ Accession of Philip II and Treaty with
the Illyrians

........................................ Withdrawal of Macedonian garrison from
Amphipolis

........................................ Peace between Athens and Philip II

358 B.C. ............................ Philip's defeat of the Paeonians and Illyrians

............................................ Death of Artaxerxes II of Persia

............................................ Accession of Artaxerxes III Ochus
(358–338 B.C.)

357 B.C. ............................ Philip intervenes in Thessaly on behalf of the
Aleudae of Larissa (winter 358/7 B.C.)

............................................ Athens recovers the Chersonesus and Euboea

............................................ Alliance of Macedon and Epirus: Philip II
marries Olympias

............................................ Outbreak of the Social War (357–355 B.C.)

............................................ Philip seizes Amphipolis

............................................ Outbreak of Athenian-Macedonian War

356 B.C. ............................ Philip's capture of Pydna

............................................ Macedonian-Chalcidian Alliance

............................................ Phocians seize Delphi: outbreak of Third Sacred
War (356–346 B.C.)

............................................ Athens organizes anti-Philip coalition

............................................ Birth of Alexander III (the Great)

............................................ Collapse of Northern coalition against Philip

............................................ Philip captures Potidaea

............................................ Alliance of Phocis, Sparta, and Athens against
Thebes and the Ampictyonic League

355 B.C. ............................ Macedonian intervention in Larissa, Thessaly

............................................ End of the Social War & weakening of the
Athenian Naval Confederacy

............................................ Official declaration of war by Amphictyonic
council on Philomelus and the Phocians

............................................ Siege of Methone by Philip

354 B.C. ............................ Offensive of the Phocians in central Greece

............................................ Fall of Methone and Pagae to Philip

............................................ Battle of Neon: death of Philomelus

............................................ Onomarchus assumes command of the Phocians

353 B.C. ............................ Onomarchus convenes counter-Amphictyony

............................................ Phocian Successes in central Greece

................................................ Theban-Macedonian Alliance

................................................ Chares captures Sestos

................................................ Intervention of Philip in Thessaly; defeat
of the Phocians

................................................ Onomarchus expels Philip from Thessaly

................................................ Alliance of Cersebleptes of Thrace and Athens

................................................ Olynthus requests alliance and aid from Athens

352 B.C. ............................ Onomarchus captures Orchomenus in Boeotia

................................................ Intervention of Philip in Thessaly

................................................ Philip Elected Archon of the *Koinon* of Thessaly

................................................ Battle of Crocus Plain: Philip Supreme
in Thessaly

................................................ Death of Onomarchus; Phyllus assumes
command of the Phocians

................................................ Alliance of Philip with Perinthus, Byzantium,
and Amadocus

351 B.C. ............................ Philip's Illyrian expedition

................................................ Siege of Heraeum Teichus

................................................ Warning of Philip to Olynthus

................................................ *Philippic I* of Demosthenes

350 B.C. ............................ Philip's Paeonian and Illyrian campaigns

349 B.C. ............................ Macedonian Invasion of the Chalcidice

................................................ Phocion sent by Athens to Euboea

................................................ *Olynthiacs* I–III of Demosthenes

................................................ Alliance of Athens and Olynthus

348 B.C. ............................ Phocion's victory at Tamyae

................................................ Arrival of Athenians under Charidemus
to Olynthus

................................................ Capture of Mecbyerna and Torone by Philip

................................................ Betrayal of Olynthus to Philip

................................................ Prosecution and acquittal of Philocrates for his
Appeal for Peace with Philip

347 B.C. ........................... Removal of Phalaecus from Phocian Command

........................................ Cooperation of Athens and Cersebleptes
of Thrace

........................................ Philip's intervention in central Greece

........................................ Siege of Halos

........................................ Phocians offer Thermopylae to Athens and Sparta

........................................ Athenian peace overtures to Philip

346 B.C. ........................... Athenian invitation for a *Koine Eirene* ("General
Peace" in Greece)

........................................ Exchange of Embassies between Athens
and Philip

........................................ Peace of Philocrates

........................................ Philip's advance to Thermopylae and submission
of Phocis

........................................ Philip presides over the Pythian Games at Delphi

........................................ Isocrates's *Letter to Philip*

........................................ Demosthenes, *On the Peace*

345 B.C. ........................... Amphictyonic council supports Athenian control
of Delos

........................................ Philip's campaign vs. Pleuratus and the Illyrians

344 B.C. ........................... Thessalian Revolt; Philip imposes
the Decadarchy

........................................ Demosthenes in the Peloponnesus

........................................ Mission of Python to Athens

........................................ Demosthenes, *Philippic II*

........................................ Mission of Hegesippus to Pella

343 B.C. ........................... Thebans press for Phocian Reparations

........................................ Impeachment and flight of Philocrates

........................................ Civil war in Elis and Megara

........................................ Pro-Macedonian factions seize Oreos and Eretria

........................................ Artaxerxes III reconquers (343–342 B.C.

........................................ Trial of Aeschines

........................................ Beginning of Phocian reparations

Timeline

..........................................Philip calls for *Koine Eirene*

342 B.C. ............................Intervention of Philip in Epirus

..........................................Athenian intervention in Acarnania

..........................................Macedonian backed disturbances in Euboea

..........................................Philip consolidates control of Thrace

..........................................Alliance of Philip and the Getae

..........................................Clash of Athens and Cardia in the Chersonesus

..........................................Macedonian colonies founded in Hebrus Valley

..........................................Athenian capture of Nicias, herald of Philip

341 B.C. ............................Macedonian aid to Cardia

..........................................Assault of Diopeithes on the Thracian cities

..........................................Chalcis-Athens alliance

..........................................Demosthenes, *On the Chersonesus*

..........................................Capture and execution of Hermias

..........................................Demosthenes, *Philippic III and IV*

..........................................Philip crushes Thracian kings Taras
and Cersebleptes

..........................................Athens takes Oreos and Eretria

..........................................Athenian missions to Byzantium, Perinthus,
Selymbria, Chios, Rhodes, and Persia

..........................................Philip's campaign on the Thracian Euxine Shore

340 B.C. ............................Athenian approval of the Euboean League

..........................................Siege of Perinthus by Philip

..........................................Letter of Philip; Macedonian fleet in Propontis

..........................................Siege of Selymbria by Philip

..........................................Macedonian capture of the Athenian grain fleet

..........................................Athens declares war on Philip II

..........................................Alexander defeats the Maedi

..........................................Chares bottles up Philip's fleet

..........................................Phocion replaces Chares

339 B.C. ............................ Escape of the Macedonian fleet

.......................................... Scythian campaign of Philip

.......................................... Amphictyonic council condemns Amphissa for sacrilege: outbreak of Fourth Sacred War (339–338 B.C.) and election of Philip as Hegemon

.......................................... Theban seizure of Nicaea

.......................................... Philip occupies Cytinium and Elataea

.......................................... Alliance of Thebes and Athens

.......................................... Skirmishes in Gravia Pass and along Cephisus River

338 B.C. ............................ Philip bypasses Gravia Pass; Parmenio captures Amphissa

.......................................... Battle of Chaeronea: collapse of the Athenian-Theban Alliance

.......................................... Philip's Settlements with Athens and Thebes

.......................................... Isocrates, *Letter III*

.......................................... Philip Calls for a *Koine Eirene* at Corinth

.......................................... Murder of Artaxerxes III: succession crisis in Persia

337 B.C. ............................ Proclamation of *Koine Eirene* at Corinth

.......................................... Creation of the League of Corinth

.......................................... Declaration of war upon Persia

.......................................... Marriage of Philip and Cleopatra

.......................................... Exiles of Olympias and Alexander

.......................................... Philip's campaign vs. Pleurias and the Illyrians

.......................................... Marriages of Attalus and Amyntas

.......................................... "Pixodarus" affair

336 B.C. ............................ Invasion of Asia Minor by Parmenio

.......................................... Assassination of Philip II

.......................................... Accession of Alexander the Great

.......................................... Accession of Darius III as Great King of Persia

.......................................... Alexander's descent into Greece

.......................................... Election as *tagos* of Thessaly

......................................... Alexander elected supreme general of the League
of Corinth

335 B.C. ............................ Campaigns in Thrace and Illyria

......................................... Alexander defeats Triballians and defeats Getae
on the Danube

......................................... Defeat of the Illyrians at Pelion

......................................... Revolt of Thebes and incipient rebellions
in Greece

......................................... Alexander enters Greece and sacks Thebes

334 B.C. ............................ Invasion of Asia Minor: Alexander visits Troy

......................................... Battle of the Granicus: Alexander conquers
western Asia Minor

......................................... Alexander frees Ionian cities and occupies Sardes

......................................... Creation of first Macedonian satrapy of Lydia

......................................... Sieges of Miletus and Halicarnassus

......................................... Alexander advances to Gordion

......................................... Memnon of Rhodes commands Persian fleet in
Aegean Sea.

333 B.C. ............................ Alexander loosens the "Gordian knot"

......................................... Darius III assembles army at Babylon and
advances to Amuq Plain in Syria

......................................... Agis III of Sparta raises mercenaries and calls for
freedom of the Greeks

......................................... Alexander crosses the Taurus, enters Cilicia, and
crosses Belan Pass

......................................... Death of Memnon at Mytilene; failure Persian
naval offensive

......................................... Battle of Issus: defeat and flight of Darius III

......................................... Capture of Royal Tent of Darius III and
royal family

......................................... Darius III offers peace terms to Alexander
Conquest of Syria and Phoenicia

332 B.C. ............................ Sieges of Tyre and Gaza

......................................... Alexander enters Egypt and hailed as pharaoh
at Memphis

331 B.C. ............................ Foundation of Alexandria; reorganization of Egypt

............................................ Alexander visits Oracle of Zeus Ammon at Siwah

............................................ Battle of Gaugamela or Arbela

............................................ Destruction of Persian army and flight of Darius III into Media

............................................ Alexander enters Babylon

............................................ Antipater defeats and slays Agis III at Battle of Megalopolis

............................................ Collapse of Greek revolt under Sparta

330 B.C. ............................ Alexander defeats Uxians and occupies Susa and Persepolis

............................................ The Burning of Persepolis: end of the Panhellenic War

............................................ Alexander advances to Ecbatana, and Darius III flees east

............................................ At Ecbatana, Alexander dismisses Greek allies

............................................ Parmenio, satrap of Media, holds treasury of 180,000 talents at Ecbatana

............................................ Bessus deposes Darius III and proclaimed Great King

............................................ Alexander's Pursuit of Bessus and murder of Darius III at Hecatompylos.

............................................ Alexander's conquest of Areia and Drangiana

............................................ Trials and executions of Philotas and Parmenio

............................................ Reorganization of the Macedonian cavalry under Hephaestion and Craterus

329 B.C. ............................ Alexander crosses Hindu Kush and invades Bactria and Sogdiana

............................................ Alexander crosses the Oxus and betrayal and capture of Bessus

............................................ Alexander founds Alexandria Eschate and campaigns against Scythians

............................................ Rebellion of Sogdians under Spitamenes and Sogdian Siege of Maracanda

Timeline

................................... Spitamenes defeats Macedonian relief column on Polytimetus River

................................... Alexander raises siege of Maracanda and wages war of pacification

................................... Betrayal and murder of Spitamenes by his allies the Massagetae

................................... Alexander winters at Bactra; execution of Bessus

328 B.C. ......................... Murder of Cleitus the Black; rising Macedonian opposition to Alexander

................................... Conquest of Sogdianan under Oxyartes and Chorienes.

................................... Capture of Sogdian Rock and Marriage of Roxane

................................... Raising of Iranian cavalry and Training of the Epigonoi ordered.

................................... Disputes over the *proskynesis* and Persian ceremony at court

................................... Conspiracy of Pages and Death of Callisthenes

327 B.C. ......................... Alexander crosses the Hindu Kush and invades India

................................... Pacification of Sajaur and Swat valleys, and assault on Aornus (Pir6:40 PM4/8/2010sar)

................................... Submission of Gandhara; Alexander received by King Taxiles

326 B.C. ......................... Battle of the Hydaspes; defeat of Porus

................................... Founding of Nicaea and Bucephela

................................... Conquest of the Land of the Five Rivers.

................................... Mutiny of Macedonians on Hyphasis (Beas) River

325 B.C. ......................... Construction and launching of fleet on the Indus

................................... Pacification of the Mallians and Oxydracae

................................... Alexander nearly killed in assault on city of the Mallians

................................... Return march through the Gedrosian Desert

................................... Fleet under Nearchus sails Indian Ocean and Persian Gulf

324 B.C. ............................ Alexander at Babylon

........................................... Reorganization of empire

........................................... Decrees for restoration of exiles and
for deification

........................................... Mutiny of Macedonians at Opis

........................................... Death of Hephaestion

323 B.C. ............................ Outbreak of the Lamian War; rising of Athens,
Thessalians, and Aetolians

........................................... Antipater in Lamia besieged by Athenian-
Thessalian-Aetolian army

........................................... Death of Alexander at Babylon

........................................... Conference of Babylon: division of Empire

........................................... Regency under Perdiccas, Antipater, and Craterus

........................................... Birth of Alexander IV and joint rule with Philip
III Arrhidaeus

........................................... Revolt of Greek Mercenaries in Bactria
(323–322 B.C.)

322 B.C. ............................ Perdiccas invades Cappadocia; Antigonus flees
to Macedon

........................................... Leonnatus is slain while relieving Antipater
in Lamia

........................................... Battle of Crannon: Craterus and Antipater crush
Greek rebels

........................................... Dissolution of Hellenic League

........................................... Antipater offers marriage alliances to Craterus,
Ptolemy, and Perdiccas

........................................... Outbreak of Civil War: Perdiccas and Eumenes
of Cardia (championing royal family) against
Antipater, Antigonus, Craterus and Ptolemy

321 B.C. ............................ Perdiccas invades Egypt to defeat Ptolemy

........................................... Murder of Perdiccas in Egypt; Seleucus declared
satrap of Babylon

........................................... Eumenes defeats and slays Craterus in
Asia Minor

.......................................... Conference of Triparadisos: Antipater declared
regent of the empire and takes custody of Kings
Philip III Arrhidaeus and Alexander IV

320 B.C. ........................... Antigonus clears Asia Minor of Perdiccan forces

.......................................... Eumenes besieged in Nora in Cappadocia

319 B.C. ........................... Death of Antipater; Polyperchon regent of empire

.......................................... Ptolemy occupies Coele-Syria; Cassander
invades Greece

.......................................... War between Polyperchon and Eumenes
(championing royal family) against Ptolemy,
Cassander and Antigonus

318 B.C. ........................... Battle of Megalopolis: Cassamder defeats
Polyperchon and overruns Macedon and Greece

.......................................... Cassander besieges Athens

.......................................... Eumenes with Silver Shields invades Phoenicia,
then withdraws eastward

.......................................... Antigonus pursues Eumenes east (319–316 B.C.)

317 B.C. ........................... Athens surrenders to Cassander

.......................................... Demetrius of Phalerum installed as tyrant
of Athens

.......................................... Polyperchon, reduced to Peloponnesus, declares
"Freedom of the Greeks"

.......................................... Olympias invades Macedon; suicide of Philip III
and Eurydice

.......................................... Cassander beseiges Olympias in Pydna

.......................................... Eumenes defeats Antigonus at Paractacene
in Media

316 B.C. ........................... Cassander takes Pydna; Olympias executed

.......................................... Cassander master of Macedon and Greece

.......................................... Battle of Gabiene: Eumenes betrayed
to Antigonus

.......................................... Execution of Eumenes

315 B.C. ........................... Flight of Seleucus from Babylon to Ptolemy

.......................................... Antigonus supreme in the east and reorganizes
the "Upper Satrapies"

............................................ War between Antigonus and Demetrius against Ptolemy, Cassander, and Lysimachus

............................................ Siege of Tyre (315–314 B.C.)

............................................ Antigonus declares "Freedom of the Greeks" and organizes Nesotic League

314 B.C. ........................... Tyre surrenders to Antigonus

............................................ Polyperchon raises Greece on behalf of Antigonus

313 B.C. ........................... Ptolemy moves his capital to Alexandria

312 B.C. ........................... Antigonus frustrated by winds in crossing Bosporus

............................................ Ptolemy invades Coele-Syria; battle of Gaza

............................................ Seleucus retakes Babylon

311 B.C. ........................... Truce between Antigonus and the allies Ptolemy, Lysimachus, and Cassander

............................................ War of Antigonus against Seleucus

............................................ Seleucus founds Seleucia ad Tigrim and consolidates his power in Iran (311–308 B.C.)

310 B.C. ........................... Cassander murders Alexander IV and Roxane: end of Argead family

............................................ Ptolemy annexes Cyprus

............................................ Outbreak of war between Antigonus and Ptolemy

309 B.C. ........................... Reconciliation of Cassander and Polyperchon

............................................ Cassander supreme in Macedon and Greece

............................................ Reconciliation between Ptolemy and Demetrius

............................................ Reconciliation between Antigonus and Seleucus

308 B.C. ........................... Ptolemy intervenes in Greece against Cassander

............................................ Ptolemaic forces seize Corinth and Sicyon

............................................ Ptolemy declares "Freedom of the Greeks"

............................................ Ptolemy withdraws to Egypt

307 B.C. ........................... Demetrius Poliocretes invades Greece

............................................ Demetrius restores Athenian democracy and expels Demetrius of Phalerum

............................................ General war in Greece

Timeline

306 B.C. ............................ Battle of Salamis: Demetrius defeats Ptolemy

............................................ Antigonid annexation of Cyprus

............................................ Antigonus and Demetrius take title
king (*basileus*)

............................................ Failure of Antigonus's invasion of Egypt (fall)

305 B.C. ............................ Demetrius besieges Rhodes (305–304 B.C.)

............................................ War between Seleucus and Chandragupta
(305–303 B.C.)

............................................ Ptolemy, Cassander, and Lysimachus assume
title king

303 B.C. ............................ Demetrius drives Cassander out of Greece

............................................ Treaty between Seleucus and Chandragupta

............................................ Seleucus surrenders Indus valley for
500 elephants

302 B.C. ............................ Ptolemy, Lysimachus, Seleucus, and Cassander
renew grand alliance against Antigonus
and Demetrius

............................................ Demetrius restores Hellenic League

............................................ Lysimachus invades Asia Minor

301 B.C. ............................ Battle of Ipsus: defeat and death of Antigonus

............................................ Partition of Alexandrine Empire

............................................ Cassander supreme in Greece and Macedon

............................................ Lysimachus occupies Western Asia Minor and
refounds Ephesus

............................................ Seleucus secures Upper Satrapies and founds
Antioch in Syria as new capital

............................................ Ptolemy illegally annexes Coele-Syria

300 B.C. ............................ Marriage alliance between Ptolemy
and Lysimachus

299 B.C. ............................ Marriage alliance between Seleucus
and Demetrius I

298/7 B.C. ........................ Death of Cassander and then his son Philip IV

297/6 B.C. ........................ Zipoetes declares himself King of Bithynia

............................................ Civil war in Macedon between Antipater IV
and Alexander V

| | |
|---|---|
| 296 B.C. | Demetrius invades Greece |
| 295 B.C. | Great siege of Athens (295–294 B.C.) by Demetrius |
| 294 B.C. | Surrender of Athens and Imposition of Oligarchy |
| | Ptolemy occupies Cyprus; Seleucus takes Cilicia |
| | Lysimachus annexes the Ionian cities |
| | Demetrius Poliorcetes king in Macedon |
| | Seleucus invests Antiochus I with co-regency and rule of the "Upper Satrapies" from Babylon |
| 293 B.C. | Demetrius founds Demetrias in Thessaly |
| | Getae defeats and temporarily captures Lysimachus |
| 292 B.C. | Revolt in Boeotia |
| | Outbreak of war between Demetrius and Pyrrhus, king of Epirus |
| | Demetrius invades Aetolia, allied to Pyrrhus |
| 291 B.C. | Pyrrhus obtains Corcyra as dowry from Agathocles of Syracuse |
| | Ptolemy secures Nesotic League in central Aegean |
| 288/7 B.C. | Invasion and partition of Macedon between Pyrrhus and Lysimachus |
| | Ptolemy annexes Tyre and Sidon from Demetrius |
| 287 B.C. | Athens revolts under Olympichus; restoration of the Athenian democracy |
| | Demetrius invades Asia Minor, capturing Ephesus and Sardes, and advances east into Cilicia |
| | Antigonus II Gonatas regent in Europe |
| 286 B.C. | Anabasis of Demetrius and his surrender to Seleucus |
| 285 B.C. | Lysimachus expels Pyrrhus from Western Macedon |
| | Lysimachus controls Greece, Macedon, Thrace, and Asia Minor |
| | Ptolemy II created co-king with Ptolemy I |

.......................................... Ptolemy Ceraunus joins court of Lysimachus

284/3 B.C. .......................... Dynastic crisis at court of Lysimachus

.......................................... Arrest and execution of Agathocles

283 B.C. ............................. Deaths of Demetrius I and Ptolemy I

282 B.C. ............................. Seleucus invades Asia Minor (late summer)

281 B.C. ............................. Battle of Corupedium: defeat and death
of Lysimachus

.......................................... Ptolemy Ceraunus murders Seleucus and is
declared king of Macedon

.......................................... Antiochus I succeeds to Seleucid empire

280 B.C. ............................. Gauls invade Macedon and Thrace

.......................................... Defeat and death of Ptolemy Ceraunus

.......................................... Refounding of Achaean League

.......................................... Clash between Antiochus I and Ptolemy II

279 B.C. ............................. Gallic invasion of Greece repelled at Delphi

.......................................... Gauls establish kingdom of Tylis in Thrace

.......................................... Ptolemaieia celebrated in Alexandria

.......................................... Nicomedes succeeds as king of Bithynia and
invites Gauls into Asia Minor

278 B.C. ............................. Gauls (Galatians) invade Asia Minor

.......................................... Reconciliation between Antiochus I
and Antigonus II

277 B.C. ............................. Battle of Lysmacheia: Antiognus II Gonatas
defeats Gauls and hailed king of Macedon

276 B.C. ............................. Aetolians annex Dolopia; Aegium joins
Achaean League

.......................................... Antigonus II secures Thessaly

.......................................... Philataerus begins minting coins at Pergamum

275 B.C. ............................. Marriage of Ptolemy II to Arsinoe II

274 B.C. ............................. Outbreak of First Syrian War (272–272 B.C.)

.......................................... Pyrrhus occupies Macedon

272 B.C. ............................. Death of Pyrrhus in Argos

.......................................... Antigonus II supreme in Macedon and Greece

# Glossary

**Achaemenid**: Denotes the dynasty that ruled Persia between 559 and 330 B.C.

**acropolis**: High point of a Greek city, where springs and temples were located. The Acropolis of Athens, rebuilt in the 5th century B.C., is considered the showcase of such citadels.

**Aeolian**: A Greek dialect, likely a mixture of West and East Greek elements, spoken in Thessaly and Boeotia, and Aeolian colonies established on the island of Lesbos, and in the Troad and Aeolis on the northwestern shores of Asia Minor.

*Agema*: The elite infantry guard of the Macedonian king. In Bactria, Alexander the Great created a cavalry agema which replaced the *ile basilike*, "royal squadron," commanded by Cleitus the Black.

*agger*: In Roman military parlance denotes a great ramp built as an incline plane against the wall of a besieged city.

**agora**: The market place of a Greek city; it evolved into the civic center with public building for the boule, law courts, and assembly.

**Agrianians** (or Agrianes): Thracian javelin men recruited into an elite unit; at Gordion in 333 B.C., the unit was raised from 500 to 1,000 men.

**Ai Khanoum**: Possibly Alexandria on the Oxus and the later Eucratidia is on the confluence of the Oxus (Amu Darya) and Kokcha rivers in Bactria (modern Afghanistan). In 1964–1974, the French archaeological team under Paul Bernard uncovered a Greek city between the 4th and 2nd centuries B.C.

*Amphictyony* ("league of neighbors"): The federal council of 22 members based on tribal affiliation rather than city-states that governed the sanctuary of Delphi. The member peoples (*ethnos*; pl. *ethne*) were Aenians, Oetaeans, Dolopes, Phthian Achaeans, Magnesians, Malians, Perrhaebians, Thessalians,

Phocians, Opuntian Locrians, Ozolian Locrians, Opuntian Locrians, the Pythians (the priestly families of Delphi), Boeotians (represented by Thebes), Dorians (represented by Sparta), and Ionians (represented by Athens). In 346 B.C., the Phocians lost their two representatives and their votes awarded to Philip II. In 279 B.C., the Phocians were readmitted after their defense of Delphi against the Galatians.

**amphora**: A large ceramic container with a pointed bottom so that it could be placed upright in sand boxes and used for the grain, wine, and oil.

**Anabasis** ("March Up Country": The narrative account of Xenophon of the expedition of Cyrus the Younger and the retreat of the Ten Thousand Greek mercenaries in 401–399 B.C.

**Anatolia**: The Asiatic peninsula of modern Turkey. Specifically it denotes the interior half of the peninsula dominated by the high plateau.

**Antigonid**: The dynasty of Macedonian kings descended from Demetrius Poliocretes, son of Antigonus I and Phila, daughter of Antipater. From Antigonus II Gonatas (281–239 B.C.) on, Antigonid kings ruled Macedon down to 168 B.C.

**Archaic Age** (750–480 B.C.): The period between the composition of the epic poems of Homer and the defeat of King Xerxes of Persia. This period witnessed the emergence of the *polis* (city-state) and a distinct Hellenic civilization.

**archon**: An elected official of a Greek city; the eponymous archon gave his name to the official year. At Athens from 681 B.C., a board of nine archons comprised an eponymous archon, polemarch, *basileus* (king-priest) and six *thesothetai* (keepers of the laws).

**Areopagus** ("Hill of Ares": The hillock to the northwest of the Acropolis of Athens where the aristocratic council, composed of ex-archons, state as a court.

**arête**: The bravery expected of Homeric heroes and, later, hoplites of city-states; the term was extended by philosophers to mean virtue.

**Argead**: The royal family of Macedon since late 8th century B.C. King Alexander I (498–454 B.C.) established the claim that the Argead family was descended from Temenus, a legendary hero of Argos who was himself descended from Heracles. Thereafter, the members of the Argead house were accepted as Greek.

**aristocracy** ("rule of the best"): Was government by the landed noble families who monopolized high office and membership on the council (boule). Aristocrats, who served as the cavalry, reduced the power of hereditary kings in favor of aristocratic republics in the 8th century B.C.

**Asia Minor**: The Asiatic peninsula of modern Turkey today; Greeks were settled on the northern, western, and southern shores since the Dark Ages (1225–900 B.C.).

**Attalid**: The Greek-speaking dynasty that ruled Pergamum between 282 and 133 B.C. The dynastic name was taken from Attalus I (241–197 B.C.) who first took the title king in 239 B.C.

**autonomia**: "Autonomy" is the cherished right of each city-state to live under its own laws.

**barbarian** (pl. barbaroi; Greek *barbaros*): Any designated non-Greek foreigners who did not live in a polis and so under the rule of law. The term did not denote peoples with an inferior culture.

**basileus** (pl. basileis): The name for king in archaic and classical Greece. The kings as described in Homer (c. 750 B.C.) were reduced to elected religious officials except at Sparta. At Sparta, two hereditary kings from two separate families, Agiad and Eurypontid, reigned as commanders and priests. In classical literature, "the king" denoted the Great King of Persia. The Greek title was used by Argead kings of Macedon and then the great kings of the Hellenistic Age.

**boule** (pl. boulai): The council of a city-state that summoned and set the agenda of the assembly. In aristocracies, oligarchies, and timocracies, the council was the prime governing body often composed of ex-magistrates selected from the propertied classes. At democratic Athens after the reforms of Cleisthenes in 508–506 B.C., the boule reflected the democratic assembly. Each year 500 members, 50 from each tribe, were chosen by sortition to serve on the council. Service was restricted to citizens of thirty years and older; only two terms were permitted in a lifetime. From 457 B.C., the property qualification for membership on the boule was removed.

**Boeotarch**: One of the seven political and military officials of the federal Boeotian League, in the 4$^{th}$ century B.C. Representation was based on population so that Thebes had four Boeotarchs. Epaminondas and Pelopidas each held this office.

**Boeotian League**: A federal league of the 11 cities of Boeotia that dated from the 6$^{th}$ century B.C. The member states, represented based on population, sent a total 60 delegates to sit on the federal council (boule) at Thebes. Seven Boeotarchs acted as the executive and military officials. The federal council had to submit final ratification treaties and declarations of war to the councils of each member city. In 379 B.C., the constitutions of the Boeotian cities were changed from oligarchic (with voting by the propertied classes only) to democratic.

**Cadmea**: The citadel of Thebes named after the legendary Cadmus, son of King Agenor of Tyre and brother of Europa. Cadmus was credited with founding Thebes and introducing the alphabet to Greece.

***cataphractus*** (pl. *cataphracti*): A heavy cavalryman wearing chain or lamellar armor, who fought primarily as a lancer. The Iranians of the Upper Satrapies excelled as cataphracti.

***chiliarch*** ("commander of 1,000"): The title given to the chief administrator of the empire; it was the Greek translation of the Persian *hazarapatish*. In 324 B.C., Hephaestion was appointed the first chiliarch; next Perdiccas held the position in 323–320 B.C.

**chora** ("hinterland"): The countryside of a polis. Attica was the hinterland of the polis Athens, and all free residents were Athenian citizens. Sparta controlled Laconia and Messenia, and residents in these hinterlands were either *perioikoi* or helots.

**cleurchy** (Greek *kleourchos*; pl. *kleourchoi*): Cleurchy was (1) an overseas colony of Athenians who retained their Athenian citizenship, or (2) Greek veterans settled in the Fayyum by the Ptolemaic kings of Egypt.

**Companion Cavalry** (*hetairoi*): Comprised of heavily armored Macedonian nobles and squires trained to fight in squadrons (*ilai*) and armed with a thrusting spear (*xyston*).

**daric**: The gold coin struck by the Great Kings of Persia. The daric (8.35 grams) was exchanged against 20 silver sigloi (singular siglos; 5.35 grams.). The gold daric was equivalent to 25 Attic silver drachmae.

**Delian League**: The alliance to pursue the naval war against Persia organized by the Athenian general Aristides at the behest of the Chians, Samians, and Mytileneans in 477 B.C. The league's delegates met on the island of Delos. In 454 B.C., the league's treasury was removed to Athens, and this action marked the conversion of the Delian League into the Athenian Empire. The league was abolished in 404 B.C.

**Delos**: An island of the Cyclades in the Aegean Sea, with a celebrated sanctuary of Apollo whose cult was common to all Ionians. In 426 B.C., the Athenian general Nicias conducted a purification of the sanctuary and reorganization of the festivals.

**Delphi**: The sanctuary of Apollo on the southwestern spur of Mount Parnassus and seat of the oracle on the site of the *omphalos*, "the navel of the world," where Apollo slew the serpent Pytho and instituted the Pythian Games. The shrine was common to all the Greeks after the First Sacred War (c. 590–585 B.C.).

**demagogue**: Denoted the radical democratic orators who dominated the Athenian assembly.

**democracy**: The rule of the people (*demos*). It was a constitution under which all male citizens in the sovereign assembly had the right to vote and sit on popular juries. At Athens, after 461 B.C., property qualifications were eliminated for the council and office. In 508–506 B.C., Cleisthenes reformed Athens into the first democracy.

*demos* (pl. *demoi*): The sovereign body of citizens.

**diadem**: The pearl necklace worn as a headband to denote Persian royalty; it was adopted by Alexander the Great after 330 B.C.

*Diadochoi* ("Successors"): Denoted the Macedonian generals of Alexander the Great, who carved out kingdoms for themselves in 323-301 B.C.

**dike** ("justice"): Initially denoted "the way" and then personified as the goddess Dike, daughter of Zeus in Hesiod's *Theogony*. Dike was the goal of the rule of law in the polis.

**diolkos** ("across portage"): The four-mile track way for conveying ships across the Isthmus of Corinth since the 7th century B.C. The modern canal linking the Gulf of Corinth and the Saronic Gulf largely follows the route of the diolkos

**Dorian**: The West Greek dialect spoken in the southern and eastern Peloponnsus (Messenia, Laconia, Argolid, Corinth, Megara, Sicyon, and Aegina, on the islands of Thera and Melos in the Cyclades, the Dorian cities of Crete, Cos, Cnidus, and Rhodes, and in the Dorian settlements of Sicily, southern Italy, and Cyrene (today eastern Libya).

**drachma** (pl. drachmae): The principle silver coin struck by Greek cities. The drachma was divided into six obols. Cities struck multiples and fractions of the drachma; hence, cities struck decadrachma (ten drachmae), tetradrachma (four drachma), didrachma (two drachma), and hemidrachma (half-drachma). City currencies were based upon a drachma of varying weight so that coins were exchanged in markets by weight. The two principle standards were the Aeginetic and Attic. The Aeginetic standard was based on a heavy drachma (6.10 grams) and used by Aegina, the Peloponnesus, and central Greece. The lighter Attic drachma (4.30 grams) was used by Athens, Corinth, and cities in the Aegean and Sicily. Philip II adopted the Attic standard for his gold currency. Alexander the Great adopted the Attic standard for Macedonian silver coins. *See also* **stater**.

*ekkleseia* (pl. *ekkleseiai*): The assembly of Athens comprising all free adult males from 18 years of age. The assembly, requiring a quorum of 6,000, was the sovereign body that met at the Pynx, a hill to the west of the agora.

*eleutheria* ("freedom"): The right of a polis to pursue its own foreign policy and aims.

**Epanorthosis**: The amendment to the Peace of Philocrates proposed by Demosthenes in 343 B.C. It provided for the revision of the text from "each holds what he has" to "each holds what is his," thereby allowing Athens reopen claim to Amphipolis. Philip II rejected it and thereafter made no further concessions to Athens.

**Ephebe** (pl. *epheboi*; Greek *ephebos*): The legal classification of Greek male adolescents (16 to 20 years) who were in training as hoplites. They were eligible to be called up for home defense.

*Ephemerides* ("Royal Diaries"): The daily reports of the court of Alexander the Great kept by the Greek secretary Eumenes of Cardia and so the putative source for many details reported in the later historical and biographical accounts on Alexander.

*ephor* ("overseer"): One of five annually elected officials who supervised the training of citizens (*agoge*), public morals, and social activities at Sparta. The creation of the board was dated to 754 B.C. The ephors assumed many of the judicial and civil powers once held by the kings.

*Epigonoi* ("Offsprings"): The 30,000 Iranian youths who were drilled in Macedonian arms to fight as phalangites in 330–324 B.C.

**epigraphy**: The scholarly study of inscriptions.

**Erythraean Sea**: Greek for Indian Ocean.

*euergetes* (pl. *euergetai*): A benefactor of a Greek city-state; kings in the Hellenistic Age were *eunomia* ("well governed"): Denoted the ideal of each city-state to be governed by the rule of law; Sparta was exalted as the model of eunomia.

*eupatridai* ("well descended"): Denoted the noble families of early Athens who alone could be elected to the board of archons and so enter the Areopagus.often hailed by this title.

**Eurypontid**: The junior royal family of Sparta which traced its descent to the legendary Heraclid Procles who, with his elder twin Eurysthenes, led the Dorians into the Peloponnesus two generations after the Trojan War.

**Euthydemid**: The Greek dynasty descended from Euthydemus (c. 223–200 B.C.) that ruled over Sogdiana and Bactria down to 130 B.C. Agathocles (190-180 B.C.) established a branch of the dynasty ruling in northwestern India.

**Fetters of Greece**: The strategic points of Demetrias, Chalcis, and the Acrocorinth garrisoned by Macedonian kings in 322–196 B.C.

**gerousia**: The council of Sparta comprised of 28 elected elders from 60 years and the two hereditary kings.

**Gordian knot:** Attached the cornel shaft to the oxcart of Gordius, who was received as king of Phrygia when he arrived at the capital Gordion in the cart. His successor, Midas, dedicated the cart to Zeus, and an oracle noted that he who would loosen the intricate knot would become lord of Asia. In 334 B.C., Alexander either cut the knot with his sword or pulled out the pole pin, thereby fulfilling the oracle.

**harmost**: A Spartan governor imposed in the allied cities of the former Delian League.

**Hecatomnid**: The dynasty of Carian lords descended from Hecatomnus (c. 404–358 B.C.), who ruled over southwestern Asia Minor down to 326 B.C.

*hegemon* ("leader"): The leading city-state in an alliance. In 546 B.C., Sparta emerged as the first hegemon in the Greek world at the head of the Peloponnesian League. Athens was the hegemon of the Delian League organized in 477 B.C.

**Hellene**: Greek name for themselves from the time of Hesiod (c. 700 B.C.).

**Hellenic League**: *See* **League of Corinth**.

**Hellenistic** ("Greek-like"): Denotes (1) the period after the death of Alexander the Great (323–31 B.C.) or (2) the mixed Hellenic-Near Eastern civilization of the same period.

*Hellenotamias* (pl. *Hellenotamiai*; "treasurers of the Hellenes"): The 10 Athenians elected by the Athenian assembly annually to administer the funds of the Delian League.

**Hellespont**: The Greek name for the Dardanelles, the straits separating Asia Minor from Europe.

**helot**: A slave in the Spartan state; most helots were the private property of their masters, and not state slaves as often surmised in modern scholarly accounts.

**hetairoi**: *See* **Companion Cavalry**.

**hipparchy**: The tactical unit (1,000 men) created by Alexander the Great in his reorganization of the cavalry after 330 B.C.

*homonoia* ("concord"): The ideal to unity and peace among the Greeks promoted by Panhellenists.

**hoplite** (pl. *Hoplitai*; Greek hoplites): The heavily armored Greek citizen equipped with the large shield (*hoplon*) and thrusting spear, who fought in a phalanx.

**hypaspists**: The elite Macedonian infantry totaling 1,500 and later 3,000 men. They usually assumed the position between the phalanx and Companion Cavalry in Alexander's battles. Although their arms and armor are uncertain, they were likely the best phalangites comparable to Grenadiers in European armies of the 18th and early 19th century.

*Hypomnemata* ("Notebooks"): The final plans of Alexander the Great, according to Diodorus Siculus, published by Perdiccas at Babylon immediately after the king's death. These included grandiose building projects, transfers of populations within the empire, and the conquest of the lands of the Western Mediterranean.

*Ile* (pl. *ilai*; "squadron"): The tactical unit (200 to 300 men) of the Companion cavalry. The royal squadron (*ile basilike*) was the royal bodyguard.

**Ionia**: Designated the western shore of Asia Minor from Smyrna (modern Izmir) to Halicarnassus (modern Bodrum), where Ionian Greeks had settled. Ionia also included the neighboring islands, notably Samos and Chios, also settled by Ionian speakers.

**Ionian**: The East Greek dialect spoken in Attica, Euboea, Ionia, the Chalcidice, most of the Aegean island, and the Ionian colonies of the Hellespontine regions, Black Sea, Sicily, and southern Italy. Attic, the Athenian language within this dialect, emerged as the literary language of the Greek world in the 5th and 4th centuries B.C.

**Ionian Revolt**: The abortive rebellion of Ionians (499–494 B.C.), instigated by Aristagoras, tyrant of Miletus, against Persian rule. The rebellion spread to the Hellespontine regions, Caria, Lycia, and Greek Cyprus.

**isegoria**: The right of all citizens to access to the Athenian assembly.

**isonomia**: The right of equal treatment under the laws of all Athenian citizens.

*isopoliteia* ("equal citizenship"): A grant of shared citizen rights to an individual or a polis. In 392 B.C., Argos and Corinth voted *isopoliteia* between their citizens. The union was dissolved by the Peace of Antalcidas in 387/6 B.C.

**Isthmus of Corinth**: The narrow land bridge that connects the Peloponnesus to Central Greece.

*kairos*: The opportune time, considered a gift of the gods.

*kaloi k'agathoi*: ("good and beautiful"): Designated aristocrats who maintained the conceit that they alone by descent had the right to rule. The term is equivalent to those of gentle blood in 18th-century Great Britain.

**katioikes** (pl. *katioikai*): A Greco-Macedonian veteran of the Attalid or Seleucid kings settled in a new founded Hellenic city.

**kausia**: The traditional broad-brimmed riding hat of Macedonians.

**Koine Eirene** ("Common Peace"): Was proclaimed in treaties of the 4th century B.C. It declared a cessation of hostilities among all belligerents, recognized all signatories as legitimate governments, and provided for adjudication of disputes. The first such common peace was declared in the Peace of Antalcidas in 387/6 B.C.

**Koine Greek**: The "common" Greek spoken in the Hellenistic world; it was a simplified dialect of Attic Greek.

**koinon** (pl. *koina*): A regional religious league.

**League of Corinth** (or Hellenic League): A federal league of Greek states established by Philip II of Macedon in 337 B.C. with the aim of avenging the invasion of Xerxes in 480 B.C. A federal council or *synedrion* governed from Corinth, and Philip II and later Alexander the Great each was elected supreme commander of league forces (*strategos autokrator*). In 322 B.C., Antipater and Craterus disbanded the league. In 303/2 B.C., Antigonus I and Demetrius Poliocretes briefly re-established the league.

**liturgy** (pl. *leitourgiai*; Greek *leitourgia*,): A designated public task, the cost of which citizens annually assumed. Liturgies included the constructing and equipping of a trireme or many social activities and amenities of the polis. By the 4th century B.C., liturgies at Athens represented a voluntary taxation of the property classes to maintain public life.

***medimnos*** (pl. *medimnoi*): A dry measure of 48 choenikes equivalent to 25 kilograms or 55 lbs. An adult male annually required six to seven medimnoi of wheat.

***Medize*** ("to side with the Medes"): Refers to those Greeks who sided with the Persians.

***Melophoroi*** ("apple-bearers"): Formed the infantry bodyguard (1,000 men) of the king of Persia. They were so named because their spear-butts ended in a golden apple.

***metropolis*** (pl. *metropoleis*; "mother city"): The founding city of a Greek colony. In Ptolemaic Egypt, it referred to the major township of a nome that was the center of the Greek community.

**mora** (pl. *morai*): A tactical unit of 400 to 500 men in a hoplite phalanx.

***Museion*** ("Museum"): The scholarly academy and library at Alexandria most likely founded by Ptolemy II (283–246 B.C.).

**mystery rites**: Initiation rites to a cult. The Eleusinian mysteries, performed annually in the Telesterion of Eleusis to the Athenian citizens, was a ritual drama of Hades's carrying off of Persephone. Mystery cults were cults with such initiation rites and dramas, and they did not represent enthusiastic, irrational cults that undermined civic and family cults in the Hellenistic and Roman ages.

**navarch**: The Spartan office of admiral, held one year, on election by the Spartan assembly. It was adopted to designate admiral of a royal fleet with Alexander the Great.

**nomos** (pl. *nomoi*): The law passed by the assembly and distinct from sacred law (*themis*).

**numismatics**: The scholarly study of coins and medals.

**obol**: One-sixth of the silver drachma; two obols was the per diem wage paid to jurors and councillors at Athens. *See also* **drachma.**

**oligarchy** ("rule of the few"): The government in the hands of the propertied classes (with the emphasis on birth in an aristocracy). The propertied classes monopolized high office and the boule.

**Olympia**: The sanctuary of Olympian Zeus on the Alpheus River in Elis. The Panhellenic Olympic Games were held at the sanctuary every fourth year.

**Panhellenic**: Refers to "all-Greek," specifically denoting of Pythia, Olympia, Nemea, and Isthmia which formed the four-year cycle of Panhellenic Games.

**Panhellenism** and **Panhellenist**: Refer to the policy and Athenian intellectuals, inspired by Isocrates (436–338 B.C.). Panhellenists called for the end of inter-state war and unity of the Greeks in a national campaign against Persia.

**Peace of Antalcidas** or **King's Peace** (386 B.C.): Ended the Corinthian War (396–386 B.C.) and represented a diplomatic success for Sparta at the price of returning the Ionian cities to the Great King Artaxerxes II of Persia. Sparta maintained her hegemony in Greece, and Athens was recognized as independent.

**Peace of Callias** (449 B.C.): The peace that ended the war between Athens and the Great King Artaxerxes I. Athenian domination was recognized in the Aegean Sea, but Athens withdrew support from rebels against the Great King in Cyprus and Egypt.

**Peace of Philocrates** (346 B.C.): Ended the war between Philip II and Athens based on each the principle that each signatory kept those territories in its possession at the time of the ratification of the treaty. Hence, the Athenians recognized Philip's conquests of Amphipolis and the Chalcidice. The Phocians were excluded from the treaty.

**Peloponnesian League**: The modern designation for the alliances (*symmachia*) between Sparta and her allies concluded in the late 6th and early 5th century B.C.

**Peloponnesus** ("Island of Pelops"): The three-pronged peninsula of southern Greece attached to central Greece by the Isthmus of Corinth.

*perioikoi* ("dwellers around"): The free residents of Laconia and Messenia who lived under their own laws but owed military service to the Spartan state. Residents of similar classification were found in Thessaly and Dorian Crete.

*periplous* ("sailing around"): Refers to the tactics employed by Athenian triremes, based on speed and timing, to flank and ram an opposing trireme.

**Periplus**: A navigational manual describing sailing distances and times. Onesicritus, helmsman of Nearchus, wrote a periplus of a voyage on the Erythraean Sea in 324 B.C. A detailed *Periplus of the Erythaean Sea* survives from the early 1st century A.D. and reports the sailing conditions and trade between Rome and India.

**phalanx**: Refers to a dense formation of heavy infantry, either Greek hoplites (usually drawn up eight deep) or Macedonians armed with *sarissai* and drawn up 16 men deep. The Macedonian phalanx comprised of *taxeis* (1,536 men) or "regiments," each of which was divided into three pentacosiarchies (singular pentakosiarchy), each of 512 men.

*Philippic*: One of three orations of Demosthenes delivered to the Athenian assembly calling for opposition to Philip II. The *Philippics* (351, 344, and 341 B.C.) are masterpieces of denunciation of a tyrant.

*philoxenia*: The mutual inherited guest friendship between families of different poleis. The guest friend (*philoxenos*) stood as surety in all legal matters as well as offered shelter and hospitality to visiting guest friends.

*phoros* ("carried"): The assessed tribute in silver paid by members of the Delian League in lieu of military service. Aristides fixed the first assessment at 460 talents; by 425 B.C. the tribute might have been as high as 1,500 talents. In the Second Athenian Naval Confederacy, such tribute was prohibited.

polis (pl. poleis): The city-state where citizens governed themselves by the rule of law. Hellenes alone were seen as living in a polis, and so this political conceit was the means by which Hellenes distinguished themselves from all others who were barbarians. The Panhellenist Isocrates (426–338 B.C.) raised the point that barbarians, who adopted the life of the polis, could join the Hellenic community.

*pothos* ("longing" or "yearning"): The emotion that inspired Alexander the Great.

*primus inter pares* ("first among equals": The Latin denoting a monarch who rules with the consent of his nobles.

*proskynesis* ("kissing towards"): An act of obeisance performed by Persians to the Great King, but in Greece and Macedon such reverence was accorded to gods. Those of high rank gave a kiss on the cheek to the Great King; those of lower rank had to bow and prostrate. Callisthenes thwarted Alexander's effort to introduce the ritual in 328 B.C.

*proxenos* (pl. *proxenoi*): A citizen who was the official guest friend of all citizens of another city-state. *Proxenoi* presented the embassies of a guest city to their own city's boule and assembly.

***prytaneion***: The circular building in the agora which housed the *prytany* on call. *See also **tholos***.

***prytanis*** (pl. *prytaneis*; "president"): One of 50 members of the *prytany* or one-tenth of the Boule of 500 at Athens.

***prytany***: Designated both the official month (40 days) and the one-tenth of the boule on call during the official month. Each *prytany* comprised 50 men chosen by lot from one of the ten tribes. Each *prytany*, when presiding over its month (determined by sortition), was on call 24 hours. The *prytany* thus acted as the executive committee of the boule and received all foreign delegations wishing to speak to the Athenian assembly.

**Ptolemaic**: The Greek-speaking Macedonian dynasty descended from Ptolemy I (323–283 B.C.) who ruled Egypt down to 30 B.C.

***pythia***: The prophetess who delivered the oracle at Delphi, often selected for their perceived powers that put them in contact with the divine world. It has been suggested that these powers were heightened by ethylene gas vapors issuing forth from beneath the sanctuary.

***quinquereme*** (Greek *penteres*; Latin *quinqueremis*;"ship of five banks of oars"): The heavy warship that replaced the trireme in the $4^{th}$ century B.C. The ship had 90 oars on each side divided into three banks of thirty oars. Two men rowed for each oar on the lower banks so the crew of 300 rowers manned a *quinquereme* (as opposed to 180 rowers of a trireme).

**Rosetta stone**: A trilingual inscription (in hieroglyphic Egyptian, demotic Egyptian, and Greek) that records a decree of Ptolemy V in 196 B.C. French engineer Captain Pierre-François Bouchard discovered the stone in 1799. It was captured by the British in 1801 and sent to the British Museum. In 1822–1824, the French philologist Jean-François Champollion used the text as the basis for deciphering hieroglypics.

**Sacred Band**: The elite hoplite unit of Thebes, composed of 150 homosexual couples organized by Gorgidas in 378 B.C. The unit was annihilated at the Battle of Chaeronea in 338 B.C.

**satrap**: The Persian governor of the Achaemenid Empire; Darius I (521–486 B.C.) reorganized the empire into 30 satrapies.

**satrapy**: A Persian province, and the basis for fiscal and military obligations.

**Second Athenian Confederacy**: The naval league organized by Athens in 378/7 B.C. In contrast to the Delian League, the Athenian assembly shared equal power with federal council or *synedrion* of allies. Restrictions were placed on Athenian power. Tribute (*phoros*) levied by Athens was replaced by contributions (*syntaxis*) voted on by the allies. In 337 B.C., Athens dissolved the league.

**Second Sophistic**: An archaizing literary and cultural movement among Greek intellectuals in between the late 1st and early 3rd centuries A.D.

**Seleucid**: The Greek speaking Macedonian dynasty descended from Seleucus I (312–281 B.C.) that ruled the Asian provinces of Alexander the Great. In 63 B.C., the Roman imperator Pompey the Great annexed Syria and ended the dynasty.

**Silver Shields** (*Argyraspides*): Apparently the *hypaspists* reformed by Alexander the Great in India. In 321 B.C., Eumenes of Cardia won over this unit of 3,000 men, but in 316 B.C., after the Battle of Gabiene, they betrayed Eumenes to Antigonus I. Antigonus I disbanded the unit. *See also* **hypaspists**

**Social War** (357–355 B.C.) War between Athens and her rebellious allies Chios, Rhodes, Cos, and Byzantium, which were supported by Mausolus, dynast of Caria. The war ended in Athenian recognition of the independence of the rebel allies. With Athens distracted by this war, Philip II was free to expand in Thessaly and Thrace.

*somatophylax* (pl. *somatophylakes*): The personal "bodyguard " of the Macedonian king. The bodyguards usually numbered seven. In 324 B.C., they were Lysimachus, Peithon, Leonnatus, Perdiccas, Ptolemy, Peucestas, and Aristonous.

**stasis** ("standing"): Civil war within a polis along ideological or class lines. Thucydides (III. 77-85) gives the most perceptive analysis of a *stasis* on Corcyra in 427 B.C.

**stater**: Denotes (1) the principal silver coin struck by Greek cities, usually a didrachma or tetradrachma or (2) the principle gold coin. Alexander the Great struck a gold stater (8.50 grams) on the Attic weight standard that became the international gold denomination of the Hellenistic world. It was exchanged at 20 silver drachmae or five tetradrachmae.

*strategos* (pl. *strategoi*): One of the 10 generals annually elected to the Athenian board (*strategeia*) instituted in 501/0 B.C. Generals were appointed to specific commands by the assembly and subject to discipline by the popular courts.

*strategos autokrator*: Supreme commander, voted to Philip II and Alexander the Great by *synedrion* of the League of Corinth. The Phocians too had such an office.

**symposium** ("drinking along with"): The social settings of many of the dialogues of Plato in which aristocrats and sophists debated intellectual issues. At the Macedonian court, the symposium was a far more raucous and violent social event.

**syncretism** ("mixing with"): The religious approach of identifying foreign gods with their Greek counterparts.

*synedrion*: The governing council of a federal league, such as that of the Second Athenian Confederacy in 378/7 B.C. or the League of Corinth in 337 B.C.

*synoikismos* (*synoecism*; "dwelling with"): The political unification of lesser settlements or even poleis into a single polis. In Athenian legend, Theseus had effected the *synoecism* of Attica.

*syntaxis* (pl. *syntaxeis*; "contribution": The voluntary contribution of money or supplies voted by members of federal leagues to the hegemon.

***tagos***: The commander elected by the federal representative of the Thessalian League; between 352 and 196 B.C., the king of Macedon was regularly so elected.

**talent**: A measure of weight for large sums of money (coins or bullion).

***taurobolium***: The sacrifice of a bull to Cybele, Magna Mater, which was condemned as a perversion of baptism by the Christian author Prudentius in c. 400 A.D.

***taxiarch*** (Greek *taxiarches*): The commander of a *taxis*, the tactical unit of the Macedonian phalanx.

***taxis*** (pl. *taxeis*; "regiment"): A unit of 1,536 Macedonian *phalangites*. Each *taxis* was recruited by region, but it was designated by the name of its commander or taxiarch. Each taxis was divided into three *pentakosiarchies* (each of 512 men), or "battalion." In 334 B.C., Alexander the Great invaded Asia Minor with six *taxeis* of the phalanx then commanded by Perdiccas, Coenus, Amyntas, Philip, Meleager, and Craterus.

**Ten Thousand**: The Greek mercenary hoplites, who numbered as many as 13,000. They served in the expedition of Cyrus the Younger, slain at the Battle of Cunaxa in 401 B.C. The Ten Thousand marched out of the Persian Empire. A total of 8,600 survivors reached Trapezus in 399 B.C., and 6,000 returned to Western Asia Minor to join the Spartan forces led by Thibron against the Persians.

***testudo*** ("tortoise"): Latin for a formation when infantry lock shields around and above them as a protection from missile weapons, especially in sieges.

**tetradrachma**: A silver coin of four drachmae. The Athenian tetradrachma (17.25 grams) was the prime fiscal and trade coin in the Aegean world. The obverse carried the head of Athena; the reverse the owl with the first three letters of the ethnic, "of the Athenians."

**theoric fund** (Greek *theorika)*: From at least 395 B.C. state surpluses, except in war, were to be set aside for distribution to citizens at festivals.

The administration of the theoric fund acquired control over Athenian state finances after the Social War (357–355 B.C.).

**thete** (pl. *thetai*; Greek *tes*: The lowest Athenian property class under the Solonian constitution which composed of citizens with an annual income of less than 200 *medimnoi*. The rowed in the Athenian fleet.

**timocracy**: Government by honor, denoted a constitution whereby rights of citizenship were based on honor or rank (time). The aristocrats held high offices and sat on the council. Men of hoplite rank voted and held minor offices. The lower classes had only voting rights in the assembly.

**Triparadisus, Conference of** (321 B.C): Ended the first war among the Diadochoi. Antipater and the Macedonian veterans agreed to a new division of the satrapies, confirming Lysimachus, Antigonus, and Ptolemy, and appointing Seleucus satrap of Babylonia. Antipater took possession of the royal family and retired to rule the empire as regent.

**trireme** (Greek *tries*): The principle warship, using ramming tactics. It was devised by the Phoenicians in the late 7th or early 6th century B.C.

**trophy** (Greek *trophaion*; "turning"): A hoplite panoply raised on a pole to mark the spot where the enemy had turned and fled in battle.

**tyrant** (pl. *tyrannoi*; Greek *tyrannos*): An Anatolian title of royalty used by Greeks to designate any man who seized power unconstitutionally. Aristotle noted that early tyrants seized power in the name of the hoplites against aristocracies. Tyrants who failed to establish royal dynasties were replaced either by oligarchy or democracy. Tyrant is thus the equivalent of the modern English dictator.

# Biographical Notes

**Abdalonymus** (332–312 B.C.): King of Sidon. Crowned by Hephaestion after Straton II 342–333 B.C.) was deposed. Abdalonymus brought the Sidonian fleet into action against Tyre. He might have commissioned the "Alexander Sarcophagus."

**Abisares**: Eponymous king of the Sanskrit kingdom of Abhisara, which lay beyond the Hydaspes (Jhelum) in modern Kashmir. After Alexander the Great defeated Porus at the Hydaspes in 326 B.C., Abisares submitted to Alexander.

**Abulites** (c. 377–326 B.C.): Persian noble and satrap of Susiana. Surrendered to Alexander in 330 B.C. and retained his satrapy. In 324 B.C., he and his son Oxathres were executed on grounds of treason.

**Ada** (r. 351–326 B.C.): Hecatomnid Queen of Caria. Married her brother Idrieus (351–344 B.C.), satrap of Caria and Lycia. In 344–340B.C., Ada ruled as satrap in her own right, but she was overthrown by her brother Pixodarus. King Artaxerxes III restored Ada and, in 334 B.C., she submitted to Alexander the Great. Alexander entrusted Ada with Halicarnassus and the satrapy of Caria, and she adopted Alexander as her son and heir.

**Aelius Aristides** (117–181 A.D.): Orator of the Second Sophistic and citizen of Smyrna. Wrote *Sacred Tales*, explaining his convalescence at the Asclepieion of Pergamum in 133–146. He penned rhetorical treatises and numerous orations, including one in praise of Rome.

**Aeschines** (c. 397–322 B.C.): Athenian orator and rival of Demosthenes. Served as a hoplite and secretary of the boule before he entered politics after the fall of Olynthus in 348 B.C. In 347 B.C., he addressed the Arcadian assembly of Megaopolis for an alliance against Philip II. He was on the first embassy to Philip II in 346 B.C. and supported peace so that he henceforth clashed with Demosthenes. In 343 B.C., Demosthenes unsuccessfully prosecuted Aeschines for treason. In 336–330 B.C., Aeschines countered with a suit against Demosthenes; both speeches *On the Crown* survive.

Demosthenes won the suit so that Aeschines was fined and retired to Rhodes to teach rhetoric.

**Agathocles** (d. c. 284/3 B.C.): Son of Lysimachus and Thracian princess Macris. In 287 B.C., Agathocles repelled an attack of Demetrius Poliocretes. He and his wife, Lysandra, daughter of Ptolemy I, clashed with Arsinoe, who turned Lysimachus against his son and heir Agathocles. In c. 284, Agathocles was arrested and later strangled in prison. Lysandra with her children and Ptolemy Ceraunus fled to Seleucus.

**Agesilaus II** (b. 427 B.C.; r. 400–360 B.C.): Eurypontid king of Sparta; half-brother of Agis II. Was selected in preference to Leotychidas, the reputed son of Alcibiades and Queen Timea. Agesilaus proved a charismatic ruler who presided over the rise and fall of the Spartan hegemony and was a model for Hellenistic kings. In 396–395 B.C., he campaigned in Asia Minor against the Persians. Recalled to Sparta in 394 B.C., he marched from the Hellespont to the Isthmus of Corinth, en route defeating the Boeotian army at Coronea. He conducted the war of attrition against Argos in the Corinthian War (394–386 B.C.). He turned the military service owed by Spartan allies into payment of money and so hired mercenaries. In 361–360 B.C., he served as mercenary captain in the army of Pharaoh Nectanebo II (360–343 B.C.) and died on his return to Sparta.

**Agesipolis I** (r. 394–380 B.C.): Agiad king of Sparta. Succeeded his father Pausanias. As a minor in 394 B.C., he was under the guardianship of his senior relative Aristodemus. In 385 B.C., he first commanded against Mantinea, and he consistently deferred to Agesilaus II.

**Agis III** (r. 338–331 B.C.): Eurypontid king of Sparta. Son of Archidamus III, opposed Philip II and Alexander the Great. In 333 B.C., Agis negotiated with Pharnabazus and Autophradates for support to liberate Greece from Macedonian rule, but news of Battle of Issus ended the plan. In 331 B.C., Agis III, with an army of 2,000 cavalry and 20,000 hoplites, including 8,000 veteran mercenaries, besieged Megalopolis in a bid to reclaim Spartan hegemony. Antipater with an army of over 40,000 relieved Megalopolis and defeated and slew Agis III.

**Agis IV** (263–241 B.C.; r. 245–241 B.C.): Was a Eurypontid king who effected political reform in Sparta by redistributing land in Laconia for 4,500 citizens and 15,000 perioikoi, thereby restoring Spartan military power. Agis IV postured as restoring the Lycurgan system, but his reforms provoked aristocratic opposition and his overthrow. He was arrested and strangled in prison.

**Alexander I** (r. 498–454 B.C.): Argead king of Macedon, preserved his kingdom from destruction during the invasion of Xerxes and sought to extend his sway over the western districts of Macedon and the Greek cities of the shore. Alexander was accepted as a Hellene, and so members of the Argead royal family were allowed to participate in Panhellenic games.

**Alexander I** (b. c. 370 B.C.; r. 352–331 B.C.): King of Epirus, also known as **Alexander the Molossian**. He overthrew his uncle Arybbas. Although he received his sister Olympias, repudiated by Philip II, he agreed to an alliance and marriage to his niece Cleopatra, daughter of Philip II and Olympias in 336 B.C. In 334–331 B.C., he crossed to Italy at the request of Taras and campaigned against the Samnites and Lucanians in emulation of his nephew Alexander the Great. He was assassinated by Lucanian exiles near Pandosia.

**Alexander II** (r. 370–368 B.C.): King of Macedon and second son of Amyntas II and Eurydice. Faced Illyrian invasions and the pretender Pausanias backed by the Athenian general Iphicrates. Alexander's capture of Larissa, in Thessaly, provoked an intervention by Thebans under Pelopidas who expelled Alexander from Thessaly in 369 B.C. Alexander II was assassinated at a festival the next year.

**Alexander III, the Great** (b. 356 B.C.; r. 336–323 B.C.): Argead king of Macedon, son of Philip II and Olympias, succeeded his father as king of Macedon and general of the League of Corinth. The greatest of generals, he secured Macedon and his control over the Greek league in 336–335 B.C. In 334–324 B.C., Alexander conquered the Persian empire, and transformed the face of the ancient world. His great battles Granicus (334 B.C.), Issus (333 B.C.), Gaugamela (331 B.C.), and the Hydaspes (326 B.C.) were masterpieces of the battle of encirclement, but Alexander also excelled in siege warfare and campaigns of pacification. In generalship, his only equal is Napoleon.

Alexander initiated his conquest of Asia as the commander of the Hellenic League in a war of retribution against Persia, but he was truly motivated by his longing (*pothos*) to emulate Achilles and Heracles. After his visit of the oracle of Siwah in 331 B.C., he became convinced of his divine destiny. After the death of Darius III, Alexander claimed the role of Great King. His policies of accommodating the Persian nobility alienated many Macedonians in 330–327 B.C. The difficult campaigning in India broke the will of the Macedonian army which refused to cross the Hyphasis and clamored to return home in 326 B.C.

In 324 B.C., Alexander the Great faced the daunting task of administering a world empire. His desire for divine honors and Exiles Decree drove the Greeks into rebellion by the time of his death in 323 B.C. His sudden death resulted in a succession crisis for he had left no obvious heirs. His Sogidan wife, Roxane, was with child, the posthumous Alexander IV, and his half-brother Philip Arrhidaeus was not competent. Yet, even though his generals divided the empire, Alexander the Great had wrought a new Hellenistic world.

**Alexander IV** (323–310 B.C.): The posthumous son of Alexander the Great and Roxane, who was born in September 323 B.C. He was declared joint king with Philip III Arrhidaeus. Alexander IV and Roxane passed successively into the custody of Perdiccas (r. 323–321 B.C.), Antipater (r. 321–319 B.C., who removed them to Pella), and finally Polyperchon (r. 319–317 B.C.). In 317 B.C., Olympias and King Aeacidas of Epirus invaded Macedon and put Alexander IV in power. Olympias's excesses lost her support so that Cassander reoccupied Macedon, forced Olympias to surrender (316 B.C.), and took possession of Alexander IV and Roxane. In 311 B.C., the other Diadochoi recognized Cassander as regent of Alexander IV until he attained his majority. In 310 B.C., Cassander ordered both Alexander IV and Roxane murdered.

**Alexander V** (r. 297–294 B.C.): King of Macedon and third son of Cassander and Thessalonice. Shared the throne with his brother Antipater. In 295 B.C., Antipater murdered his mother Thessalonice and warred on Alexander V, who summoned as allies Pyrrhus and Demetrius Poliocretes. Demetrius expelled Antipater and then murdered Alexander and seized the Macedonian throne.

**Alexander of Pherae** (r. 369–358 B.C.): Son of Jason and tyrant. Aspired to dominate Thessaly. The lesser cities Larissa, Lamia, and Pharsalus appealed to the Boeotians. In 364 B.C., Boeotians under Pelopidas defeated Alexander at Cynocephalae, but Pelopidas fell in the battle. Alexander was compelled to ally with the Boeotian League and renounced his ambitions in Thessaly. In 362–358 B.C., he clashed with the Athenians in the North Aegean. He was assassinated at the instigation of his wife Thebe.

**Amphoterus**: Son of Alexander and was the brother of Craterus and navarch of Alexander's fleet in 333–331 B.C. *See* **Craterus**.

**Amyntas** (d. 330 B.C.): Son of Andromenes, taxiarch of the phalanx in 334–330 B.C., was a friend of Philotas. He along with his younger brothers Simmias, Polemo, and Attalus were acquitted of charges of treason in 330 B.C. Amyntas fell in action soon after; his brothers disappear from the sources.

**Amyntas**: Son of Nicolaus, a Macedonian noble. Named satrap of Bactria to replace Artabazus in 328 B.C.

**Amyntas III** (r. 393–369 B.C.): King of Macedon. Succeeded to a troubled kingdom, and he sought alliances with Olynthus against the Illyrians and then with the Spartans against Olynthus in 382–379 B.C. After 378 B.C., he aligned with Jason of Pherae and Athens. In 371 B.C., at a Panhellenic congress, Amyntas III recognized Athenian claims to Amphipolis. He was succeeded by his three sons Alexander II (r. 369–368 B.C.), Perdiccas III (r. 368–359 B.C.), and Philip II (r. 359–336 B.C.).

**Amyntas IV** (r. 368–359 B.C.): Son of Perdiccas III and was an infant at the time of his father's death. The Macedonian nobility and assembly passed over

Amyntas and acclaimed as king Philip II. Amyntas was married to Cynane, daughter of Philip II and the Illyrian princess Audata. There is no evidence that Philip ever ruled as regent for his nephew. In 336 B.C., Amyntas, perhaps twenty-five years of age, was executed on orders of Alexander the Great because his cousin was a possible pretender.

**Amyrtaeus** (r. 404–399 B.C.): Egyptian Amenirdisu. Pharaoh of Egypt overthrew Persian rule in the Delta and was proclaimed pharaoh of Dynasty XVIII. Amyrtaeus, ruling from Sais, faced Persian resistance in Upper Egypt. He was overthrown by Nepheritres (399–393), who founded Dynasty XIX and secured Upper Egypt.

**Anaxarchus of Abdera** (fl. c. 340–315 B.C.): Greek philosopher and student of atomist philosopher Democrtius (c. 460–370 B.C.) was friend to Alexander the Great. In Bactria in 328–327 B.C., he argued in favor of divine honors for Alexander the Great against the objections of Callisthenes. He was executed by Nicocreon, king of Salamis, Cyprus.

**Antigonus I Monophthalmus** (b. c. 382; r. 306–301 B.C.): "The One-eyed." A senior general of Alexander the Great, he was entrusted with the strategic satrapy of Phrygia (central Asia Minor) in 333–323 B.C. Antigonus held open the lines of communication between Europe and Alexander's advancing army. At the conference at Babylon in 323 B.C. he received an enlarged satrapy of Phrygia, Lycia, and Pamphylia, but he quarreled with Perdiccas and joined Antipater in Macedon (323 B.C.). He campaigned successfully against the outlawed Eumenes of Cardia in 320–316 B.C. and so emerged as the candidate to unite the empire. His first war against Cassander, Ptolemy, and Lysimachus in 315–311 B.C. ended in stalemate; the second one in his defeat and death at Ipsus (r. 309–301 B.C.). He was the greatest of Alexander's generals and remembered by Greeks and Asians for his responsible government and set the style for Hellenistic monarchies.

**Antigonus II Gonatas** (b. c. 320–329 B.C.; r. 283–239 B.C.): Of Demetrius Poliocretes and Phila (daughter of Antipater). Took charge of Greece when Demetrius invaded Asia Minor in 287 B.C. By 280 B.C. He controlled Corinth, Sicyon, Piraeus, and Demetrias. At the Battle of Lysimacheia (277 B.C.) he destroyed 20,000 Gauls, and he was hailed king by the

Macedonians. In 274–272 B.C., he defeated Pyrrhus in a war for the mastery of Macedon. He defeated the Greek states in the Chremonidean War (268–262 B.C.). Despite his loss of Corinth in 243 B.C., Antigonus left Macedon a great power. Stoic philosopher, honest administrator, relentless general, and humane king, Antigonus was one of Macedon's greatest monarchs.

**Antiochus I Soter** (b. 324 B.C.; r. 281–261 B.C.): Son of Seleucus and the Sogdian princess Apame, he ruled the Upper Satrapies from c. 294/3 B.C. with his wife and former stepmother Stratonice. In 281 B.C., he was accepted as king after the murder of his father Seleucus, and he faced a Gallic invasion of Asia Minor. His war to recover Coele-Syria from Ptolemaic control (First Syrian War, 274–271 B.C.) ended in stalemate.

**Antiochus III Megas** (b. 241 B.C.; r. 223–187 B.C.): "The Great." Seleucid king styled himself as a conqueror in the guise of Alexander the Great. In 209–205 B.C., Antiochus led an eastern expedition into Bactria and India to reassert Seleucid hegemony. By his victory at Panium in 200 B.C., Antiochus conquered Ptolemaic possessions in the Levant and Asia Minor. But the king's Alexandrine pretensions led to a war with Rome in 192–188 B.C. The consul Lucius Cornelius Scipio decisively defeated Antiochus at Magnesia in 189 B.C. and so broke Seleucid power.

**Antipater** (397–319 B.C.): Leading general and diplomat under Philip II. Negotiated the peace with Athens in 337 B.C., and he acted as senior advisor to Alexander the Great. In 334–325 B.C., he administered Macedon and Greece during Alexander's absence. In 331 B.C., he defeated King Agis III at Megalopolis and forced Sparta into the Hellenic League. In 323–322 B.C. he was besieged in Lamia by the insurgent Athenians, Aetolians, and Thessalians but, along with Craterus, he crushed the revolt at Crannon. In 321 B.C., he and Craterus invaded Asia Minor and, at Triparadisus, the Macedonian army elected him regent of the empire. He returned to Macedon with the royal family (321–319 B.C.), but he turned the running of the Asian empire to the leading satraps. Ptolemy and Antigonus grew especially powerful, and Antipater's death precipitated the second civil war among the Diadochoi.

**Antipater II** (r. 297–294 B.C.): King of Macedon. The second son of Cassander and Thessalonice. In 295 B.C., he murdered his mother and warred against his brother Alexander V. He was expelled from Macedon by Demetrius Poliocretes, fell into the hands of Lysimachus, and was executed.

**Apame** or **Apama** (d. c. 300 B.C.): Daughter of the Sogdian lord Spitamenes, married Seleucus I at Opis in 324 B.C. She was the mother of Antiochus I (281–261 B.C.) and, upon her death, Seleucus founded Apamea in Syria in her honor.

**Apelles of Colophon** (fl. c. 360–290 B.C.): As a painter, he painted portraits of Philip II and Alexander the Great. His masterpiece was Aphrodite arising from the sea and was widely copied by Greek and Roman painters and was the inspiration of Botticelli's Birth of Venus. The Alexander mosaic at Pompeii is believed to be after Apelles's painting. Apelles was credited with a painting at Ephesus depicting Alexander hurling a thunderbolt.

**Apollonius of Rhodes** (c. 295–240 B.C.): Epic poet and librarian at Alexandria (c. 260–247 B.C.), wrote the literary epic *Argonautica*, a learned retelling of Jason and the Argonauts. His work found little favor from Callimachus, but Apolloninus set the fashion for erudite, baroque poetry in the Hellenistic and Roman ages.

**Apollonius of Tyana** (c. 40–120 A.D.): Pythagorean philosopher, is known from a novelistic life written by the sophist Philostratus (c. 172–250 A.D.) at the request of the empress Julia Domna in 217 A.D. The work was completed by 238 A.D. Philostratus presented Apollonius as a miracle worker and the Alexander the Great of philosophers, seeking wisdom by his journey to India.

**Archelaus** (r. 413–399 B.C.): Argead king of Macedon. Succeeded his father Perdiccas II and failed to bring Amphipolis or the Chalcidice under his rule. He allied with Athens, and sponsored important military, social, and economic reforms. Archelaus, patron of the tragedian Euripides, turned his court at Pella into a center of Hellenic arts and letters.

**Archidamus III** (r. 360–338 B.C.): Eurypontid king of Sparta. Supported the Phocians in the Third Sacred War (3578–346 B.C.). In 343–338 B.C., on invitation of Taras, Archidamus intervened in southern Italy against the Lucanians. He was defeated and slain at Manduria in Apulia.

**Aristotle** (386–322 B.C.): Philosopher and scientist. A native of Stageira in the Chalcidice. Aristotle, dissatisfied with Plato's spiritual cosmology, sought materialist explanations and so wrote a range of subjects, notably logic, rhetoric, biology, ethics, and politics. He tutored Alexander the Great in 343–341 B.C., and thereafter retained a friendship with his brilliant student. In 336 B.C., Aristotle founded the Lyceum at Athens. His *Politics* is a brilliant exposition on Greek governments, and his logic and inductive reasoning have influenced all subsequent Western philosophy.

**Arrian** (c. 86–146 A.D.): Lucius Flavius Arrianus Xenophon. Historian and Roman senator. A native of Nicomedia. Arrian pursed a senatorial career under the emperor Trajan and was friend to Hadrian. He was consul suffectus in 129 or 130. In 134–135, he was governor of Cappadocia, and repelled an invasion of nomadic Alans. He wrote in Greek the *Anabasis* or Asian expedition of Alexander the Great based on the account of King Ptolemy I and other eye witness histories. Arrian also wrote an *Indica*, based on the *Periplus* of Nearchus, a tactical manual of his battle line against the Alans, and a *Periplus* of the Black Sea.

**Arses** (r. 338–336 B.C.): King of Persia. The young son of Artaxerxes III placed on the throne by the eunuch chiliarch Bagoas. Arses took the dynastic name Artaxerxes IV; he was murdered on orders of Bagoas.

**Arsinoe II** (c. 316–270 B.C.): Daughter of Ptolemy I and Berenice, married Lysimachus in 300 B.C. Responsible in part for the downfall and death of Agathocles, she reaped no reward for her intrigues. In 281 B.C. she was forced to marry Ptolemy Ceraunus, but she managed to escape to Egypt by 279 B.C. She married her full brother Ptolemy II (c. 275 B.C.), and she was the first Hellenistic queen to receive divine honors upon her death.

**Arsites** (r. 336–330 B.C.): Satrap of Hellespontine Phrygian under Darius III. Likely commanded the Persian army at the Grancius in 334 B.C. He committed suicide after the battle.

**Artabazus** (c. 389–325 B.C.): Persian noble, as satrap of Hellespontine Phrygia, he joined his brothers Ariobarzanes and Mithridates in a revolt against Artaxerxes III in 358–354 B.C. In 353 B.C., he fled to Philp II as exile. In 342 B.C., he was pardoned and restored to favor by Arataxerxes III and served Darius III. In 330 B.C., he submitted to Alexander the Great in Hyrcania. His daughter Barsine became a mistress of Alexander. Artabazus was respected at the Macedonian court and satrap of Bactria in 329–328 B.C.

**Artaxerxes II** (r. 404–358 B.C.): Memnon, king of Persiathe. Elder son of King Darius II and Queen Parysitis. Defeated and slew his brother Cyrus the Younger at Cunaxa in 401 B.C. In response to Spartan intervention in Asia Minor, Artaxerxes raised the Greek coalition that fought Sparta to a stalemate in the Corinthian War (396–386 B.C.). By the King's Peace of 386, Artaxerxes regained the Greek cities of Asia Minor.

**Artaxerxes III** (b. c. 425 B.C.; r. 358–338 B.C.): Ochus, king of Persia and son of Artaxerxes II. Restored Achaemenid rule in the Western satrapies with the reconquest of Egypt in 343–342 B.C. In 340–338 B.C., he assisted Athens and Cersebleptes of Thrace against Philip II. He was assassinated by the eunuch chiliarch Bagoas.

**Artaxerxes IV**. *See* **Arses**.

**Artaxerxes V**. See **Bessus**.

**Asander** (r. 334–328 B.C.): Son of Philotas. Appointed satrap of Lydia. In 328 B.C., he accompanied Nearchus with reinforcements. In 323 B.C., Asander was rewarded with the satrapy of Caria. In 317–313 B.C., Asander joined the coalition against Antigonus I. The father of Asander was not Philotas, commander of the Companions, and there is no reason to link him to the family of Parmenio.

**Attalus** (c. 390–336 B.C.): Macedonian nobleman. A senior general of Philip II. His niece Cleopatra Eurydice married Philip II in 337 B.C. In 336 B.C., he shared command with Parmenio in Asia Minor. After the assassination of Philip II, he was implicated in a plot with the Atheninas and so executed.

**Attalus I** (b. 269 B.C.; r. 241–197 B.C.): Soter, king of Pergamum, was adopted as son and heir by his second cousin Eumenes I. Attalus assumed the title king in 238 B.C., and by an adroit alliance with Rome he expanded Pergamene power at the expense of Philip V and Antiochus III.

**Attalus II** (b. 220 B.C.; r. 159–139 B.C.): Philadelphus, king of Pergamum, succeeded his elder brother Eumenes II. He was a loyal ally of Rome and phihellene monarch. He donated to Athens the magnificent Stoa of Attalus.

**Athenaeus of Naucratis**: Greek rhetorician and grammarian writing in the late 2$^{nd}$ century A.D. Penned the *Deipnosophistae*, "dinner table philosophers" (in fifteen books), which contain anecdotes drawn from 2,500 separate works.

**Autophradates**: Persian general and noble, defeated the rebel satrap Artabazus in 354 B.C. In 333 B.C., after the death of Memnon of Rhodes, Autophrates and Pharnabazus succeeded to joint command of the Persian fleet in the Aegean.

**Azelmilk** (r. c. 340–332 B.C.): Greek Azemilcus, king of Tyre and loyal vassal of Darius III. Refused permission for Alexander to sacrifice to Melqart and so to claim the kingship of Tyre in 332 B.C. Alexander thus took Tyre by siege.

**Bagoas** (d. 336 B.C.): Persian eunuch chiliarch intrigued in the murder of Artaxerxes III in 338 B.C., and put on the throne Arses, who was hailed Artaxerxes IV. Bagoas ruled through Arses but faced rebellions in Babylonia and Egypt and the threat of an invasion by Philip II of Macedon. Bagoas had Arses murdered, when the young king proved defiant and elevated Darius III, former satrap of Armenia, to the throne. Darius III immediately executed Bogas in the summer 336 B.C.

**Balacrus** (c. 385–324 B.C.): Bodyguard of Philip II and Alexander the Great, was appointed satrap of Cilicia in 333 B.C. He assisted Antigonus in the pacification of Asia Minor, and he was aligned with Antipater. He was fell in a campaign against rebels in Pisidia.

**Balacrus** (d. c. 328 B.C.): Macedonian officer who commanded the javelin men in 336–328 B.C. He proved his tactical skill at the Battle of Gaugamela and in operations in Bactria and Sogdiana in 329–328 B.C. He is presumed to have died before the invasion of India.

**Bardylis** (r. c. 385–358 B.C.): Or Bardyllis, king of the Illyrians. Clashed with the Molossian kings of Epirus. In 359 B.C., Bardylis defeated and slew King Perdiccas III of Macedon, but in 358 B.C. he was defeated and slain by Philip II.

**Barsaenetes** (r. 336–330 B.C.): Persian noble and satrap of Arachosia and Drangiana under Darius III, slew Darius III at Hectamopylus in 330 B.C. He fled an exile into India.

**Barsine** (c. 363–309 B.C.): Daughter of Artabazus, satrap of Hellespontine Phrygia, married Mentor of Rhodes, and then his brother Memnon of Rhodes. She fled with her father to the court of Philip II in 353–342 B.C. She was captured after the Battle of Issus and became the mistress of Alexander. In 329 or 327 B.C., she gave birth to a son Heracles, but she lost favor at court after Alexander married Roxane. She retired to Pergamum; her daughter married Nearchus in 324 B.C. In 309 B.C., Polyperchon championed Heracles as king of Macedon, but he surrendered Barsine and Heracles to Cassander who ordered mother and son executed.

**Barsine**: Daughter of Darius III. *See also* **Statira**.

**Berenice I** (c. 340–281 or 271 B.C.): Daughter of Lagus and half-sister of Ptolemy I, arrived in Egypt in 317 B.C. and soon became Ptolemy's mistress. She bore him Arsinoe II and Ptolemy II. By 285 B.C. Ptolemy divorced his first wife Eurydice, daughter of Antipater, and married Berenice, recognizing Ptolemy II as his sole heir.

**Berossus** (fl. c. 290–270 B.C.): Babylonian astronomer, wrote in Greek the *Babylonica* (in three books) a history of Mesopotamia from the Creation down to the reign of Nabonidus The work, which has not survived, was widely cited by later Greek and Roman authors.

**Bessus** (d. 329 B.C.): Satrap of Bactria, was proclaimed King **Artaxerxes V** (330–329 B.C.). Bessus commanded the Persian right flank at the Battle of Gaugamela. In 330 B.C., he deposed Darius III after the Persian army fled Ecbatana. He ordered Darius murdered lest the king fall into the hands of Alexander and so alienated many Persian nobles who submitted to Alexander. In 330 B.C., he retired to Bactria and Sogdiana, where he was declared King Artaxerxes V. In 329 B.C., Alexander surprised Bessus by an invasion from the southeast. Bessus fled to Nautaca, where he was betrayed by Spitamenes and Dataphernes. Bessus was mutilated and impaled at Ecbatana.

**Callimachus of Cyrene** (c. 310–240 B.C.): A lyric poet and scholar of the Museion at Alexandria. He was recognized as an outstanding scholar and master of the learned lyric poems, epigrams, and odes that provided the model for Hellenistic poetry. He disapproved of the revived epic of Apollonius of Rhodes.

**Callisthenes of Olynthus** (c. 360–328 B.C.): Greek historian and great-nephew of Aristotle, accompanied Alexander as the official historian of the Asia expedition. Callisthenes, notorious for his self-importance, clashed with Alexander over the issue of *proskynesis*. Callisthenes compelled Alexander to drop the ritual, and so Alexander was willing to believe Callisthenes was the inspiration behind a conspiracy of royal pages in 328 B.C. Callisthenes was arrested and died a miserable death in captivity. Callisthenes penned several historical works on Greek history in the 4th century B.C. and an account on Alexander's expedition. His friend, the peripatetic philosopher Theophrastus (c. 371–287 B.C.), eulogized Callisthenes in a treatise so that philosophical writers viewed Alexander as a tyrant enslaved by his passions. The more sensational anecdotes from Callisthenes's work were incorporated into the *Alexander Romance* of the 3rd century A.D., whose unknown author is know as Pseudo-Callisthenes and provided the source for Medieval vernacular romances on Alexander.

**Callistratus of Aphidnae** (c. 410–355 B.C.): Athenian politician and general, wrote the constitution of the Second Athenian Naval Confederacy in 378 B.C. He administered Athenian finances and urged the alliance with Sparta against Thebes. He prosecuted Timotheus for misconduct in 373 B.C. He negotiated peace with Sparta in 371 B.C. In 361 B.C., he was impeached and convicted in absentia for the loss of Oropus. He found refuge at the Macedonian court, but he returned to Athens and was arrested and executed.

**Cambyses** (r. 530–522 B.C.): King of Persia, son of Cyrus I, conquered Egypt in 525–522 B.C., but his death led to the outbreak of the Great Revolt (522–521 B.C.).

**Caracalla** (b. 188; r. 198–217 A.D.): Marcus Aurelius Antoninus, Roman emperor and son of Septimius Severus and Julia Domna. Was remembered for his savagery, notably the murder of his brother Geta in 212. Caracalla imitated Alexander the Great, and he conducted his Parthian War (214–217) as a re-creation of Alexander's expedition.

**Caranus** (d. 329 B.C.): Commander of the Greek allied infantry in 331–330 B.C., shared command with Erigyius in the campaign against Satibarzanes of Areia in 330 B.C. In 329 B.C., he was slain along with the officers Andromachus and Menedemus (and the interpreter Pharnuches of Lycia), in the defeat of their column by Spitamenes on the Polytimetus River.

**Cassander** (b. c. 358 B.C.; r. 305–297 B.C.): King of Macedon and son of Antipater, joined Alexander in 324 B.C. Antipater passed over his own son in 319 B.C. and appointed Polyperchon his successor. Ruthless, cautious, and suspicious, Cassander allied with Antigonus and drove Polyperchon out of Macedon in 319–316 B.C. He married Thessalonice to legitimize his position. He ordered the execution of Olympias in 316 B.C. Named regent of Alexander IV in 311 B.C., he murdered the young king and his mother Roxane in 310 B.C. In 305–297 B.C. he ruled as king of Macedon. After the Battle of Ipsus (301 B.C.), Cassander consolidated his hold over Greece. He died of a wasting disease in 297 B.C.

**Cersebleptes** (r. 358–342 B.C.): Or Cersobleptes, son of Cotys and Odrysian king of Thrace. Depended on the Athenian mercenary captain Charidemus. In 357 B.C., he ceded the Thracian Chersonesus to Athens, and so control of the Hellespont. Cersobleptes, allied to Athens thereafter, fought Philip II as his rival for the Balkans. In 343–342 B.C., Philip II defeated Cersobleptes and annexed Thrace as a *strategeia*, or military province.

**Chabrias** (c. 426–356 B.C.): Athenian general, defeated the Peloponnesian fleet off Aegina in 388 B.C. and then commanded the Athenian fleet that supported Cypriote King Evagoras of Salamis in his rebellion against Persia. Chabrias was hailed for his defense of Boeotia in 378 B.C. and his naval victory over the Peloponnesian fleet at Naxos in 376 B.C. He was defeated and slain in the naval battle against the rebel allies off Chios in 356 B.C.

**Chandragupta** (b. c. 340 B.C.; r. c. 320–298 B.C.): Mauryan emperor of India, Greek Sandrocottus. Of obscure origins, Chandragupta overthrew the Nanda kings of Magadha in 321 B.C., and forged the first empire in India based on the Indus and Ganges valleys. He swept the Greco-Macedonian garrisons out of the Indus valley. In 305 B.C., Seleucus I ceded to Chandragupta the Indian satrapies, Arachosia, Gedrosia and Paropamisadae in return for 500 war elephants. According to the Seleucid envoy Megasthenes, Chandragupta fielded an army of 400,000 men.

**Chares** (c. 400–325 B.C.): Athenian general, was master in commanding mercenaries but notorious for his exactions from allies. In 361 B.C., he backed oligarches who overthrew the democracy of Corcyra to the anger of the Athenian assembly. In 358 B.C., he secured the Thracian Chersonesus from Cersebleptes. During the Social War, he succeeded to the command of the fleet upon the death of Charbias in 357 B.C. He blamed his defeat at the Battle of Embata in 356 B.C. on his colleagues Iphicrates, Menestheus, and Timotheus, so he brought suit against all three. Timotheus was convicted, but Chares alienated Isocrates and Eubulus, who dominated the assembly. Chares, out of favor at home, served as mercenary captain of the rebel satrap Artabazus in 356–353 B.C. Chares commanded the mercenaries sent by Athens to Olynthus in 349 B.C. He fought at Chaeronea in 338 B.C., and urged support of Thebes in 335 B.C. He fled Athens, after the sack of Thebes. He served as a mercenary commander in the Persian fleet in 333–

332 B.C. He retired to the mercenary center Taenarum and died there still in opposition to Alexander the Great.

**Charidemus of Oreus** (c. 385–333 B.C.): Mercenary captain, served in Thrace under Iphicrates and Timotheus in 367–362 B.C. He briefly served in the revolt of Artabazus, satrap of Hellespontine Phrygia, and then took service with his brother-in-law King Cersebleptes. In 357 B.C., Charidemus was voted Athenian citizenship for his role in the return of the Thracian Chersonesus over the objections of Demosthenes. He commanded Athenian forces against Philip II in the Chersonesus in 351 B.C., and at Olynthus in 349–348 B.C. He commanded the Athenians at Chaeronea in 338 B.C. and advocated alliance with Thebes in 335 B.C. He fled to Susa, taking service with Darius III. He was executed on orders of Darius III for his outspoken critique of Persian strategy in 333 B.C.

**Clearchus** (d. 401 B.C.): Son of Ramphias, Spartan officer and senior commander of the Ten Thousand. He was harmost of Byzantium in 411–409 B.C. In 401 B.C., he was senior officer of the Greek mercenaries under Cyrus the Younger that won the Battle of Cunaxa. He and four other senior officers were treacherously executed by Artaxerxes II. In the *Anabasis*, Xenophon writes a favorable sketch of his friend Clearchus.

**Clearchus** (r. 364–352 B.C.): Tyrant of Heraclea Pontica, a student of Plato and Isocrates, was remembered as an arrogant, spiteful ruler who assumed the trappings and titles of Zeus and demanded worship.

**Cleitarchus of Alexandria**: Wrote a history of Alexander the Great (now lost) during the reign of Ptolemy II (283–246 B.C.). Diodorus Siculus (for book 17 on Alexander) and Curtius Rufus both drew on Cleitarchus's work.

**Cleitus**, grandson of King Bardylis: The Illyrian prince of Pelion who rebelled from Macedonian rule in 335 B.C. Alexander defeated Cleitus in the summer of 335 B.C. after his Thracian campaign.

**Cleitus the Black** (d. 358 B.C.): Son of Dropides (c. 375–328 B.C.), commanded the royal squadron (*ile basilike*). His sister Lanice was the nurse of Alexander. At the Battle of Granicus, Cleitus slew the satrap Spithridates, who was about to strike a fatal blow against Alexander. After the execution of Philotas in 330 B.C., Cleitus and Hephaestion shared command of the Companions. Cleitus was slain by Alexander in a drunken rage in winter quarters at Maracanda in early 328 B.C., because Cleitus objected to Alexander's pretensions and pro-Persian policy.

**Cleitus the White** (d. 318 B.C.): A taxiarch of the phalanx at the Battle of the Hydaspes in 326 B.C. In 324 B.C., he was discharged with other veterans at Opis. In 323 B.C., Cleitus commanded the imperial fleet that defeated the Athenian navy off the Echinades Islands. In 321 B.C., he was appointed satrap of Lydia. Loyal to the Argead house, he served Antipater and then Polyperchon. In 318 B.C., he defeated Cassander's navy near Byzantium but lost his ships in a surprise attack by Antigonus. Cleitus en route to Pella was ambushed and slain by soldiers of Lysimachus.

**Cleombrotus I** (r. 382–371 B.C.): Agiad king of Sparta, succeeded his brother Agesipolis. He was defeated and slain by the Thebans at the Battle of Leuctra in 371 B.C.

**Cleomenes III** (r. 236–222 B.C.): Agiad king, married Chilionis, daughter of Agis IV. In 226 B.C. he used his mercenary army to impose reform at Sparta. In 225–222 B.C., he mounted a recovery of Spartan power in the Peloponnesus, but he was defeated by King Antigonus III Doson and the Achaeans at the Battle of Sellasia in 222 B.C. Cleomenes III died an exile at the Ptolemaic court in 219 B.C., and his reforms were rescinded.

**Cleomenes of Naucratis** (d. 322 B.C.): Appointed treasurer of Egypt by Alexander the Great in 332 B.C. He exploited his position to amass a personal fortune, and Alexander overlooked the corruption. At the Conference of Babylon in 323 B.C., he was named hyparch of Egypt, becoming second to the new satrap Ptolemy. In 322 B.C., Ptolemy ordered the execution of Cleomenes and seized a treasury of 8,000 talents.

**Cleopatra** (355/4–309 B.C.): Daughter of Philip II and Olympias, was married to Alexander I of Epirus (342–330 B.C.) in 336 B.C. In 322 B.C., Olympias offered Cleopatra in marriage first to Leonnatus and then to Perdiccas. Eumenes of Cardia transferred Cleopatra to Sardes and argued on her behalf so that Perdiccas finally rejected the alternate offer of Nicaea, daughter of Antipater, in favor of Cleopatra. Perdiccas, however, was assassinated in Egypt (321 B.C.), and Cleopatra endured a house arrest in Sardes until 309 B.C., when she was murdered on orders of Antigonus I when he heard Ptolemy I was making overtures of marriage to her.

**Cleopatra VII** (b. 69 B.C.; r. 51–30 B.C.): Philopator, Ptolemaic Queen of Egypt, was the last Ptolemaic ruler. In 48 B.C., Gaius Julius Caesar supported Cleopatra against brother Ptolemy XIII. In 47 B.C., Cleopatra, Caesar's mistress, gave birth to Caesarion. In 46–44 B.C., Cleopatra visited Rome and returned to Alexandria after Caesar's assassination. In 41–31 B.C., Cleopatra became the lover and political ally of Mark Antony against Octavian. She and Mark Antony were defeated at the Battle of Actium. She committed suicide in 30 B.C. lest she be paraded in triumph at Rome.

**Cleopatra Eurydice** (d. 336 B.C.): Niece of Attalus, married Philip II in 337 B.C. After the assassination of Philip II, Olympias had Cleopatra. She is credited by Justin and her two children, Europa and Caranus, who were also murdered.

**Coenus** (c. 370–326 B.C.): Elimote noble, was the son of Polemocrates and son-in-law of Parmenio. A taxiarch in 335–331 B.C., Coenus and his regiment took the far right position in every battle. He was not compromised by the executions of Philotas and Parmenio. In 328 B.C., Coenus commanded an independent column that defeated Spitamenes at Gabae. At the Battle of the Hydaspes, in 326 B.C., he commanded a hipparchy. In July 326 B.C., Coenus articulated the grievances of the army when it mutinied on the Hyphasis. He died soon after from illness.

**Conon** (c. 444–392 B.C.): Athenian general, commanded Athenian squadrons at Naupactus in 414 B.C. and in the Hellespont in 410–407 B.C. In 406 B.C., his squadron was trapped at Mytilene so that Athens launched the relief fleet that won the Battle of Arginusae. In 405 B.C., he escaped from Aegospotami to find refuge with King Evagoras of Salamis in Cyprus. In 394 B.C., Conon defeated the Peloponnesian fleet off Cnidus and returned to Athens with money to rebuild the Long Walls and Athenian fleet.

**Craterus** (c. 370–321 B.C.): Son of Alexander and a noble of Orestis, was a talented taxiarch in 335–331 B.C. He succeeded to second in command of Alexander's army after the murder of Parmenio in 330 B.C. He distinguished himself in the hard campaigns of Bactria, Sogdiana, and India (329–325 B.C.). He was regarded as honorable, efficient, and popular with the ordinary soldiers. In 323 B.C., he was in Cilicia (southeastern Asia Minor) with 10,000 discharged veterans en route to Europe when Alexander died. He thus missed the critical conference at Babylon so that he was named guardian of Philip III and joint ruler of the European regions with Antipater. In 322 B.C., he invaded Greece, linked up with Antipater, and crushed the insurgent Greeks, thus ending the Lamian War. In 324 B.C., he had married Amastris, daughter of Oxyathres, but he divorced her in 322 B.C. to marry Phila, daughter of Antipater. He then joined his father-in-law Antipater in a war against Perdiccas (321 B.C.). Eumenes of Cardia, however, defeated and slew Craterus in a battle in Asia Minor. Craterus, the most attractive of Alexander's marshals, would have made an excellent king.

**Crates of Olynthus:** The hydraulic engineer of Alexander the Great, designed the water system of Alexandria, Egypt, in 332 B.C.

**Ctesias of Cnidus:** Greek physician to Artaxerxes II from 404 to 359 B.C. Wrote a *Persica (*now lost), a fabulous account (in 23 books) of the Persian Empire and India.

**Curtius Rufus:** Roman historian writing in Latin during the reigns of Claudius (41–54) or Vespasian (69–79). Composed a history of Alexander in ten books of which only last eight survive. The work is noted for its delight in exotica.

**Cyrus I** (r.559–530 B.C.): "The Great," king of Persia and the first Achaemenid king of Persia, conquered the Lydian and Babylonian empires.

**Cyrus the Younger** (c. 424–401 B.C.): The younger son of Darius II (465–423 B.C.) and Queen Parysatis, Cyrus cooperated with Lysander in defeating Athens in 407–404 B.C. In 401 B.C., he was slain at Cunaxa in a bid to seize the throne from his brother Artaxerxes II.

**Darius I** (r. 521–486 B.C.): King of Persia, organized the imperial administration, and crushed the Ionian Revolt (499–494 B.C.). His army was defeated by the Athenians at the Battle of Marathon in 490 B.C.

**Darius III** (b. c. 380 B.C.; r. 336–330 B.C.): Codomonus, king of Persia, was the son of Arsames (nephew of Artaxerxes III) and Sisygambis (daughter of Artaxerxes II). Bagoas, the eunuch chiliarch, elevated Darius III, formerly known as Artashata (Artaxerxes) and satrap of Armenia, as Great King after the assassination of Arses. Darius III soon after had Bagoas executed. Personally brave and generous, he was decisively defeated by Alexander the Great at Issus in 333 B.C. and Gaugamela in 331 B.C. His defeats and the capture of the royal family lost Darius legitimacy in the eyes of his nobles. In 330 B.C., Darius fled east when Alexander surprised the Persian court at Ecbatana. Darius was deposed and enchained on orders of Bessus, satrap of Bactria. Darius was murdered near Hecatompylus in Parthyae when Alexander descended upon Bessus's camp.

**Datames** (r. c. 385–362 B.C.): Satrap of Cappadocia, enjoyed the favor of Artaxerxes II, but in 370–362 B.C. he instigated revolts in Asia Minor and the Levant, "the Satraps' Revolt." Datames, defeating two royal field armies, was assassinated, and the revolt collapsed.

**Datapharnes** (d. 328 B.C.): Sogdian lord and ally of Spitamenes, shared Spitamenes's fate.

**Demades** (c. 380–319 B.C.): Athenian orator and politician of obscure origin, was often called a demagogue by his political opponents. From 349 B.C., he opposed Demosthenes and Hypdrides and so urged peace with Philip II. After the Battle of Chaeronea in 338 B.C., he negotiated the peace with Philip II. In 335 B.C., he convinced Alexander to relent in his demand to punish Demosthenes and his associates. He convinced the Athenians not to ally with King Agis III of Sparta, and moved the resolution for the divine honors of Alexander the Great in 324 B.C. After the defeat at Crannon in 322 B.C., he negotiated with Antipater the surrender for Athens. While on embassy at Pella in 319 B.C., Demades was executed by Cassander on grounds of plotting with Antigonus.

**Demaratus of Corinth** (d. 331 B.C.): Personal friend to Philip II and Alexander the Great, reconciled father and son in 336 B.C. A member of the bodyguard of Alexander the Great in 336–331 B.C. Demaratus, at the Battle of the Granicus, came to Alexander's rescue, offering his spear to the king.

**Demetrius of Phaleron** (c. 350–280 B.C.): Athenian peripatetic philosopher and politician, was first elected *strategos* in 325 B.C. He supported the conservatives led by Phocion. In 317 B.C., Cassander entrusted Demetrius as lawgiver (*nomothetes*) with the powers to rewrite the Athenian constitution. Demetrius, in tandem with his mentor Theophrastus, wrote a conservative government with franchise restricted to the propertied classes. In 317–307 Demetrius dominated Athens under his conservative constitution. When Demetrius Poliocretes captured Athens in 307 B.C., Demetrius fled to Thebes and then Alexandria.

**Demetrius** (d. 330 B.C.): Bodyguard (*somatophylax*) of Alexander the Great, was demoted and replaced by Ptolemy in 331 B.C. He was implicated in the conspiracy of Philotas and executed.

**Demetrius I** (c. 200–180 B.C.,): Greco-Bactrian king and son of Euthydemus, conquered the Punjab, and invaded the Ganges valley, capturing the former Mauryan capital Pataliputra. He founded a Greco-Indian kingdom based on the Land of the Five Rivers and Upper Ganges that endured until c. 20 B.C.

**Demetrius I Poliocretes** (b. 336; r. 306–283 B.C.): "Taker of Cities," son of Antigonus I, he married Phila, daughter of Antipater in 321 B.C. and served with his father in the East (319–316 B.C.). He was a dashing, but erratic, general who styled himself the new Alexander. In 312 B.C., he was defeated by Ptolemy at Gaza, but he later directed Antigonid forces in Greece (307; 304–302 B.C.). He won a spectacular naval victory at Salamis in 306 B.C. He wasted precious time on besieging Rhodes (305–304 B.C.), and he threw away victory at Ipsus by pursuing the enemy horse too recklessly. In 301–296 B.C. he held a precarious naval domination in the eastern Mediterranean until seized the throne of Macedon in 296 B.C. He quickly lost Macedon and most of Greece after he invaded Asia Minor in 287 B.C. In 286 B.C., he surrendered to Seleucus, who treated Demetrius as an honored captive until he drank himself to death.

**Demetrius II** (b. c. 161 B.C.; r. 145–139 and 129–125 B.C.): Nicator, Seleucid king and son of Demetrius I (162–150 B.C.), seized the throne with the support of Ptolemy VI. In 139 B.C., he was defeated and captured by Parthian King Mithradates I. Demetrius's brother Antiochus VII was proclaimed king. In 129 B.C., the Parthians decisively defeated and slew Antiochus VII, and Demetrius escaped captivity to a second reign and civil war that saw the disintegration of the Seleucid Empire.

**Demosthenes** (384–322 B.C.): An Athenian orator and foe of Philip II and Alexander the Great. His speeches, notably the *Philippics*, are masterful invective and Attic prose, but his policy of alliance with Thebes against Philip II ended in failure. Demosthenes, who had written orations for civil and criminal ligation, emerged as a political figure in 351–349 B.C., advocating alliance with Olynthus against Philip II. At Pella, in 347–346 B.C., he negotiated, along with Philocrates and Aeschines, the peace with Philip, but Demosthenes charged his colleagues with venality. In 343 B.C., he proposed the Epanorthosis, or amendment to the Peace of Philocrates, that ensured a new war with Philip II. The Greek coalition promoted by Demosthenes was defeated at Chaeronea in 338 B.C. Demosthenes rejoiced over the assassination of Philip and urged opposition to Alexander the Great in 335 B.C. and again in 323 B.C. Demosthenes committed suicide in 322 B.C. after the Athenian defeat in the Lamian War (323–322 B.C.).

**Dercyllidas**: Or Dercylidas, was Spartan harmost of Abydos in 411 B.C. In 399–397 B.C., he commanded Spartan forces in Asia Minor. He concluded on his own initiative a peace with the satrap Pharnabazus and so campaigned in Thrace. In 396 B.C. King Agesilaus II took command of the Asian expedition. Dercyllidas served as envoy to Pharnabazus. In 394 B.C., he was sent to recall Agesilaus to Sparta, and he distinguished himself in the Corinthian War (396–386 B.C.).

**Diades of Thessaly**: Military engineer of Philip II and Alexander the Great and student of Polyidus of Thessaly, he designed siege engines. He built the mole and siege works Tyre in 332 B.C. His treatise on machinery was cited by the Roman architect and writer, Marcus Vitruvius Pollio (c. 80–15 B.C.).

**Dinocrates of Rhodes** (fl. c. 335–300 B.C.): The architect and engineer of Alexander the Great, had collaborated with Demetrius of Ephesus in reconstructing the Artemision destroyed by fire in 356 B.C. In 332 B.C., he planned the city of Alexandria. He designed the funerary monument of Hephaestion in 324 B.C. He drew up plans for Alexander to build a city on Mount Athos, but the project was dropped as impractical.

**Diodorus Siculus** (c. 90–30 B.C.): Wrote a universal history in forty books down to the Gallic Wars of Julius Caesar. His account preserves a wealth of details drawn from now lost earlier historians, and his narrative is the prime source on the reign of Philip II since the history of Theopompus is lost. His 17 book is devoted to the career of Alexander the Great.

**Diodotus** (c. 250–230 B.C.): Greco-Bactrian king, was satrap of Bactria under Antiochus I (281–261 B.C.). He declared himself king in Bactria and Sogdiana. He is known only from brief comments by Justin and Strabo and his coins. It seems that the coins depict a single individual rather than father and son as previously believed.

**Diogenes of Sinope** (c. 404–323 B.C.): Founder of Cynic philosophy, studied under Antisthenes, a follower of Socrates at Athens. He lived as a beggar in the streets of Athens and later Corinth in a quest of self-sufficiency. Given his impoverished living, he was nicknamed a dog (*kynon*); hence the name Cynic. He is remembered from anecdotes reported by Diogenes Laertius, writing in the early 3rd century A.D. Most famous was Diogenes's meeting with Alexander the Great at Corinth in 336 B.C.

**Dion** (b. 408 B.C. r. 357–354 B.C.): Tyrant of Syracuse. Syracusan noble, Dion advised his brother-in-law of Dionysius I, patronized Plato at court, and educated Dionysius II (367–357 and 346–344 B.C.). His teachings lost him favor with Dionysius I so that Dion was banished to Athens. In 357 B.C., Dion returned to Syracuse and seized power. Dion proved a suspicious, brutal tyrant with divine pretensions as a favorite of Zeus.

**Dionysius I** (b. c. 432 B.C.; r. 405–367 B.C.): Tyrant of Syracuse, was an adherent of the democratic leader Hermocrates and officer in the Syracusan army in 409–406 B.C. In 405 B.C., Dionysius seized power at Syracuse, and negotiated a treaty with Carthage. In 402–397 B.C., he transformed Syracuse into the leading Hellenic city of the West with great walls. By successive wars against Carthage, he regained most of Greek Sicily by the treaty of 390 B.C. and then imposed his hegemony over the Italiot cities.

**Drypetis**: A younger daughter of Darius III, married Hephaestion in 324 B.C. See **Statira**.

**Epaminondas** (418–362 B.C.): Son of Polymnis, Theban general, forged a friendship with the democratic leader Pelopidas in 385 B.C. He was the military genius behind the Theban hegemony. In 371 B.C., as Boeotarch, Epaminondas he decisively defeated the Spartan army by a weighted attack on the left wing. In 370–369 B.C., Epaminondas invaded the Peloponnesus and concluded alliances with Argos, the Arcadian League, and Messene (the last liberated from Spartan rule). In 362 B.C., he fell mortally wounded at Mantinea, although he defeated the Athenian-Spartan coalition.

**Ephorus of Cyme** (c. 400–330 B.C.: Historian, declined to accompany Alexander the Great on the Asian expedition. Ephorus wrote a universal history (in 29 books) that is now lost. His son Demophilus wrote a thirtieth book covering 357–340 B.C. Diodorus Siculus and Strabo drew on Ephorus's work; Polybius is critical of Ephorus's accounts of battles.

**Erigyius of Mytilene** (c. 355–328 B.C.): Son of a Greek emigre and boyhood friend of Alexander the Great. He distinguished himself as a commander of the Greek allied and mercenary cavalry. In 330 B.C., he slew in single combat the satrap Satibarzanes. He died of dysentery in Sogdiana.

**Eubulus** (c. 405–333 B.C.): Athenian politician and opponent of Demosthenes, argued for peace with Philip II and so was allied with Aeschines and Philocrates. As commissioner of the Theoric Fund, he gained control over public finances. On financial grounds, Eubulus persuaded the Athenian assembly to end the Social War in 355 B.C. and to make peace with Philip II in 346 B.C. In 352 and in 348 B.C., he supported Athenian expeditions to Thermopylae and Euboea, respectively, to unite the Greeks in defense against Philip II.

**Eucratides** (c. 175–145 B.C.): Greco-Bactrian king who ruled over Bactria and Sogdiana and extended his sway over the Greek kings in Northwestern India. The city Ai Khanoum (possibly Alexandria on the Oxus) was renamed Eucratida in his honor. In c. 167 B.C., King Mithradates I of Parthia checked the western expansion of Eucratides. The murder of Eucratides precipitated a civil war and conquest by Bactria by the nomad Yuezhi, the ancestors of the Kushan emperors.

**Eudamus** (d. 316 B.C.): A Thracian veteran officer, was appointed commander of Macedonian forces in India in 326 B.C. At the conference of Babylon in 323 B.C., Eudamus was confirmed as master of the Indian satrapies. In 317 B.C., he annexed the kingdoms of Porus and Taxiles, and fought for Eumenes of Cardia. He was captured at the Battle of Gabiene and executed on orders of Antigonus Monophthalmus.

**Eudoxus of Cyzicus**. *See* **Hippalus**.

**Eumenes I** (263–241 B.C.): Attalid ruler of Pergamum   and nephew and adopted son of Philetaerus, carved out a state in the Caicus valley and defied Seleucid efforts of reconquest.

**Eumenes II** (r. 197–159 B.C.): King of Pergamum and son of Attalus I and Apollonis, fought with Rome at the Battle of Magnesia in 189 B.C. He received most of Seleucid Western Asia Minor under the Treaty of Apamea in 188 B.C. He expanded the library of Pergamum and donated to Athens the Stoa of Eumenes.

**Eumenes of Cardia** (c. 362–316 B.C.): The Greek secretary of Philip II and Alexander the Great, he kept the *Ephemerides* or *Royal Journal*. He possessed military skill second only to Antigonus. Appointed satrap of Cappadocia and Paphlagonia in 323 B.C., he served Perdiccas (323–321 B.C.) and then Polyperchon (321–316 B.C.) because each championed the Argead family. His victory over Craterus in 321 B.C. was vitiated by the murder of Perdiccas and the conference of Triparadisus where Eumenes was outlawed by the Macedonian army. In 320 and 318–316 B.C. Eumenes kept Antigonus at bay, retreating eastward into the Upper Satrapies. Despite tactical victories at Paracetacene (317 B.C.) and Gabiene (316

B.C.), Eumenes was betrayed by the elite Silver Shields, who handed him over to Antigonus. He was tried and executed, and with his death passed the last true protector of Alexander's house.

**Eurydice** (c. 337–317 B.C.): Adea, was the daughter of Amyntas and Cynana (who was a daughter of Philip II and the Illyrian princess Audata). She married Philip III Arrhidaeus despite resistance from Perdiccas, and she intrigued to rule the empire through her husband. In 317 B.C., she deserted Polyperchon for Cassander, whom she named as regent of the empire. Later in the same year, she and Philip III fell into the hands of their old rival Olympias who forced them both to commit suicide.

**Eurydice, Phila, and Nicaea**: The three daughters of Antipater. In 322 B.C. Eurydice married Ptolemy I and bore him Ptolemy Ceraunus and Lysandra. Phila married Craterus in 322 B.C. and bore him a son Craterus (later governor of Corinth for Antigonus Gonatas). She married Demetrius Poliocretes in 319 B.C. and bore him a son Antigonus Gonatas. Nicaea was offered in marriage to Perdiccas, who jilted her for Cleopatra. In 316 B.C. she married Lysimachus, and she bore Agathocles, but Lysimachus divorced her in c. 300 B.C. to marry Arsinoe II.

**Euthydemus** (r. c. 230–200 B.C.): Greco-Bactrian king, was a native of Magnesia and satrap of Sogdiana. He overthrew King Diodotus and established the Euthydemid dynasty that ruled Central Asia down to 130 B.C. In 208 B.C., he submitted to Antiochus III and concluded a marital alliance. His silver tetradrachmae became the trade coins of central Asia.

**Evagoras I** (410–374 B.C.): Teucrid king of Salamis, Cyprus, was guest friend (*philoxenos*) to many leading Athenians. Evagoras received Conon, after the Athenian defeat at Aegospotami in 405 B.C. and assisted the return of Conon in 394 B.C. In 391–381, with Athenian support, Evagoras rebelled from King Artaxerxes II and aimed to bring under his control all of Cyprus. In 381 B.C., his navy was defeated by the Persian imperial fleet, and Evagoras surrendered on favorable terms. He was assassinated and succeeded by his son Nicocles (373–360 B.C.).

**Glaucias:** Illyrian prince of the Taulantians and ally of Cleitus the Illyrian, was defeated at Pelion by Alexander the Great in 335 B.C.

**Harpalus** (d. 323 B.C.): Macedonian noble and son of Machatas, was a boyhood friend of Alexander the Great. In 331 B.C., because of his lame leg, he was appointed treasurer at Babylon. He and his mistress Pythonice were notorious for their corruption and decadence. In 324 B.C., Haraplus, fearing punishment for his misdeeds, absconded from Babylon to Athens with 5,000 talents and 6,000 mercenaries. His intrigues at Athens and Taraenum precipitated the Lamian War. He was murdered in Crete in 323 B.C. His brother Philip was first satrap of India.

**Hephaestion** (c. 356–324 B.C.): The son of Amyntor. He was a Macedonian noble and was dearest friend to Alexander. Alexander and Hephaestion were compared to Achilles and Patrocles. Hephaestion was a boyhood friend of Alexander, but little is known of him until 333 B.C., when he was named a bodyguard (*somatophylax*). He was mistaken for Alexander by Persian Queen Sisygambis. In 330 B.C., he was given joint command of the Companion cavalry. He commanded independent columns in Central Asia and India in 329–325 B.C. In 324 B.C., he was named chiliarch and married Drypetis, daughter of Darius III. He died of illness at Ecbatana in late 324 B.C. Alexander ordered an opulent funerary monument, and heroic honors were decreed the oracle of Amun at Siwah. The grief-stricken Alexander never recovered from the death of his beloved friend.

**Heracles** (329 or 327–309 B.C.): The reputed illegitimate son of Alexander the Great and Barsine, daughter of Artabazus. In 309 B.C. Polyperchon raised him as king against Cassander, but the two dynasts quickly struck a deal nominating Polyperchon as Cassander's deputy (*strategos*) in Greece. Heracles was immediately put to death.

**Herodotus** (c. 490–430 B.C.): Hailed the father of history, was born at Halicarnassus and traveled throughout the Persian empire. He wrote his history dealing with the wars between the Greeks and Persians. Herodotus's account is the main source for early Greek history as well as for contemporary peoples of the Near East.

**Herostratus of Ephesus** (d. 356 B.C.): Set fire to the Artemision of Ephesus on July 20, 356 B.C. He was executed by the civic authorities, and his memory was condemned. The event was taken as a portend of the birth of Alexander the Great. Hence, Alexander offered to pay for the reconstruction of the temple in 334 B.C.

**Hesiod** (c. 700 B.C.): Poet of Boeotia (central Greece), he wrote in epic meter the *Theogony* and *Works and Days*. The first epic recounts the myths of the Greek gods; the second was a cry for *dike* (justice) within the early Greek *polis* (city-state).

**Hippalus**: Greek navigator and merchant, is credited by the *Periplus of the Erythraean* Sea with discovering how to use the monsoon winds to sail across the Erythraean Sea (Indian Ocean) to the Indian ports in c. 117–116 B.C. He might have piloted a ship of **Eudoxus of Cyzicus**, an explorer of the Red Sea in the reign of Ptolemy VIII (182–116 B.C.), who is credited with the same discovery by Strabo.

**Hippodamus of Miletus** (c. 480–408 B.C.): Architect, mathematician, and philosopher, designed the orderly plan for a Greek city, dividing residential and public space. At the request of Pericles, he planned the Piraeus, the port of Athens. He is credited with designing the city of Rhodes, founded in 408 B.C., and the reconstruction of Miletus. The cities of Olynthus, capital of the Chalcidian League, and Priene in Ionia were built on the Hippodamian plan

**Homer** (c. 750 B.C.): Reputedly a native of Smyrna, this blind poet was credited with the composition of the *Iliad* and *Odyssey*.

**Hyperides** (389–322 B.C.): Athenian orator and politician, was a political ally of Demosthenes and prosecuted Philocrates in 343 B.C. In 336 B.C., he moved the motion voting a gold crown to Demosthenes for his public services, but in 324 B.C. he prosecuted Demosthenes for accepting bribes from Haraplus. Hyperides, who pressed for the Lamian War, was surrendered to Antipater and executed.

**Idrieus** (351–344 B.C.): Hecatomnid dynast and satrap of Caria, was a loyal vassal of Artaxerxes III and was responsible for the expansion of the sanctuary of Zeus at Labranda.

**Iphicrates** (415–353 B.C.): Athenian general, perfected the equipment and tactics of light armed infantry or peltasts. In 390 B.C., he and his peltasts annihilated a Spartan *mora* of 600 hoplites near Corinth. In 386–379 B.C., he took mercenary service with King Cotys of Thrace, and in 378–373 B.C., in the Persian army sent against Egypt. In 367–364 B.C., he failed to capture Amphipolis. In 356 B.C., he and his son Menesthenes refused to support Chares at the Battle of Embata. They were both prosecuted and acquitted.

**Isocrates** (436–338 B.C.): Athenian orator and Panhellenist, called for Greek *homonoia* (concord) and unity in his *Panegyricus* (380 B.C.), pleading for a new alliance between Athens and Sparta against Persia. Isocrates redefined Hellene as a cultural rather than racial designation. After the Social War, Iscorates opposed imperial expansion, and he came to see Philip II of Macedon as the champion of Greek unity and so penned an open letter urging the king to lead an expedition against Persia.

**Jason of Pherae** (c. 385–370 B.C.): Son of Lycophron, was tyrant and *tagos* of the Thessaly. In 374–370 B.C., he fielded an army of 10,000 mercenary hoplites and 2,000 Thessalian cavalry. He aspired to domination of mainland Greece, but was assassinated in 370 B.C.

**Justin**: Or Marcus Justianus, Latin historian of the 2nd century A.D., who composed an epitome of the history of Pompeius Trogus on Philip II and Alexander the Great. Deficient in chronology and details, Justin's epitome still contains important information.

**Kujula Kadphises**, Kushan emperor founded the Kushan Empire in central Asia based on the caravan trade and the Greco-Bactrian cities.

**Leonidas** (r. 45–64 A.D.): Alexander the Great's tutor between the ages of six and twelve, as selected by Olympias. Leonidas imposed a rigorous frugal regimen, reproaching Alexander for any displays of luxury or waste.

**Leonnatus** (c. 358–322 B.C.): Lycestrian noble related to the Argead line, he was a boyhood friend and bodyguard (*somatophylax*) of Alexander the Great. He distinguished himself in India and Gedrosia. He and Peucestas defended the wounded Alexander during the assault on the city of the Malli. Able, but headstrong, Leonnatus received Hellespontine Phrygia in 323 B.C. He accepted an offer from Olympias to marry Cleopatra, invaded Europe, raised the siege of Lamia, but he was killed in a cavalry skirmish.

**Leosthenes** (356–323 B.C.): Veteran Athenian mercenary general who served in Achaemenid armies. In 323, he along with 8,000 mercenaries at Taenarum, joined the Athenians in their rebellion against Macedonian rule. He fell in the initial fighting at Lamia.

**Lucian of Samosata** (c. 125–180 A.D.): Rhetorician and satirist of the Second Sophistic, was a native Aramaic speaker who mastered Greek. In polished Greek, he wrote satirical dialogues on the gods and heroes, a scathing account of the charlatan prophet Alexander of Abonouteichus.

**Lycophron of Pherae** (c. 356–352 B.C.): Tyrant, shared power with his brother Peitholas. He allied with Philomelus and the Phocians to assert their control over Thessaly. He fought with Onomarchus against Philip in 353–352 B.C. After the Battle of Crocus Plain, he surrendered Pherae to Philip II, and withdrew with 3,000 mercenaries into Phocis.

**Lycurgus**: Legendary lawgiver of Sparta was considered to have lived in c. 775–750 B.C. Most Spartan institutions were attributed to Lycurgus.

**Lycurgus** (c. 395–324 B.C.): Athenian orator and politician, was a student of Plato and Isocrates. In 335 B.C., he advocated an alliance with Thebes and so was perceived as an ally of Demosthenes and Hyperides. In 337–325 B.C., he supervised Athenian finances, raising annual revenues to 1,200 talents. He supervised the fortification of the Piraeus and city, repairs of public buildings, and the reform of the ephebate.

**Lysander** (c. 450–395 B.C.): Navarch of Sparta in 407–406 B.C. Lysander won the confidence of Cyrus the Younger, and, by his victory at Notium (406 B.C.), discredited Alicbiades. After the Spartan defeat at Arginusae,

Lysander was appointed command of the Peloponnesian fleet in the Aegean as *epistoleus*, secretary to the navarch, in 405–403 B.C. He ended the Peloponnesian War by his victory at Aegispotami, and imposed the Thirty Tyrants on Athens. Lysander failed to convert his success into primacy within Sparta. In 396 B.C., his royal patron Agesilaus humiliated Lysander, demoting him to carver of the meat at the royal table. In 395 B.C., Lysander fell at the Battle of Haliartus.

**Lysandra** (b. c. 305 B.C.): Daughter of Ptolemy I and Euryidice, and sister of Ptolemy Ceraunus. She was wife to Alexander V (297–294 B.C.), and then Agathocles, son of Lysimachus. In 284 B.C., upon the murder of Agathocles, she and her children fled to Seleucus. Thereafter she disappears from the sources.

**Lysimachus** (b c. 362; r. 305–281 B.C.): The son of the Thessalian immigrant Agathocles, was a boyhood friend and bodyguard of Alexander the Great. He commanded the fleet on the Hydaspes in 324 B.C. In 323 B.C. he received the satrapy of Thrace. In 315 B.C. he joined the coalition against Antigonus, and he proved essential in defeating Antigonus at Ipsus (301 B.C.). He acquired western Asia Minor as a result, and in 288–285 B.C. he gained Macedon and Greece. In c. 300 B.C., he married Arsione II, daughter of Ptolemy I, but she intrigued against Agathocles, Lysimachus's popular son by his first wife, Nicaea (daughter of Antipater). When Lysimachus was duped into the trial and execution of Agathocles, he lost support. His son's widow, Lysandra, and her brother Ptolemy Ceraunus, fled to Seleucus, who thereupon invaded Asia Minor. Lysimachus was defeated and killed at Corupedium in 281 B.C.

**Lysippus of Sicyon** (c. 390–300 B.C.): The sculptor of Alexander the Great, credited with portraits and equestrian statues of the king. Lysippus fixed the heroic godlike image of Alexander, and defined the graceful portrait art of the late Classical era.

**Mazaeus** (c. 385–328 B.C.; r. 361–336 B.C.): Persian noble. As satrap of Cilicia, he suppressed rebellions in the Levant and fought mercenary army of Pharaoh Nectanebo II. Darius III promoted Mazaeus to satrap of Syria (336–331 B.C.), and he commanded the Persian left wing at the Battle of Gaugamela in 331 B.C. He submitted to Alexander and so received

Babylonia as his satrapy (331–328 B.C.). His two sons, Artiboles (Persian Ardu-Bel) and Hydarnes (Vidarna), served in Alexander's cavalry in the eastern campaigns.

**Manetho** (fl. c. 280–250 B.C.): Egyptian priest and historian, wrote in Greek *Aegyptiaca,* a history of the pharaohs from Narmer (Menes) down to Ptolemy I, the chronological basis for Egyptian history.

**Mausolus** (r. 377–353 B.C.): Or Mausollus, Hecatomnid dynast of Caria, was noted for his great funerary monument the Mausoleum, at Halicarnassus, and building program at the sanctuary of Zeus at Labranda. He ruled as satrap of Caria and extended his sway over Lycia and the Greek cities of southwestern Asia Minor. He backed the rebel allies in the Social War (357–355 B.C.). This philhellene dynast was perceived by Athens as a greater threat than Philip II. His sister and queen Artemisa (353–351 B.C.) ruled in her own right after Mausolus's death.

**Mazaces** (r. 336–330 B.C.): Persian satrap of Egypt under Darius III, surrendered Memphis and the satrapy to Alexander the Great in 332 B.C.

**Megesthenes** (c. 350–290 B.C.): Envoy of Seleucus I to Chandragupta in 302–291 B.C., wrote an *Indica* (in four books) describing the Mauryan court at Pataliputra and the lands of the Indus and Ganges. Strabo and Arrian each used the work for his account of India.

**Meleager** (d. 323 B.C.): Veteran taxiarch of Philip II, commanded a regiment of the phalanx in 334–323 B.C. He was never promoted to cavalry commander due to clashes with Alexander in India. At the conference of Babylon in 323 B.C., he represented the interests of the infantry who called for the acclamation of Philip III Arrhidaeus and earned the enmity of Perdiccas, who ordered Meleager executed.

**Memnon of Rhodes** (c. 380–333 B.C.): Greek mercenary officer, served under his older brother Mentor in 353–340 B.C. In 340 B.C., he succeeded to his brother's lands in the Troad and married his brother's widow Barsine. Memnon checked the advance force of Macedonians under Parmenio in 336–335 B.C. In 334 B.C., the Persian satraps rejected Memnon's strategy of attrition. Appointed Persian commander in the West by Darius III, he directed the defense of Halicarnassus, and commanded the Persian fleet in the Aegean in 334–333 B.C. He died at the siege of Mytilene in August 333 B.C.

**Menander** (342–293 B.C.): Athenian comic poet, was a student of Theophrastus. He composed over one hundred comedies; only the *Dyskolos* survives. He created the New Comedy, the satire on manners that replaced the political satire of Old Comedy in the 5th century B.C.

**Menander I Soter** (r. 165–130 B.C.): Greco-Bactrian king of India, known as Milinda Panka in Buddhist sources, presided over the heyday of the Greco-Indian kingdom. He was credited with a conversion to Buddhism, and stories were circulated comparing him to the Buddhist Mauryan emperor Asoka. (273–232 B.C.). Given his coins and classical literary sources, Menander was more likely a patron of Buddhist shrines rather than a convert.

**Mentor of Rhodes** (c. 385–340 B.C.): Greek mercenary officer, served in the armies of Artabazus, satrap of Hellespontine Phrygia, in the rebellion against King Artaxerxes III in 358–354 B.C. He married Barsine, daughter of Artabazus. He fled to Egypt and took service in the mercenary army of Pharaoh Nectanebo II, serving in Phoenicia in c. 350–346 B.C. He deserted to Artaxerxes III and distinguished himself in the Persian reconquest of Egypt in 343–342 B.C. He was sent as Persian commander in the western Anatolia; he died shortly after 340 B.C. His brother Memnon married Barsine and succeeded to Mentor's position.

**Midas** (r.c. 725–696 B.C.): King of Phrygia, known as Mita in Assyrian annals. He was last of a succession of Phrygian kings who had ruled under the dynastic name Midas. Midas, a philhellene, made dedications at Delphi and was the subject of many legends among the Greeks, including the oracle of the Gordian knot. The last Midas constructed the great tumulus at Gordion. He committed suicide after the Cimmerians overran his kingdom.

**Mithridates I** (b. c. 105 B.C.; r. 171–137 B.C.): Arsacid king of Parthia, forged the Parthian empire. He defeated Greco-Bactrian King Eucratides in c.

167 B.C. In 139 B.C., he defeated and captured the Seleucid king Demetrius II and occupied Mesopotamia.

**Mithridates VI Eupator** (b. 134 B.C.; r. 121–63 B.C.):King of Pontus was regarded by the Romans as the greatest king since Alexander the Great. Mithridates fought three Mithridatic wars against Rome for mastery of Asia Minor (98–85 B.C.; 83–71 B.C.; 74–63 B.C.). In his appeals and official art, Mithridates styled himself as the new Alexander the Great.

**Mithrobazares** (336–330 B.C.): Satrap of Cappadocia under Darius III, fell at the Battle of Granicus in 334 B.C.

**Musicanus**: Sanskrit Mushika, king of the Sind, he ruled from Medieval Alor and was compelled to submit to Alexander the Great in 325 B.C. Musicanus and Sambus, with the support Brahmins, soon revolted. Musicanus was captured and crucified at Harmatelia.

**Narbazanes** (336–330 B.C.): Persian noble and chiliarch of Darius III At the Battle of Issus, he commanded the cavalry in 333 B.C. After Darius III was deposed by Bessus, Narbazanes submitted to Alexander the Great.

**Nearchus of Crete** (c. 360–300 B.C.): Son of an emigre of Crete, was a boyhood friend of Alexander the Great. In 334–328 B.C., he was satrap of Pamphylia. In 328 B.C., he was summoned to Bactria along with seamen for service in India. In 326–325 B.C., Nearchus was navarch of the fleet on the Hypdaspes and Indus. In 325 B.C., he commanded the navy sailing in support of Alexander's army marching through Gedrosia, but adverse winds delayed departure. Nearchus met Alexander on the shores of Carmania. In 324 B.C., Nearchus was rewarded with a gold crown and married to the daughter of Mentor and Barsine. He supported Antigonus I in the wars of the Diodochoi. He composed a *Periplus* of the Erythraean Sea which was used by Arrian for his *Indica*.

**Nectanebo II** (r. 360–342 B.C.): Nakhthorhebe, pharaoh of Egypt, overthrew his father Teos (362–360 B.C.) with the Greek mercenary army commanded by Agesilaus II. In 343–342 B.C., he was expelled from Egypt by the army of Artaxerxes III Ochus. He fled an exile into Nubia, and later it was rumored that Alexander the Great was the pharaoh son of Nectanebo II.

**Neoptolemus** (b. c. 390 B.C.; r. 370–360 B.C.): Aeacid king of Epirus, was the father of Alexander I of Epirus and Olympias. He ruled jointly with his brother Arybbas who succeeded to the entire kingdom in 360–352 B.C.

**Nicaea**: Daughter of Antipater. *See also* **Eurydice**.

**Nicanor** (d. 330 B.C.): Son of Parmenio, distinguished himself as a taxiarch against the Getae in 335 B.C. In 334–330 B.C., He commanded the hypaspists. And he died of disease shortly after the pursuit of Darius III.

**Nicocreon** (r. 331–311 B.C.): Teucrid king of Salamis, Cyprus, rebuilt Tyre and entertained Alexander the Great there in 331 B.C. In 315–311 B.C., he sided with Ptolemy, and was rewarded with rule over the entire island.

**Nicomedes I** (r. 279–255 B.C.): King of Bithynia forged the Hellenistic kingdom of Bithynia, founding the capital Nicomedia. In 277 B.C., he hired the Galatians as mercenaries, and transported 10,000 Celtic warriors and their families into Asia Minor. Upon their discharge, the Galatians raided the cities of Western Asia Minor until they were driven by Antiochus I into northwestern Phrygia which they settled and renamed Galatia.

**Olympias** (c. 378–316 B.C.): The daughter of King Neoptolemus of Epirus and descendant of the Homeric hero Achilles. She married Philip II in 357 B.C. This indomitable, ambitious queen clashed violently with Philip II, who exiled and divorced her in 337 B.C., but she returned to favor when Alexander the Great ascended the throne in 336 B.C. Alexander was devoted to his mother, but Olympias alienated most Macedonians by her violent temper, erratic political intrigues, and barbaric ways. While Alexander conquered Asia, Olympias quarreled with the regent Antipater, whom she learned to detest. In 331 B.C. she returned to Epirus from where she schemed against Antipater. In 317 B.C., she invaded Macedon on behalf of her grandson Alexander IV, captured and drove to suicide her hated rivals Eurydice and Philip III, and purged the court of Pella. Her bloody regime enabled Cassander to rally support and recover Macedon. Besieged in Pydna in 317–316 B.C., Olympias was forced to surrender, and Cassander prudently ordered her execution despite promises of safe conduct.

**Onesicritus** (c. 360–290 B.C.): Pilot and helmsman, was a native of the Aegean island Astypalaea. He accompanied Nearchus to Bactria in 328 B.C. He was the pilot of Alexander's flagship on the Hydaspes and Indus in 326–325 B.C. In 324 B.C., he was helmsman of the flagship of Nearchus. He was rewarded with a gold crown and composed a work on the education of Alexander. Arrian and Strabo criticized Onesicritus for mixing fable with facts, for he was likely the source of Plutarch's anecdote of the visit of the Amazons to Alexander.

**Onomarchus** (d. 352 B.C.): Son of Euthycrates, was elected commander (*strategos autokrator*) by the Phocians after the death of Philomelus. In 353 B.C., he defeated and expelled Philip II from Thessaly. In 352 B.C., at Crocus Plain, Philip II decisively defeated the Phocian mercenary army. Onomarchus committed suicide.

**Oxyarthes** (d. c. 303 B.C.): Achaemenid noble and brother of King Darius III (r. 336–330 B.C.), distinguished himself at the Battle of Issus in 333 B.C. In 330 B.C., he submitted to Alexander the Great, after Bessus had deposed and then murdered Darius III. Enjoying high favor at Alexander's court, Oxyarthes directed the execution of Bessus in 329 B.C. His daughter Amastris (c. 306–284 B.C.) was promised in marriage to Craterus by Alexander the Great. Craterus repudiated Amastris, who was married to Dionysius, tyrant of Heraclea Pontica (c. 353–305 B.C.)

**Oxyrates** (d. c. 305 B.C.): Bactrian lord and father of Roxane, supported Bessus in 330–329 B.C. After Alexander captured the Sogdian Rock in 327 B.C., Oxyartes submitted. He was promoted to satrap of Parapamisadae, which he held to his death shortly before 305 B.C.

**Pammenes** (d. c. 353 B.C.): A talented general and protégé of Epaminondas. He hosted Philip II, who was sent as a hostage to Thebes in c. 368–364 B.C. Pammenes distinguished himself in the Peloponnesian campaign in 370–369 B.C. and commanded Boeotian forces in the Third Sacred War in 355–354 B.C., defeating Philomelus at Neon. In 354–353 B.C., he commanded 5,000 Boeotian hoplites sent to assist the rebel satrap Artabazus. Pammenes was arrested and apparently executed on orders of Artabazus.

**Parmenio** (c. 400–330 B.C.): Macedonian noble and most trusted general of Philip II, was ordered to secure the bridgehead in Asia Minor in 336–335 B.C. Parmenio, loyal to Alexander the Great, commanded the left wing at the Battles of Granicus, Issus, and Gaugamela. His sons Philotas and Nicanor commanded the Companion cavalry and hypaspists, respectively. In Arrian's account, Parmenio is presented as the cautious foil to Alexander, but the senior general was respected for his ability and loyalty. In 330 B.C., he took charge of the treasury of 180,000 talents and garrison at Ecbatana. When his son Philotas was executed for treason, Alexander ordered the judicial murder of Parmenio lest the senior general raise a rebellion.

**Parysatis**: A younger daughter of Darius III, married Alexander the Great in 324 B.C. *See* **Statira**.

**Patrocles** (c. 312–261 B.C.): Macedonian general and navigator, explored the Caspian Sea on order of Seleucus I. In c. 280 B.C., Patrocles proved the Caspian Sea was a great inland lake that did not flow into a great eastern ocean. Strabo cited his account.

**Pausanias** (c. 64–120 A.D.): Geographer and local historian, wrote a *Description of Greece* in ten books with a wealth of information about local shrines, cults, and traditions of the Greek world.

**Pausanias of Orestis** (d. 336 B.C.): Macedonian noble and assassin of Philip II, was disgraced by Attalus, a leading general of Philip II, failed to receive satisfaction for his humiliation. At Aegeae in 336 B.C., Pausanias slew Philip II, but while making his escape Pausanias was killed by Leonnatus and Perdiccas. The Lycenstrian brothers, Heromenes and Arrhabaeus, were executed for complicity; the third brother, Alexander, was pardoned. While modern scholars suspect the complicity of Olympias or Alexander, none of the sources state this.

**Peithon** (c. 355–316 B.C.): Noble from Eordaea, was a bodyguard of Alexander the Great. Friend of Perdiccas, he was an able but arrogant officer who supported Perdiccas's bid for the throne and so was named satrap of Media at the Conference of Babylon in 323 B.C. In 321 B.C., he murdered Perdiccas and took charge of leading the army out of Egypt to Triparadisus. Satrap of Media since 323 B.C., Peithon effectively controlled the easternmost portions of the empire until he was arrested and executed by Antigonus.

**Pelopidas** (410–364 B.C.): Theban democratic politician and associate of Epaminondas, expelled the Spartan garrison on the citadel of Thebes in 379 B.C. and reorganized the Boeotian League. He was the political genius behind the Theban hegemony, and he fell at the Battle of Cynocephalae, in Thessaly in 364 B.C., defeating Alexander of Pherae.

**Perdiccas** (c. 365–321 B.C.): Son of Orontes, noble from Orestis, was a boyhood friend and bodyguard of Alexander. He was an able taxiarch who distinguished himself in the capture of siege of Thebes in 335 B.C. and operations in Bactria. After the death of Hephaestion (324 B.C.), he was appointed chiliarch, or chief administrator of the empire. In June 323 B.C., he could have taken the throne, but he adopted a compromise, thereby enabling his enemies Ptolemy, Antipater, Craterus, and Antigonus to form a coalition against him by late 322 B.C. In 321 B.C. he invaded Egypt to destroy Ptolemy, but Ptolemy's defense and a mutiny led to his murder by Peithon and Seleucus.

**Perdiccas III** (b. c. 380 B.C.; r. 368–359 B.C.): Argead king of Macedon, was the second son of Amyntas III and Eurydice. He and 4,000 Macedonians were slain in battle against Bardylis, king of the Illlyrians.

**Perseus** (b. 212 B.C.; r. 179–167 B.C.): Antigonid king of Macedon, the dashing son of Philip V, posed as a new Alexander the Great. The Roman Senate, suspicious of the popular king, provoked the Third Macedonian War (172–168 B.C.). The consul Lucius Aemilius Paullus defeated Perseus at

Pydna in 168 B.C. The Macedonian kingdom was abolished in place of four autonomous republics in alliance with Rome.

**Peucestas** (c. 358–290 B.C.): Boyhood friend of Alexander the Great, was a trierarch of the fleet to the Hydaspes in 326 B.C. He and Leonnatus saved the wounded Alexander at the city of the Malli in 325 B.C. Peucestas was rewarded as a special eighth bodyguard (*somatophylax*). In 324 B.C., Peucestas, who took a Persian wife and adopted Persian manners, was appointed satrap of Persia. In 317–316 B.C. Peucestas sided with Eumenes of Cardia against Antigonus, but he and Eumenes quarreled over strategy. After the Battle of Gabiene, Peucestas took service with Antigonus I, and the Demetrius Poliocretes.

**Phalaecus** (d. 343 B.C.): Elected supreme general of the Phocians in 351 B.C. With the treasures of Delphi exhausted, Phalaecus negotiated a surrender to Philip II that ended the Third Sacred War in 346 B.C. Phalaecrus and his mercenaries were hired by Cnossus in Crete, in a war against Lyttus, which hired Peloponnesian mercenaries under King Archidamus III. Phalaecus was defeated and killed at a siege of Cydonia.

**Pharnabazus** (d. c. 373 B.C.): The Persian satrap of northwestern Asia Minor in 413–395 B.C. with his capitals at Dascylium and Gordion. He cooperated with the Spartans.

**Pharnabazus** (c. 370–320 B.C.): Persian noble, son of Artabazus, was the brother-in-law of Memnon of Rhodes and succeeded to command of the Persian fleet in August 333 B.C. He secured Tenedos, Samothrace, Siphnos, and Andros, reoccupied Miletus, and entered into negotiations with King Agis III of Sparta. When the news of the defeat of Darius III at Issus reached the Aegean, Pharnabazus withdrew. His fleet defected to Alexander the Great. In 330 B.C., he and his father Artabazus submitted to Alexander in Hyrcania.

**Phayllus** (d. 351 B.C.): Son of Euthycrates, was elected supreme general of the Phocians after the death of his brother Onomarchus. He garrisoned Thermopylae and so checked the advance of Philip II in 352 B.C. In 351 B.C., he invaded the Peloponnesus to assist Sparta, but he died of illness.

**Phila**: Daughter of Antipater. *See also* **Euryidice.**

**Philetaeru** (b. c. 343 B.C.; r. 281–263 B.C.): Ruler of Pergamum, Paphlagonian eunuch, served Antigonus I, and then Lysimachus, who entrusted Philetaerus with the citadel of Pergamum and a treasury of 9,000 talents. In 282 B.C., Philetaerus deserted to Seleucus and was confirmed in his position. As a Seleucid agent, Philetaerus expanded his control over the Caicus valley and transmitted his position to nephew Eumenes I.

**Philip** (d. 326 B.C.; r. 326–327 B.C.): Macedonian noble of Elimeia and son of Machatas, was appointed the first satrap of India, ruling from Taxila He was assassinated by his mercenaries, and Eudamus was appointed the new satrap. He was the brother of Haraplus.

**Philip II** (r. 359–336 B.C.): Argead king of Macedon, a brilliant king of Macedon in is own right, was the father of Alexander the Great. Philip transformed Macedon into the leading Hellenic power. In 357 B.C., he seized Amphipolis, and henceforth was at war with Athens. In 353 B.C., he intervened unsuccessfully in Thessaly against the Phocians, but in 352 B.C. defeated the Phocians at Crocus Plain and was elected *tagos* of the Thessalian League. His conquests in Thessaly and Thrace alarmed Olynthus, which allied with Athens. In 349–348, Philip conquered the Chalcidice. Athens was compelled to conclude with Philip the Peace of Philocrates in 346 B.C., and Philip ended the Third Sacred War soon after by separate peace. After 343 B.C., Philip clashed repeatedly with the Athenians, inspired the orator Demosthenes. In 338 B.C., he defeated the coalition army of Athens and Thebes at the Battle of Chaeronea and so united the Greek city-states into the League of Corinth. He was assassinated before he could lead his war against Persia.

Philip had seven wives. In 359 or 358 B.C., he married Phila, daughter of the noble Derdas II of Elimaea and Audata, an Illyrian princess (by whom he had a daughter Cynane). In 358 B.C., he married Philinna of Larissa, mother of Philip III Arrhidaeus. In 356 B.C., he married **Olympias**, daughter of the Molossian King Neoptolemus of Epirus. She was Philip's queen and mother of Alexander the Great and Cleopatra. In 352, he married Nicesipolis of Pherae, mother of **Thessalonice**. In 339 B.C., he married Medea, princess of the Getae. In 337 B.C., Philip repudiated Olympias and married **Cleopatra Eurydice** (d. 336 B.C.), niece of Attalus. Justin and Satyrus report that Cleopatra had two children, a daughter Europa and son Caranus, who were murdered on orders of Olympias in 336 B.C.

**Philip III Arrhidaeus** (b. c. 357–317 B.C.; r. 323–317 B.C.): The retarded son of Philip II and Philinna of Larissa, a Thessalian aristocrat. Olympias is reputed to have fed him poisoned mushrooms when Philip was a child so as to stunt his intellect. In 323 B.C. the Macedonian phalanx at Babylon unexpectedly declared him king. In 322 B.C. he was married to Eurydice, who managed her husband until their deaths in 317 B.C.

**Philip IV** (297 B.C.): King of Macedon, oldest son of Cassander and Thessalonice, ruled briefly after his father's death and died prematurely of illness.

**Philip V** (b. 238 B.C.; r. 221–179 B.C.): Antigonid king of Macedon, son of Demetrius II and Chryseis, succeeded his stepfather Antigonus Doson (229–221 B.C.). Philip, known for his acid wit and ambitious plans, fought the Greek states in the Social War (220–217 B.C.). In 215 B.C., he allied with the Carthaginian general Hannibal in Italy, and so Philip battled Rome, supported by the Aetolians, Athens, and Attalus I of Pergamum, in the First Macedonian War (215–205 B.C.). Rome again declared war on Philip V in Second Macedonian War (200–196 B.C.). In 197 B.C., Titus Quinctius Flamininus defeated Philip at Cynocephalae and so broke Macedonian power.

**Philip of Acarnania**: Physician and friend to Alexander the Great, cured Alexander from the fever contracted after the king had swum in the cold waters of the Cyndus in 333 B.C. Alexander drank the medicinal potion after handing to Philip a letter from Parmenio warning the king that Philip was bribed to poison the king. Philip extracted the arrow from Alexander's shoulder during the siege of Gaza in 323 B.C.

**Philocrates** (b. c.385 B.C.; d. after 343 B.C.): Athenian orator and politician, favored peace with Philip II after the fall of Olynthus. In 347–346 B.C., he headed the first Athenian embassy to negotiate a settlement with Philip II that ended in the Peace of Philocrates in 346 B.C. Aeschines and Demosthenes each objected to concessions in the initial peace. Philocrates was impeached by Demosthenes in 343 B.C. on grounds of bribery on the second embassy sent to secure Philip's ratification of the peace. Philocrates chose exile to execution.

**Philomelus** (d. 354 B.C.): Son of Theotimus, was the supreme general (*strategos autokrator*) of the Phocians in the Third Sacred War (355–346 B.C.). In summer 356 B.C., countered an ultimatum from the Boeotians and Thessalians by occupying Delphi and using the treasures to hire 5,000 mercenaries. Athens and Sparta concluded alliances with Phocis. The Amphictyony declared a sacred war on the Phocians in fall 355 B.C. In 354 B.C., Philomelus was defeated and killed at the Battle of Neon.

**Philotas** (c. 370–330 B.C.): Son of Parmenio, was promoted to command of the Companion cavalry in 336 B.C. Philotas distinguished himself in 334–331 B.C., but he was noted for his boastful self-importance. Craterus and Hephaestion each viewed Philotas as a rival. In autumn, Philotas was arrested and convicted for failure to bring a conspiracy to the attention of Alexander. Philotas, after his conviction, might well have denounced the king's policies. The execution of Philotas compelled Alexander to order the judicial murder of Parmenio.

**Phocion the Good** (c. 402–318 B.C.): Athenian general, was respected for his frugal habits and loyalty. He was elected to a record forty-five generalships. Phocion was conservative in his politics and meticulous in his military operations. He served as a junior officer under Chabrias. In 351–349 B.C., he served as mercenary commander for King Artaxerxes III in the campaign to subdue Cyprus. He distinguished himself twice in Euboea, in 348 and 341 B.C. He commanded the Athenian relief force to Byzantium in 340 B.C. Phocion favored peace with Macedon. In 335 B.C., he secured for Athens generous terms from Alexander the Great. Phocion opposed the Lamian War and represented Athens to Antipater in 322 B.C. The Athenians blamed Phocion for the harsh terms imposed by Antipater. In 319 B.C., Phocion urged an alliance with Cassander, but Polyperchon occupied Athens and ordered the execution of Phocion.

**Phoebidas**: Spartan officer, seized the Cadmea, acropolis of Thebes in 382 B.C., while en route to Olynthus. He was acquitted for misconduct by the intervention of King Agesilaus II.

**Phraates III** (r. 70–58 B.C.): Arsacid king of Parthia, exploited the wars between Rome and Mithridates VI so that he occupied and consolidated Parthian rule over Mesopotamia.

**Phrataphernes** (d. 316 B.C.): Persian noble and satrap of Parthyae and Hyrcania under Darius III 336–330 B.C.), fought at the Battle of Gaugamela. After the death of Darius III, Phrataphernes submitted to Alexander the Great, and was confirmed in his satrapy (330–321 B.C.). He participated in the Bactria, Sogdian, and Indian campaigns. In 330 B.C., he, along with Erigyius and Caranus, defeated the rebel satrap Satibarzanes of Areia. In 328–327 B.C., he punished the rebel Autophrades, satrap of the Mardians and Tapurians.

**Pindar** (522–443 B.C.): A Boeotian lyric poet. His victory odes to victors in the Olympic or Nemean games are masterpieces of verse and imagery. The odes of Pindar reflect the Greek aristocratic society. Out of respect for the poet, Alexander the Great spared the home of Pindar when Thebes was sacked in 335 B.C.

**Pixodarus** (340–334 B.C.): Hecatomnid dynast of Caria and satrap, was the third son of Hecatomnus. Pixodarus expelled Queen Ada from Halicarnassus and ruled as satrap. In 337 B.C., he sought a matrimonial alliance with Philip II, offered his daughter to Philip Arrhidaeus. On his own initiative, Alexander, resentful of what he perceived to be a slight by his father, offered himself in marriage. The irate Philip banished Alexander's friends from court and cancelled the alliance.

**Plutarch of Chaeronea** (c. 46–120 A.D.): Philosopher and biographer, was a native of Chaeronea, in Boeotia. Plutarch was a prodigious scholar, writing the parallel biographies of noble Greeks and Romans, which are invaluable sources for the leading figures of the 4th century B.C. as well as preserving a wealth of information on the Hellenistic world. He also wrote important Middle Platonic philosophical works.

**Pnytagoras** (c. r. 351–332 B.C.): King of Salamis, Cyprus submitted to Alexander the Great, and brought his fleet into action against Tyre in 332 B.C.

**Polyaenus**: Macedonian rhetorician who wrote in Greek *Stratagems* (in eight books) which was dedicated to the Roman emperors Marcus Aurelius (161–180) and Lucius Verus (161–169). The work contains many anecdotes about commanders in Antiquity.

**Polybius** (c. 203–120 B.C.): Historian and statesman of the Achaean League, was a native of Megalopolis in the Peloponnesus. In 168 B.C, he was deported to Rome because he had supported King Perseus of Macedon. As an honored prisoner, Polybius attached himself the circle of Publius Cornelius Scipio Aemilianus, and wrote a insightful history explaining the rise of Roman power. But he is a major source for Hellenic history and provided an invaluable summary of Callisthenes's account of the Battle of Issus in 333 B.C.

**Polyidus of Thessaly**: Military engineer of Philip II, devised covered battering rams (*poliorceticus krios*) and the great movable tower or Helepolis. His battering rams were first used at the siege of Byzantium in 340 B.C.

**Polyperchon** (c. 394–303 B.C.): Son of Simmias was a Macedonian noble. He was a tough veteran of Philip II, who commanded a regiment (*taxis*) of Alexander's phalanx. He was popular with the men. In 319 B.C. Antipater named Polyperchon as his successor, but Polyperchon lacked the political tack to run Greece and the prestige to hold together the empire. Cassander drove Polyperchon out of Macedon in 319–317 B.C. so that Polyperchon was reduced to several strongholds in the Peloponnesus. In 309 B.C., he allied with Antigonus and championed Heracles, illegitimate son of Alexander and Barsine. But Polyperchon struck a deal with Cassander (after deserting the Antigonid cause) and agreed to rule as Cassander's *strategos* over the Peloponnesus. Barsine and Heracles were surrendered to Cassander and executed.

**Pompeius Trogus**: Gnaeus Pompeius Trogus, was a Latin writer and native of Gallia Narbonensis of the first century B.C. He wrote a Macedonian history in 42 books, *Historiae Philippicae*. He made use of the works of Theopompus, Ephorus, and Polybius. His work has survived in an epitome by Justin. *See* **Justin**.

**Porus** (d. 317 B.C.): The Pauravas rajah, ruled a kingdom between the Hydaspes (Jhelum) and Acesines (Chenab) rivers in the Punjab. In June 326 B.C., he was defeated and captured by Alexander at the Battle of the Hydaspes. Alexander restored Porus to his kingdom, and Porus provided elephants and 5,000 men for Alexander's campaign to the Hyphasis (Beas). Porus ruled as a Macedonian vassal until 317 B.C., when he was assassinated on orders of the Seleucid general Eudemus or the Mauryan emperor Chandragupta.

**Ptolemy I** (b. c. 367; r. 305–283 B.C.): Son of Lagus and Arsinoe I, was a boyhood friend and bodyguard of Alexander. He served brilliantly in Sogdiana in 328–327 B.C. and in India. In 323 B.C., he shrewdly took Egypt as his satrapy, and so he aimed for partition. He opposed Perdiccas (323–321 B.C.) and then Antigonus (315–301 B.C.) as agents of unity. After Ipsus in 301 B.C., Ptolemy went on to build a great state including Egypt, Coele-Syria, Cyrene, Cyprus, the Nesiotic League, and Greek cities of southern Asia Minor. An accomplished author, he wrote a history of Alexander the Great which was the main source for Arrian. Ptolemy founded the cult of Serapis and patronized Greek culture. An efficient administrator, but average general, he studiously avoided battle whenever possible. He alone survived to die at an advanced age in his bed and was deified.

**Ptolemy II Philadelphus** (b. 308 B.C.; r. 283–246 B.C.): Son of Ptolemy I and Berenice, was elevated as joint king with his father in 285 B.C. He created the efficient Ptolemaic administration and tax system of Egypt. Despite his physical weakness, he conducted a successful foreign policy in Greece, Syria, and the wider Hellenic world. In c. 275 B.C., he married his sister Arsinoe II, whose influence over Ptolemy II is exaggerated. Ptolemy built the famous lighthouse of Alexandria (Pharos), the museum, and the library.

**Ptolemy III Euergetes** (b. c. 285 B.C.; r. 246–221 B.C.): Son of Ptolemy I and Arsinoe I, was the greatest warrior of the dynasty, winning the Third Syrian War (246–241 B.C.) and so extending Ptolemaic naval domination in the eastern Mediterranean. In 244 B.C., he married Berenice II (267–221 B.C.), daughter of Magas of Cyrene and so acquired Cyrene.

**Ptolemy IV Philopator** (b. c. 240 B.C.; r. 221–205 B.C.): Son of Ptolemy III and Berenice II, proved a lazy, depraved king. In 217 B.C., his minister Sosibius fielded an Egyptian phalanx of 20,000 men and so defeated the Seleucid King Antiochus III at Raphia. The victory proved a pyrrhic one because the Egyptians in the Thebaid rose in rebellion, and Ptolemaic power declined rapidly.

**Ptolemy V Epiphanes** (b. c. 210 B.C.; r. 205–181 B.C.): Son of Ptolemy IV and Arsinoe III, succeeded at age five. At the Battle of Panium in 200 B.C., Antiochus III defeated the Ptolemaic army and occupied Ptolemaic Levantine and Anatolian possessions. The king is best remembered for the edict preserved on the Rosetta Stone in 196 B.C.

**Ptolemy Ceraunus** (d. 279 B.C.; r. 281–279 B.C.): "The Thunderbolt" and king of Macedon, was the son of Ptolemy I and Eurydice. He left Alexandria for the court of Lysimachus in c. 285 B.C. and joined the faction of Agathocles and his wife Lysandra. In 283/2 B.C., he fled to Seleucus and helped convince him to invade Asia Minor. In 281 B.C. he murdered Seleucus, declared himself king of Macedon and married his half-sister, Arsinoe II (whom he then tried to murder). He fell fighting the Gauls in the winter of 279 B.C.

**Pyrrhus** (319–272 B.C.): Known as "the Red King." He was the son of King Aeacidas of Epirus (331–317 B.C.) and ruled as a minor under regents (307–302 B.C.) until he was expelled by Cassander. Initially linked to Demetrius by an alliance (for his sister Deidamia married Demetrius I), he was sent to Egypt as a hostage by Demetrius in c. 299 B.C. With Ptolemaic support, Pyrrhus returned to Epirus in 296 B.C. and spent the next twenty-years trying to regain his lost heritage of Macedon, contesting Demetrius Poliorcetes, Lysimachus, and Antigonus II Gonatas. In 280–275 B.C., Pyrrhus intervened to aid Taras (Tarentum) in southern Italy against the Romans. His costly victories over the Romans gave rise to the phrase "pyrrhic victory." Upon his return to Greece, he warred against Antigonus II, and he met his death street fighting in Argos in 272 B.C.

**Pytheas of Massilia**: Greek navigator, writer, and explorer of Northern Europe in c. 315–310 B.C., visited Gaul, Britian, and Thule or the northern Norwegian coast of Halogaland and the Lofoten islands. He gives the first accurate information on Scandinavia. He also calculated the attitude of the sun, latitudes, and the angle of the poles, and he noted the action of the moon on causing the tides.

**Python of Byzantium**: Greek diplomat and student of Isocrates, took service at the court of Pella in the 350s B.C. Python represented Philip at both the Peace of Philocrates and in the negotiations over the Epanorthosis in 343 B.C.

**Roxane** (c. 343–310 B.C.): Daughter of the Bactrian lord Oxyartes, married Alexander the Great in 327 B.C. and bore Alexander IV in 323 B.C. She was a pawn in the hands of Perdiccas, Antipater, Polyperchon, and finally Cassander. Cassander ordered her death in 310 B.C.

**Sambus**: Sanskrit Sambhu, king of the lower Indus, ruled from Sindimana (modern Sehwan). He joined in the rebellion of Musicanus and the Brahmins in 325 B.C. He escaped from Harmatelia, and his fate is unknown.

**Satibarzanes** (d. 330 B.C.): A Persian noble and satrap of Areia under Darius III (336–330 B.C.). In 330 B.C., he slew Darius III at Hectamopylus, but he submitted to Alexander the Great and was confirmed in his satrapy. Satibarzanes, receiving 2,000 cavalry from Bessus, rebelled when Alexander had departed for Drangiana. Erigyius and Caranus, along with Artabazus, were detached to crush the revolt. Erigyius slew Satibarzanes in single combat.

**Scylax of Caryanda**: A Carian skipper commissioned by King Darius I to navigate the Indus River in 515–513 B.C. Scylax sailed from Caspatyrus in Gandhara down the Indus into the Erythaean Sea (Indian Ocean) and then along the southern shores of Arabia into the Red Sea and thence to Suez. His voyage proved the Indus did not flow into the Nile. A *periplus* composed in the 3rd century B.C. was attributed to Scylax and used by Strabo.

**Seleucus I Nicantor** (b. 358 B.C.; r. 305–281 B.C.): Had an undistinguished career under Alexander the Great and, in 323 B.C., he received only command of the cavalry. He aided Peithon in the murder of Perdiccas and was thus rewarded with the satrapy of Babylon. He refused to submit to Antigonus in 315 B.C. and fled to Ptolemy. After the Battle of Gaza, Seleucus, with a flying column, audaciously retook Babylon and consolidated his hold over Iran despite efforts by Antigonus to destroy him in 311–308 B.C. At Ipsus he held the center and defeated Antigonus. In 301 B.C., he built his new capital at Antioch, in Syria, and shifted the locus of his empire to the west. After the Battle of Corupedium (281 B.C.), Seleucus occupied Asia Minor, but he was murdered by Ptolemy Ceraunus as soon as he landed in Europe.

**Seusippus** (c. 407–339 B.C.): An Athenian philosopher and nephew of Plato and scholarch of the Academy (347–339 B.C.). He rejected the theory of forms proposed by Plato and was known for his works on ethics and metaphysics.

**Seuthes III** (c. 330–300 B.C.): Tributary king of the Odrysians in Thrace who rebelled against Alexander the Great in 325 B.C. Antipater crushed the revolt, but Seuthes later defied Lysimachus, satrap of Thrace, and so allied with Antigonus. In 320 B.C., Seuthes relocated its capital to a new city Seuthopolis (modern Kazanluk).

**Simonides of Ceos** (556–468 B.C.): Lyric poet, was patronized by Hipparchus, tyrant of Athens (526–514 B.C.), the Aleuadae of Larissa in Thessaly, and after 490 B.C. by Hiero I, tyrant of Syracuse. His odes praise athletic victors and the gods. In 477 B.C., he celebrated the fallen at the Battle of Plataea in an ode recently recovered and published.

**Sisygambis** (d. 323 B.C.): Daughter of King Artaxerxes II, married Arsames of Ostanes, and their son was Darius III. She, along with Statira, the wife of Darius III, and her grandchildren were captured by Alexander the Great after Issus. She never forgave Darius III for his desertion and so refused to be rescued when Persians plundered Alexander's camp at Gaugamela. She starved herself to death in grief over the death of Alexander.

**Sphodrias**: Spartan officer and harmost at Thespiae, failed to seize the Piraeus, port of Athens, by a night attack in 379 B.C. The outraged Athenian assembly supported Phoebidas and the democrats of Thebes to overthrow Spartan rule in Boeotia. Sphodrias was acquitted of misconduct by the intervention of King Agesilaus II.

**Spitamenes** (c. 370–328 B.C.): A Sogdian lord (c. 370–328 B.C.) who supported Bessus in 330–329 B.C. But he betrayed Bessus to Alexander the Great. Spitamenes headed the rebellion that erupted in the Upper Satrapies when Alexander founded Alexandria Eschate on the Jaxartes River. In 329 B.C., Sptiamenes inflicted the only serious defeat suffered by Alexander's army against a detachment of the Polytimetus River. In 328 B.C., Coenus defeated Spitamenes at Gabae so that Spitamenes was betrayed and murdered by his followers. His daughter Apame married Seleucus Nicanor in 324 B.C.

**Spithridates** (d. 334 B.C.): Or Spithrobates, was a Persian satrap of Lydia. In the cavalry battle at the Grancius, he raised his sword to slay Alexander the Great, but Cleitus the Black intervened, and severed Spithridates's right arm. The satrap fell mortally wounded.

**Stasansor of Soli** (d. 316 B.C.): A Greek mercenary officer who joined Alexander's army in 333 B.C. In 327 B.C., he and the Persian noble Phratapherness commanded the detachment that crushed the revolt of Arsamens, satrap of Areia, in 329 B.C. Stasanor was appointed first satrap of Areia and then transferred to Drangiana furnished supplies and camels for the return march in 324 B.C. In 321–316 B.C., he was satrap of Sogdiana.

**Statira** (c. 340–322 B.C.): Also known as Barsine, daughter of King Darius III and the elder Queen Statira, was captured by Alexander the Great after the Battle of Issus in 333 B.C. She and her Drypetis were educated as Macedonians at Susa in 330–324 B.C. In 324, Statira (along with a younger sister Parysatis) married Alexander and her sister Drypetis married

Hephaestion. She was murdered on orders of Perdiccas, perhaps because she was with child and perceived as a threat to Roxane and Alexander IV.

**Strabo of Amasia** (c. 64 B.C.–24 A.D.): Geographer and philosopher, traveled widely in the Roman world. He wrote a history (now lost) and Geographica (in 17 books) that is an invaluable source that quotes many otherwise lost works.

**Stratonice** (c. 317–250 B.C.): Seleucid Queen, was the daughter of Demetrius Poliorcetes and Phila. She married Seleucus I in c. 300 B.C. In 294 B.C., Seleucus divorced Strationice when he learned that his son Antiochus I was in love with his stepmother. Antiochus I married Stratonice, and their son Antiochus II succeeded. Antiochus I founded the city Stratonicea in Caria in honor of his wife.

**Taxiles**: Was the ruler of Taxila (Sanskrit Takshashila) in Gandhara) from at least c. 330 B.C. His personal name was Omphis (Sanskrit Ambhi). Taxiles invited Alexander the Great into India and provided elephants, soldiers, and supplies to the Macedonian army. He had died by 317 B.C. because the Thracian commander Eudamus ruled Taxila.

**Teos** (r. 360–362 B.C.): Or Tachos, Pharaoh of Egypt, was the elder son and successor of Nectanebo I. He was overthrew by his brother Nectanebo II with a mercenary army commanded by Agesilaus II. Teos fled to King Artaxerxes II of Persia.

**Thais**: Athenian courtesan (*hetaira*) and mistress of Ptolemy, convinced Alexander and his friends, drunk from symposium, to burn the palace of Persepolis in 330 B.C.

**Theophrastus** (371–297 B.C.): Peripatetic philosopher and a native of Eresus on the island Lesbos, succeeded to the Lyceum of Aristotle. He wrote works on logic, botany, physics, and ethics. His students included Demetrius of Phaleron and the comic poet Menander. Theophtrastus wrote a eulogy to his friend Callisthenes, the historian, and so ensured the condemnation of Alexander as a tyrant by later philosophical writers.

**Theopompus** (b. c. 378 B.C.): Historian and native of Chios, composed a *Hellenica*, or history of Greece, from 411 to 394 B.C. Some scholars identify the fragmentary *Hellenica Oxyrrhynica* as portions of this lost work. Theopompus also wrote a now lost *Philippica*, an account of the reign of King Philip II of Macedon (359–336 B.C.). He was a student of Isocrates, and so knew the leading political and literary figures at Athens. Through Alexander's influence, Theopompus returned to settle at Chios in 333 B.C. His work was used by Pompeius Trogus, and so indirectly by Justin. Plutarch and the rhetorician Athenaeus of Naucratis also cite the *Philippica*.

**Thessalonice** (351–295 B.C.): Daughter of Philip II and the Thessalian aristocrat Nicesipolis, she married Cassander in 316 B.C. and bore him three sons: Philip IV, Antipater II, and Alexander V. After the deaths of Cassander and Philip IV in 297–296 B.C., she ruled as regent of Macedon, but she foolishly favored her youngest son, Alexander V, thereby precipitating a civil war that opened Macedon to conquest by Demetrius Poliorcetes. She was murdered by her second son Antipater II.

**Thibron** (d. 391 B.C.): Spartan commander. In 399 B.C., he commanded the Peloponnesian army sent to defend the Ionian cities against Persia. He enlisted 6,000 veterans of the Ten Thousand. His indifferent command led to his recall in 398 B.C. In 391 B.C., Thibron was killed in a punitive expedition against Struthas, satrap of Sardis.

**Timotheus** (c. 410–354 B.C.): Son of Conon, proved an able commander and loyal Athenians, but was aloof and even arrogant in his manner. He was political ally to his mentor Isocrates. Between 378 and 356 B.C., he was elected general (*strategos*). He commanded expeditions to Corcyra in 373 B.C. and to the Chalcidice and Hellespont in 365-363. Twice, in 365 and in 364–363, he unsuccessfully besieged Amphipolis. He clashed with Chares over strategy in the Social War (357–355 B.C.). Timotheus, Iphicrates, and Menestheus failed to support Chares at the Battle of Embata in 356 B.C. Chares, blaming the defeat on his colleagues, brought suit against all three generals. Only Timotheus was convicted and fined 100 talents, and so went into voluntary exile.

**Tissaphernes** (d. 395 B.C.): Persian satrap of Sardes from 413 B.C., sought to exploit the war between Sparta and Athens. In 412 B.C., he secured under the Treaty of Miletus the Ionian cities in return for financial assistance to the Spartan fleet. In 407 B.C., Cyrus the Younger replaced Tissaphernes, who relocated to Nysa in the Maeander valley. His embarrassing defeats at the hands of Agesilaus II in 396–395 B.C. led to the satrap's assassination.

**Trajan** (r. 98–117 A.D.): Roman emperor was adopted by Nerva (96–98 A.D.), and hailed the best of emperors (*optimus princeps*). By his conquests of Dacia, Armenia, and Mesopotamia, Trajan expanded the Roman Empire to its greatest extent. Trajan inspired Arrian to write his Anabasis on Alexander the Great. And in his Parthian War (114–117 A.D.), Trajan compared his exploits to those of Alexander.

**Vima Kadphises** (r. 78–126 A.D.): Kushan emperor, extended his sway over northwestern India. He promoted the trade along the Silk Road and minted the first gold coins featuring Hindu and Buddhist types. His reign witnessed the brilliant Greco-Buddhist sculptures of Gandhara.

**Xenophon** (427–355 B.C.): Athenian mercenary general, historian, and philosopher, was a student of Socrates and friend of King Agesilaus II of Sparta. Xenophon, who served with Cyrus the Younger, recorded the march of the Ten Thousand (401–399 B.C.) in his *Anabasis*. Xenophon wrote a narrative Greek history, *Hellenica*, covering 411–362 B.C. that lacks the precision and insight of Thucydides's work. His *Cyropaedia* (Education of Cyrus) and *Agesilaus* are also important historical sources. He also penned technical military works, philosophical dialogues, and apology for Socrates at his trial in 399 B.C. The *Constitution of the Spartans* and *Constitution of the Athenians*, attributed to Xenophon, were penned by authors using his name as pseudonym.

**Xerxes** (r. 486–465 B.C.): Achaemenid king of Persia, invaded Greece in 480 B.C. and suffered a decisive defeat at the Battle of Salamis that compromised the integrity of his empire. The Athenian tragedian Aeschylus produced the *Persians* (472 B.C.) dramatizing the defeat of Xerxes as a tragic hero.

**Zeno of Caunus**: Son of Agregophon, was secretary to the financial minister in the reigns of Ptolemy II (283–246 B.C.) and Ptolemy III (246–222 B.C.). Zeno left an archive of over 2,000 letters and documents that is the major source for Ptolemaic administration.

**Zeno of Citium** (334–262 B.C.): Founder of Stoic philosophy, preached a doctrine of *apatheia* or detachment from emotion to achieve a harmonious life. Zeno based his views on a rational cosmology directed by the Logos, identified with Zeus or Jupiter, whose "spark" was within and animated all beings.

# Bibliography

**Sources in Translation**

Aeschines. *The Speeches of Aeschines*. Translated by C. D. Adams. Loeb Classical Library. Cambridge, MA: William Heinmann Ltd., 1919. Definitive translation of the public orations of Demosthenes's principal opponent.

Arrian. *The Campaigns of Alexander*. Rev. ed. Translated by A. de Sélincourt. Harmondsworth, Middlesex, England: Penguin Classics, 1976. Recommended modern translation of the major narrative source on the campaigns of Alexander the Great.

————. *History of Alexander and Indica*. Translated by P. A. Brunt. Vol. 1. Loeb Classical Library. Cambridge, MA: William Heinmann Ltd., 1976. Revised translation with Greek text and excellent notes.

————. *History of Alexander and Indica*. Translated by P. A. Brunt. Vol. 2. Loeb Classical Library. Cambridge, MA: William Heinmann Ltd, 1983. Recommended translation for book VIII or the *Indica* of Arrian. Excellent commentary.

Austin, M. M. *The Hellenistic World from Alexander to the Roman Conquest: A Selection of Ancient Sources in Translation*. Cambridge, MA: Cambridge University Press, 1981. Superb collection of narrative and documentary sources, many of them not otherwise translated.

Burtt, Minor. *Attic Orators*. Vol. 2. *Lycurgus, Dinarchus, Demandes, Hyperides*. Loeb Classical Library. Cambridge, MA: William Heinmann Ltd., 1954. The standard translation with Greek texts of political orations in period 351–322 B.C.

Cornelius Nepos. *The Book on Great Foreign Generals*. Translated by J. C. Rolfe. Loeb Classical Library. Cambridge, MA: William Heinmann Ltd, 1929. Translation of Latin source with anecdotes on Alexander, Greek commanders, and Persian kings.

Curtius Rufus, Quintius. *The History of Alexander the Great*. Translated by J. C. Yadley. Harmondsworth, Middlesex, England: Penguin Books, 1984. Recommended translation with excellent notes and commentary on colorful Latin account of Alexander the Great.

———. *History of Alexander*. 2 vols. Translated by J. C. Rolfe. Loeb Classical Library. Cambridge, MA: William Heinmann Ltd., 1946. Translation with Latin text and sound notes.

Demosthenes. *Orations*. Vols. 1–3. Translated by J. H. Vince. Loeb Classical Library. Cambridge, MA: William Heinmann Ltd., 1930, 1926, and 1939. Definitive translation and Greek text of the political speeches of the Athenian politician.

Diodorus Siculus. *Library of History*. Vol. 6, bks. XIV–XV.19. Translated by C. H. Oldfather. Loeb Classical Library. Cambridge, MA: William Heinmann Ltd., 1954. The translation of narrative of the early 4th century B.C.

———. *Library of History*. Vol. 7, bks. XV.20–XVI.65. Translated by C. L. Sherman. Loeb Classical Library. Cambridge, MA: William Heinmann Ltd.,1952. The translation of the narrative of the later 4th century B.C. and early reign of Philip II.

———. *Library of History*. Vol. 8, bks. XVI.66–XVII. Translated by C. Bradford Wells. Loeb Classical Library. Cambridge, MA: William Heinmann, Ltd.,1963. The translation of narrative of the reigns of Philip II and Alexander the Great.

———. *Library of History*. Vol. 9, bks. XVIII–XIX.65. Translated by R. M. Geer. Loeb Classical Library. Cambridge, MA: William Heinmann, Ltd.,1947. Translation of the main account of the Diadochoi.

Harding, Philip, trans. and ed. *From the End of the Peloponnesian War to the Battle of Ipsus*. Cambridge: Cambridge University Press, 1985. Recommended translation of narrative and documentary sources of the 4th century B.C., including many inscriptions.

Heckel, Waldemar and J. C. Yardley. *Historical Sources in Translation: Alexander the Great*. Oxford: Basil Blackwell, 2004. Excellent translation of literary sources on Alexander, including many never before translated and organized by themes.

Isocrates. *Orations*, vols. 1–2. Translated by George Norlin. Vol. 3 translated by La Rue Van Hook. Loeb Classical Library. Cambridge, MA: William Heinmann Ltd., 1929, 1945, and 1961. Definitive translation of the public orations with Greek text.

Justin. *Epitome of the Philippic History of Pompeius Trogus*. Translated by J. X. Yardley. Philadelphia: American Philological Association, 1994. The first translation of this Latin work on the reigns of Philip II and Alexander the Great.

Plutarch. *The Age of Alexander*. Translated by I. Scott-Kilvert. Harmondsworth, Middlesex, England: Penguin Classics, 1973. Recommended modern translation of the lives relevant to Alexander the Great with the only life of Eumenes included.

———. Lives, vol. 8. *Sertorius and Eumenes; Phocion and Cato the Younger*. Translated by B. Perrin. Loeb Classical Library Series. Cambridge, MA: William Heinmann Ltd., 1919. Best translation of the life of Eumenes of Cardia.

———. Lives, vol. 7. *Demosthenes and Cicero; Alexander and Caesar*. Translated by B. Perrin. Loeb Classical Library Series. Cambridge, MA: William Heinmann Ltd., 1919. Alternate translation to the two most important lives in the Penguin translation.

———. *On Sparta*. Translated by R. J. A. Talbert. Harmondsworth, Middlesex, England: Penguin Classics, 2005. Excellent collection of sources on Sparta. Modern translation

McKechine, P. R. and S. J. Kern, trans. *Hellenica Oxyrhynchia*. Warminster: Phillips and Aries, 1988. Translation of the history of uncertain authorship on the early 4th century B.C. recovered on a papyrus.

Moore, J. M., trans. *Aristotle and Xenophon on Democracy and Oligarchy*. Berkeley: University of California Press, 1975. Recommended translation of the literary sources on the constitutions of Athens, Sparta, and Thebes with excellent commentary and notes.

Saunders, A. N. W., trans. *Greek Political Oratory*. Harmondsworth, Middlesex, England: Penguin Classics, 1978. Excellent modern translation of the major political speeches of Demosthenes and Isocrates.

Xenophon. *A History of My Times*. Translated by Rex Warner. Harmondsworth, Middlesex, England: Penguin Classics, 1979. The recommended modern translation of the *Hellenica* covering events from 410 to 362 B.C.

———. *The Persian Expedition*. Translated by Rex Warner. Harmondsworth, Middlesex, England: Penguin Classics, 1972. Recommended modern translation on The March of the Ten Thousand in 401–399B.C.

**Commentaries and Studies on Sources**
Atkinson, J. E. *A Commentary on Curtius Rufus' Historiae Alexandri*. Bks. 3 and 4. Amsterdam: J. C. Gibben, 1980. Scholarly analysis and commentary on Latin text.

———. *A Commentary on Curtius Rufus' Historiae Alexandri*. Bks. 5–7.2. Amsterdam: Hakkert, 1994. Scholarly analysis and commentary on Latin text.

Baynham, E. J. *Alexander the Great: The Unique History of Quintus Curtius Rufus*. Ann Arbor: University of Michigan Press, 1995. Study on sources and limitations of Curtius Rufus.

Bosworth, A, B. *A Historical Commentary on Arrian's History of Alexander*. Oxford: Oxford University Press, 1980. Definitive scholarly commentary on text of Arrian.

Hamilton, J. R. *Plutarch, Alexander: A Commentary*. Oxford: Clarendon Press, 1969. Definitive scholarly commentary on text.

Hammond, N. G. L. *Three Historians of Alexander the Great: The So-called Vulgate Authors, Diodorus, Justin, and Curtius.* Cambridge: Cambridge University Press, 1983. Analysis of sources and transmission of information about Alexander the Great.

Hornblower, J. *Hieronymus of Cardia.* Oxford: Oxford University Press, 1981. Discussion of the lost work of an author who was a source of Diodorus Siculus.

Pearson, Lionel. *The Lost Histories of Alexander the Great.* New York: The American Philological Association, 1960. Definitive scholarly study on the lost contemporary accounts of Alexander the Great.

Stadter, Philip A. *Arrian of Nicomedia.* Chapel Hill: University of North Carolina Press, 1980. Discussion of merits of Arrian as a source as well as his public life.

**Numismatics**
Bellinger, A. R. *Essays on the Coinage of Alexander the Great.* New York: American Numismatic Society; Numismatic Studies no. 11, 1963. Scholarly analysis of the coinage and finances of Alexander the Great.

Holt, Frank L. *Alexander the Great and the Mystery of the Elephant Medallions.* Berkeley: University of California Press, 2003. Study of the silver medallions minted to celebrate the Battle of the Hydaspes in 326 B.C. with excellent plates.

Kraay, Colin M. *Archaic and Classical Greek Coins.* Berkeley: University of California Press, 1976. Recommended introduction to Greek coinages.

Martin, Thomas R. *Sovereignty and Coinage in Ancient Greece.* Princeton: Princeton University Press, 1985. Thoughtful study on the use of coins as money.

Mørkholm, Otto. *Early Hellenistic Coinage from the Accession of Alexander the Great to the Peace of Apamea (336–186 B.C.)*. Cambridge: Cambridge University Press, 1991. Posthumous publication of the coinages of Alexander and the Hellenistic monarchies along with fine maps and plates.

Price, Martin Jessop. *The Coinage in the Name of Alexander the Great and Philip Arrhidaeus*. 2 vols. London: The British Museum. 1991. Definitive corpus of the coinage of Alexander the Great.

————. *The Coinage in the Name of Alexander the Great and Philip Arrhidaeus*. 2 vols. London: The British Museum. 1991. Definitive corpus of the coinage of Alexander the Great.

### References
*The Cambridge Ancient History*. Vol. 6. Edited by J. B. Bury, S. A. Cook, and Adcock. Cambridge: Cambridge University Press, 1927. Still best political narrative account of 404–301 B.C.

*The Cambridge Ancient History*. Vol. 6, 2nd ed. rev. Edited by D. M. Lewis, J. Boardman, S. Hornblower, and M. Ostwald. Cambridge: Cambridge University Press, 1994. Excellent chapters on social, economic, and intellectual life, as well as on the regions of the Persian Empire.

*The Cambridge Ancient History*. Vol. 7, pt 1, 2nd ed. rev. Edited by F. W. Walbank and A. E. Astin. Cambridge: Cambridge University Press, 1984; best detailed introduction to the early Hellenistic world.

*The Cambridge Economic History of the Greco-Roman World*. Edited by W. Scheidel, I. Morris, and R. Saller. Cambridge: Cambridge University Press, 2007. Series of important articles on continuity and limitations of ancient economic life.

Haywood, John. *Historical Atlas of the Classical World 500 B.C.–A.D. 600*. New York: Barnes and Noble Books, 1998. Recommended atlas.

Morkot, Robert. *The Penguin Historical Atlas of Ancient Greece*. New York: Penguin Books, 1996. Atlas with excellent historical notes and illustrations.

**Bibliography**

Talbert, Richard J. A. *Barrington Atlas of the Greek and Roman World*. 2 vols. Princeton: Princeton University Press, 2000. The definitive atlas of all ancient sites; indispensable for scholarly work.

**Persian Empire**
Allen, Lindsay. *The Persian Empire*. Chicago: Chicago University Press, 2005. Recommended new study on the Persian Empire.

Briant, Pierre. *From Cyrus to Alexander: A History of the Persian Empire*. Translated by Peter T. Daniels. Winona Lake, Indiana: Eisenbaums, 2002. Monumental study by the distinguished French scholar recognized as the expert on Achaemenid Persia.

*The Cambridge History of Iran*, vol. 2. *The Median and Achaemenian Periods*. Edited by I Gershevitch. Cambridge, Cambridge University Press, 1985. Superb reference work with a wealth of bibliography on sources.

Cameron, G.G. *Persepolis Treasury Tablets*. Chicago: University of Chicago Press, 1948. The sources fundamental for Achaemenid administration.

Cook, J. M. *The Persian Empire*. New York: Schocken Books, 1983. Recommended introduction to Persia.

Dandamaev, M.A. and B.G. Lukonin. *The Culture and Social Institutions of Ancient Iran*. Translated by P. L. Kohl. Cambridge: Cambridge University Press, 1989. Superb essays representing the best of Russian scholarship.

Olmstead, A.T. *History of the Persian Empire*. Chicago: University of Chicago Press, 1948. Dated but still useful narrative of Persia with use of Greek literary sources.

Stronach, David. *Pasargadae*. Oxford: Oxford University Press, 1978. The scholarly study on the ritual capital published by the excavator.

Weiskopf, Michael. *The so-called "Great Satraps' Revolt," 366–360 B.C.* Historia Einzelschriften 63. Stuttgart: Franz Steiner Verlag, 1989. Learned analysis of the revolt and Persian administration in the 4th century B.C.

**Ancient India**

Chakravarti, P. C., *The Art of War in Ancient India*. New York: Macmillan, 1978. Recommended introduction.

Marshall, J. *Taxilia*. Cambridge: Cambridge University Press, 1951. Scholarly study of the site published by the excavator. The main source for knowledge of cities in the Indus valley in the time of Alexander the Great.

Mookerji, R. M. *Chandragupta Maurya and His Times*, 3rd ed. Delhi: Motilal Banarsidas, 1960. Definitive study of first Mauryan emperor.

Raychaudhuri, H. C. *Political History of Ancient India*. Calcutta: University of Calcutta Press, 1953. Cosmo Publications Reprint, 2006. Dated but useful study of the Indian kingdoms.

Smith, Vincent A. *The Early History of India from 600 B.C. to the Muhammadan Conquest Including the Invasion of Alexander the Great*. Oxford: Oxford University Press, 1924. Excellent survey of historical developments in India.

Spear, P. and M. Wheeler, *The Oxford History of India*, 4th ed. Oxford: Oxford University Press, 1981. Recommended reference work on early India.

**Greece, 404–322 B.C.**

Austin, M. M. *Greece and Egypt in the Archaic Age*. Cambridge: Cambridge Philological Society, 1970. Scholarly monograph with far-ranging implications for the relations between the Greeks and Egypt.

Boardman, John. *The Greeks Overseas: Early Greek Colonies and Trade*. 4th ed. London: Thames and Hudson, 1999. Superb introduction to the breadth of Greek civilization and relationships with the peoples of the Mediterranean and the Near East.

Buchanan, J. J. *Theorika: A Study of Monetary Distributions to the Athenian Citizenry during the Fifth and Fourth Centuries B.C.* Locust Valley, N.Y.: Augustina Press, 1962. Definitive scholarly study on Athenian finances in the 4th century B.C.

Bibliography

Buckler, John. *The Theban Hegemony, 371–362 B.C.* Cambridge, MA: Harvard University Press, 1980. Well-written study on Thebes and Boeotian League.

Buckler, John and Hans Beck. *Central Greece and the Politics of Power in the Fourth Century B.C.* Cambridge: Cambridge University Press, 2008. A series of important articles on the Theban hegemony, Athenian naval confederacy, and Philip II.

Cargill, Jack. *The Second Athenian League: Empire or Free Alliance.* Berkeley: University of California Press, 1981. The well-written account on the league; excellent discussion of sources and technical problems.

Cartledge, Paul. *Agesilaos and the Crisis of Sparta.* Baltimore: Johns Hopkins University Press, 1987. Diffuse account of the Spartan hegemony, premised on the traditional view of Sparta as an oppressive state.

Davis, J. K. *Athenian Propertied Families, 600–300 B.C.* Oxford: Oxford University Press, 1971. Definitive reference work for all leading Athenians.

Forrest, W. G. G. *A History of Sparta, 950–192 B.C.* London: Hutchinson, 1968. Well-written but dated account of Sparta based on a Marxist view of Sparta as an oppressive state.

Hamilton, Charles D. *Agesilaus and the Failure of Spartan Hegemony.* Ithaca: Cornell University Press, 1991. Excellent biography on the king with a balanced account on Spartan policy. Economic and social analysis premised on an oppressive Sparta.

———. *Sparta's Bitter Victories: Politics and Diplomacy in the Corinthian War.* Ithaca: Cornell University Press, 1979. The definitive detailed study on a crucial war.

Hansen, Mogens. *The Athenian Democracy in the Age of Demosthenes: Structure, Principles, and Ideology.* Translated by J. A. Crook. Norman: University of Oklahoma Press, 1999. Articles on Athenian democracy by the leading constitutional and political historian.

————. *Eisangelia: The Sovereignty of the People's Court in Athens in the Fourth Century B.C. and the Impeachment of Generals and Politicians.* Odense: Odense University Press, 1975. Indispensable scholarly study on Athenian political trials.

Harris, Edward M. *Aeschines and Athenian Politics.* New York: Oxford University Press, 1995. The first serious work on Aeschines's political role.

Hirsch, S. W. *The Friendship of the Barbarian: Xenophon and the Persian Empire.* Hanover, NH: University Press of New England, 1985. Perceptive study on the relationship between Greeks and Persians in the 4th century B.C.

Hodkinson, Stephen. *Property and Wealth in Classical Sparta.* London: Duckworth, 2000. Groundbreaking study on Spartan society that has overturned traditional views on Sparta as an arrested, oppressive state and society.

Hornblower, S. *Mausolus.* Oxford: Oxford University Press, 1982. Scholarly study on the Carian dynasty and opponent of Athens.

Jaeger, W. *Demosthenes: The Origin and Growth of His Policy.* Berkeley: University of California Press, 1938. Dated study of Demosthenes as the heroic democratic foe to Philip II of Macedon.

Jones, A. H. M. *The Athenian Democracy.* Oxford: Basil Blackwell, 1957. A series of essays on specific topics rather than a true introduction.

Lane Fox, Robin, ed. *The Long March: Xenophon and the Ten Thousand.* New Haven: Yale University Press, 2004. Popular account of Xenophon and the march.

Larsen, J. A. O. *Greek Federal States.* Oxford: Clarendon Press, 1968. Dated scholarly study on the operation of federal leagues. Emphasis on constitutional procedures.

————. *Representative Government in Greek and Roman History*. Berkeley: University of California Press, 1955. Recommended survey of federalism in antiquity.

Lee, John W. *A Greek Army on the March: Soldiers and Survival in Xenophon's Anabasis*. Cambridge: Cambridge University Press, 2008. Study on the conditions of service and experience of mercenary service.

Lewis, D. N., *Sparta and Persia*. Leiden: E. J. Brill, 1977. Superb essays on Spartan-Persian relations by a distinguished epigraphist and historian.

Mosley, D. J. *Envoys and Diplomacy in Ancient Greece*. Historia Einzelschriften 22. Wiesbaden: Franz Steiner Verlag, 1973. Thoughtful scholarly monograph on the means and limitations of conducting diplomacy.

Mossé, Claude. *Athens in Decline, 404–86 B.C.* Boston: Routledge and Kegan Paul, 1973. Excellent introduction to Athens with emphasis on economic history.

Ober, Josiah. *Fortress Attica: Defense of the Athenian Land Frontier 404–322 B.C.* Mnemosyne Supplement 48. Leiden: E. J. Brill, 1985. Controversial thesis based on archaeological evidence of Athenian policy of defense in the 4th century B.C.

Pickard-Cambridge, Sir Arthur Wallace. *Demosthenes and the Last Days of Greek Freedom, 384–322 B.C.* New York: G. P. Putnam's Sons, 1914. Classic account of the heroic Demosthenes as conceived in the 19th century.

Roberts, Jennifer T. *Accountability in Athenian Government*. Madison: University of Wisconsin Press, 1982. Important study on political trials and factional politics in late classical Athens.

Ryder, T. T. B. *Koine Eirene: General Peace and Local Independence in Ancient Greece*. Oxford: Oxford University Press, 1965. Scholarly study on the treaties and diplomacy of 4th century B.C.

Sealey, Raphael. *Demosthenes and His Time: A Study in Defeat*. Oxford: Oxford University Press, 1993. Recommended new study on Demosthenes.

Sinclair, R. K. *Democracy and Participation in Athens*. Cambridge: Cambridge University Press, 1988. Best introduction on the Athenian democracy.

Strauss, Barry. *Athens after the Peloponnesian War: Class, Faction, and Policy, 403–386 B.C.* Ithaca: Cornell University Press, 1986. Important study on Athenian recovery in the early 4th century B.C.

Trittle, Lawrence, A. *Phocion the Good*. London: Croom Helm, 1988. Modern biography of the leading Athenian general and conservative.

Waterford, Robin. *Xenophon's Retreat*. Cambridge, MA: Belknap, 2006. Modern popular account on the Ten Thousand.

Westlake, H. D. *Thessaly in the Fourth Century B.C.* London: Methuen, 1938. Series of scholarly articles on this ill documented but important subject.

Worthington, Ian. *Demosthenes: Statesman and Orator*. New York: Routledge, 1995. Modern scholarly biography, strong on Demosthenes's role as an orator.

**Warfare in Greek World:**
Adcock, F. E. *The Greek and Macedonian Art of War*. Berkeley: University of California Press, 1987. Classic introduction and recommended.

Anderson, J. K. *Military Theory and Practice in the Age of Xenophon*. Berkeley: University of California Press, 1970. Crucial scholarly study on changes in Greek warfare.

*The Cambridge History of Greek and Roman Warfare*. 2 Vols. Edited by P. Sabin, H. van Wees, and M. Whitby. Cambridge: Cambridge University Press, 2007. Recommended reference work.

Griffith, G. *The Mercenaries of the Hellenistic World.* Cambridge: Cambridge University Press, 1947. Classic study on mercenary service.

Hanson, Victor D. *The Western Way of War: Infantry Combat in Classical Greece.* 2nd ed. Berkeley: University of California Press, 2009. Provocative study on experience of combat. Recommended as a must.

————, ed. *Hoplites: The Classical Greek Battle Experience.* New York: Routledge Press, 1993. Series of important scholarly articles.

Jordan, B. *The Athenian Navy in the Classical Period.* Berkeley: University of California Press, 1975. The classic account.

Lawrence, A. W. *Greek Aims in Fortification.* Oxford: Oxford University Press, 1979. Excellent study based on archaeology.

Marsden, Edward W. *Greek and Roman Artillery: Historical Development.* Oxford: Oxford University Press, 1999. The definitive scholarly study.

Morrison, J. S. and J. F. Coates. *Greek and Roman Oared Ships, 399-30 B.C.* Oxford: Oxbow Books, 1996. Recommended study on changes in naval warfare.

Parke, H. W. *Greek Mercenary Soldiers from Earliest Times to the Battle of Ipsus.* Oxford: Oxford University Press, 1933.

Pritchert, W. K. *The Greek States at War.* Volumes 1-5.. Berkeley: University of California Press, 1975-1991. Scholarly studies of warfare and society in widest context; series of thoughtful articles rather than a synthesis of the sources.

Trittle, Lawrence A. *From Melos to My Lai: War and Survival.* London: Routledge, 2000. Recommended on the experience of combat penned by leading scholar and veteran.

## Early Macedon

Adams, W. Lindsay and Eugene Borza, eds. *Philip II, Alexander the Great and the Macedonian Heritage.* Lanham, NY: University Press of America, 1982. Seminal collection of articles on Macedon.

Andronikos, Manlios. *Vergina: The Royal Tombs.* Athens: Ekdoite Athenon, 2004. Defintive study of the tombs and objects from Tomb II by the excavator.

Borza, Eugene N. *Before Alexander: Constructing Early Macedonia.* Publications of the Association of Ancient Historians. Claremont, CA: Regina Books, 1999. Introductory study of sources and scholarship.

————. *In the Shadow of Olympus: The Emergence of Macedon.* Rev. ed. Princeton: Princeton University Press, 1992. Brilliant and well-written account of Macedon. The seminal study by the leading historian of Macedon.

Carney, E. D. *Women and Monarchy in Macedonia.* Norman: Oklahoma University Press, 2000. Study of the social role of high-ranking women.

Errington, R. Malcolm. *A History of Macedonia.* Berkeley: University of California Press, 1990. Older narrative account; superceded by Borza's study.

Hammond, N. G. L. and G. T. Griffith. *A History of Macedonia.* Vol. 2: 550–336 B.C. Oxford: Oxford University Press, 1979. Excellent scholarly study with the most detailed account of the reign of Philip II.

Howe, T. and R. Reames, eds. *Macedonian Legacies: Studies in Ancient Macedonian History and Culture in Honor of Eugene N. Borza.* Edited by T. Howe and J. Reames. Claremont, CA: Regina Books, 2009. Important series of articles.

Yalouris, Nicholas, Katerina Rhomiopoulou, and Manlios Andronikos. *The Search for Alexander: An Exhibition.* Boston: New York Graphic Society and The Greek Ministry of Culture and Sciences, 1980. Lavishly illustrated catalogue of the objects found in excavation at Vergina and other sites.

## Philip II

Buckler, John. *Philip II and the Sacred War*. Leiden: E. J. Brill Academic Publishers. Mnemosyne Supplement no. 109, 1997. Definitive scholarly account.

Carney, Elizabeth. *Olympias, Mother of Alexander the Great*. New York: Routledge, 2006. Definitive modern study.

Cawkwell, George. *Philip of Macedon*. London: Faber and Faber Ltd., 1978. Sympathetic biography. Controversial use of the works of Demosthenes.

Ellis, J. K. *Philip II and Macedonian Imperialism*. London: Thames and Hudson, 1976. Scholarly study essential for use of sources and chronology.

Pearlman, S., ed. *Philip and Athens*. Cambridge: Heffer Press, 1973. Important collection of articles and essays.

Worthington, Ian. *Demosthenes: Statesman and Orator*. New York: Routledge, 1995. Newest account with judicious view on Philip II.

## Alexander the Great

Badian, E. "Alexander the Great and the Loneliness of Power." In *Studies in Greek and Roman History*. Cambridge, MA: Harvard University Press, 1964, pp. 192–205. Seminal article within the collection of essays by a leading ancient historian that defines the diabolical tyrant Alexander.

———"Alexander the Great and the Unity of Mankind." Historia 7 (1958), 425–455. Important article in learned journal published in Wiesbaden. This article expels the romantic notions of Alexander's aims.

———*The Deification of Alexander the Great: Protocol of the Twenty-First Colloquy 7 March 1976*. Claremont, CA: Center for Hermeneutical Studies in Hellenistic and Modern Culture, 1976. Important conference papers on precedents for the deification of Alexander the Great.

Baldry, H. C. *The Unity of Mankind in Greek Thought.* Cambridge: Cambridge University Press, 1965. Discussion of the sources, notably philosophical works, for an emergence of wider notion of unity of mankind in the Hellenistic Age.

Bieber, Margaret. *Alexander the Great in Greek and Roman Art.* Chicago: Argonaut, 1964. Classic study on depictions of Alexander by leading art historian.

Bosworth, A. B. *Alexander and the East: The Tragedy of Triumph.* Oxford: Clarendon Press, 1996. Serious scholarly study arguing for a tyrannical Alexander, but the thesis is over-argued and ultimately not convincing.

―――. *Conquest and Empire: The Reign of Alexander the Great.* Cambridge: Cambridge University Press, 1988. Superb narrative account with excellent studies on special topics.

Bosworth, A. B. and E. J. Baynham, eds. *Alexander the Great in Fact and Fiction.* Oxford: Oxford University Press, 2000. Delightful work that underscores the popularity of Alexander the Great.

Cary, Max. *The Medieval Alexander.* Cambridge: Cambridge University Press, 1956. The scholarly account of medieval romances and views on Alexander.

Cary, M. and E. H. Warmington. *The Ancient Explorers.* Rev. ed. Baltimore: Penguin Books, 1963. Excellent introduction of exploration in the ancient role with a sense of the impact of Alexander on expanding geographic knowledge.

Chroust, Anton-Hermann. *Aristotle.* 2 vols. London: Routledge and Kegan Paul, 1973. Recommended introduction to the philosopher's works.

Cohen, Ada. *The Alexander Mosaic: Stories of Victory and Defeat.* Cambridge: Cambridge University Press, 2000. Most recent, and recommended, study of this celebrated depiction of Alexander the Great.

Dahmen, Karsten. *The Legend of Alexander the Great on Greek and Roman Coins*. New York: Routledge, 2007. A useful introduction to later images of Alexander.

Dodge, Theodore Ayrault. *Alexander: A History of the Origin and Growth of the Art of War from Earliest Times to the Battle of Ipsus with a Detailed Account of the Campaigns of the Great Macedonian*. Boston, 1890; reprint New York: De Capo, 1996. Dated but still useful analysis on Alexander's role in warfare by soldier and military writer.

Eggermont, P. H. L. *Alexander's Campaigns in Sind and Baluchistan and the Siege of the Brahmin town of Harmatelia*. Leuven: Leuven University Press, 1971. Learned analysis of the sources and geography of campaigns in the lower Indus in 325 B.C.

Ehrenberg, Victor. *Alexander and the Greeks*. Translated by R. Fraenkel vonVelsen. Westport, CT: Hyperion Books, 1980. Scholarly account on the subject.

Engels, Donald. *Alexander the Great and the Logistics of the Macedonian Army*. Berkeley: University of California Press, 1978. Seminal study on logistics in the ancient world. Indispensable for the campaigns of Alexander.

Fuller, J. F. C. The *Generalship of Alexander the Great*. New York: Minerva Books, 1960. Analysis of Alexander's generalship by leading British general and military thinker. Recommended. Still the most plausible explanation of the cavalry action at the Battle of the Hydaspes in 326 B.C.

Green, Peter. *Alexander the Great*. New York: Praeger Publishers, 1970. Idiosyncratic but interesting account of Alexander the Great. The reconstruction of the Battles of Granicus and Issus are not plausible.

Griffith, G. T., ed. *Alexander the Great: The Main Problems*. Cambridge: Cambridge University Press, 1966. Useful study on the state of scholarly inquiry at the time.

Habicht, Christian. *Athens from Alexander to Antony*. Translated by D. L. Schneider. Cambridge, MA: Harvard University Press, 1997. Superb study of political, cultural, and economic life of Athens from 336 to 30 B.C. Recommended.

Hamilton, J. R. *Alexander the Great*. Pittsburgh: University of Pittsburgh Press, 1974. Recommended well-written introductory account.

Hammond, N. G. L. *The Genius of Alexander the Great*. Chapel Hill: University of North Carolina Press, 1998. Recommended summation of Alexander's military genius by a distinguished British scholar based on a lifetime of mastery of the sources and the archaeology of the Balkans.

Harl, Kenneth W. "Alexander's Cavalry Battle on the Granicus," in *Polis and Polemos: Essays on Politics, War, and History in Ancient Greece in Honor of Donald Kagan*. Edited by C. D. Hamilton and P. Krentz. Claremont: Regina Books, 1997, pp. 303–326. Most recent analysis of the battle based on the topography and sources.

Heckel, Waldemar. *The Conquests of Alexander the Great*. Cambridge: Cambridge University Press, 2008. Popular summary with useful tables. Maps are schematic and narrative is abbreviated and disappointing.

————. *The Last Days and Succession of Alexander the Great: A Prosopographical Study*. Historia Einzelschriften 56. Stuttgart: Franz Steiner Verlag, 1988. Seminal scholarly study on the final aims of Alexander.

————. The *Marshals of Alexander's Empire*. New York: Routledge, 1992. The definitive reference work on commanders of Alexander.

Heckel, Waldemar and L. A. Trittle, eds. *The Age of Alexander*. Claremont, CA: Regina Books, 2003. A useful collection of articles on Alexander.

Heisserer, A. J. *Alexander and the Greeks of Asia Minor*. Norman: Oklahoma University Press, 1980. The definitive scholarly study based on the inscriptions with texts, translation, and commentary.

Holt, Frank L. *Alexander the Great and Bactria: Formation of a Greek Frontier in Central Asia*. Mnemosyne Supplement. Leiden: E. J. Brill, 1988. Scholarly study based on archaeology, topography, and sources.

————. *Into the Land of Bones: Alexander the Great in Afghanistan*. Berkeley: University of California Press, 2005. Recommended study on Alexander's campaigns in Central Asia.

Lane Fox, Robin. *Alexander the Great: A Biography*. New York: Dial Press, 1974. Lively, popular account but criticized for use of sources.

Lloyd, G. E. R. *Aristotle: The Growth and Structure of his Thought*. London: Cambridge University Press, 1968. Recommended introduction.

Marsden, E. W. *The Campaign of Gaugamela*. Liverpool: Liverpool University Press, 1964. Definitive scholarly study on the battle.

McCrindle, J. W. *Ancient India: Its Invasion by Alexander the Great*. London: Metheun, 1894. Still important collection of sources and discussion of the routes of invasion.

Milns, R. D. *Alexander the Great*. New York: Pegasus, 1968. Fine popular introduction.

Mitchell, F. W. *Lykourgan Athens, 338–322 B.C.* Lectures in Memory of Louise Semple, Second Series. Cincinnati: University of Cincinnati Press, 1970. Important scholarly essays on the reforms in Athens during the time of Alexander the Great.

Nikolitsis, N. T. *The Battle of the Granicus: A Source-Critical Study*. Stockholm: Swedish Institute in Athens, 1973. Careful topographical study of the battlefield.

O'Brien, John. *Alexander the Great: The Invisible Enemy*. New York: Routledge, 1994. Controversial study arguing for Alexander as an alcoholic.

Parker R. A. and J. Cerny. *A Saite Oracle Papyrus from Thebes*. Providence, RI: Brown Egyptological Studies, no. 4, 1962. Definitive scholarly study on the oracle.

Robinson, C. A. *The History of Alexander the Great*. 2 vols. Baltimore: Johns Hopkins University Press, 1977. Important scholarly study with special studies in the second volume on sources and controversies on Alexander.

Stark, Freya. *Alexander's Path from Caria to Cilicia*. New York: Harcourt, Brace and World, Inc., 1956. Perceptive remarks on Alexander in the Asia Minor from celebrated traveler and writer.

Stein, Sir Aurel. *On Alexander's Track to the Indus: Personal Narrative of Explorations of the Northwest Frontier*. London: Macmillan and Company, 1929. Still the most important survey of the Indian routes taken by Alexander. Written by a celebrated British officer and explorer.

Stewart, A. *Faces of Power: Alexander's Image and Hellenistic Politics*. Berkeley: University of California Press, 1993. Recommended study on depiction of Alexander in art.

Tarn, W. W. *Alexander the Great*. 2 vols. Cambridge: Cambridge University Press, 1948. The definitive scholarly portrayal of the heroic Alexander. Excellent supplementary studies in the second volume.

Thomas, Carol G. *Alexander the Great in His World*. Oxford: Basil Blackwell, 2006. Recommended introduction to the world of Alexander.

Wheeler, Mortimer. *Flames over Persepolis: Turning-point in History*. New York: William Morrow, 1968. Well-written, popular account of Alexander in Iran.

Wilcken, Ulrich. *Alexander the Great*. Translated by G. C. Richards. New York: W. W. Norton and Company, 1967. Still the most perceptive biography on Alexander.

Wood, Michael. *In the Footsteps of Alexander the Great: A Journey from Greece to Asia.* Berkeley: University of California Press, 2001. Idiosyncratic but interesting account of a personal journey that reveals the popularity of Alexander in the Near East.

## Hellenistic World

Allen, R. E. *The Attalid Kingdom: A Constitutional History.* Oxford: Clarendon Press, 1983. Political narrative of the Attalid state.

Aperghis, G. G. *The Seleukid Royal Economy: The Finances and Financial Administration of the Seleukid Empire.* Cambridge: Cambridge University Press, 2002. Scholarly study on the administration and organization of the empire.

Bagnall, Roger S. *The Administration of Ptolemaic Possessions outside of Egypt.* Leiden: E.J. Brill, 1976. Important study also for Ptolemaic diplomacy and political ambitions.

Bar-Kochva, B. *The Seleucid Army: Organisation and Tactics in the Great Campaigns.* Cambridge: Cambridge University Press, 1976. Important study on major battles of the Hellenistic age and the conditions of mercenary service.

Berthold, R. M. *Rhodes in the Hellenistic Age.* Ithaca: Cornell University Press, 1984. The recommended modern narrative.

Bevan, Edwyn R. *The House of Ptolemy: A History of Hellenistic Egypt under the Ptolemaic Dynasty.* Oxford: Oxford University Press, 1927. Dated but lively political narrative.

———. *The House of Seleucus: A History of the Hellenistic Near East under the Seleucid Dynasty.* Oxford: Oxford University Press, 1902. Dated but lively political narrative.

Billows, Richard A. *Antigonos the One-Eyed and the Creation of the Hellenistic State.* Berkeley: University of California Press, 1991. Excellent modern biography as well as an analysis of the foundations of Hellenistic states

Bingen, Jean. *Hellenistic Egypt: Monarchy, Society, Economy, and Culture.* Berkeley: University of California Press, 2007. Recommended survey.

Bosworth, A. B. *The Legacy of Alexander: Politics, Warfare, and Propaganda under the Successors.* Oxford: Oxford University Press, 2002. Recommended study on the wars of the Diadochoi and political appeals.

Bowman, Alan K. *Egypt after the Pharaohs, 332 B.C.–A.D. 642.* Berkeley: University of California Press, 1986. Superbly written introduction. Recommended.

Burkert, Walter. *Ancient Mystery Cults.* Cambridge, MA: Harvard University Press, 1987. The most thoughtful scholarly study on mystery cults. Judicious in use of sources.

Cary, Max. *A History of the Greek World, 323–146 B.C.* 2$^{nd}$ ed. rev. London: Metheun, 1952. Classic narrative of the Hellenistic world.

Cohen, Getzel M. *The Hellenistic Settlements in Europe, the Islands, and Asia Minor.* Berkeley: University of California Press, 1996. The reference study on founding of Greek cities.

————. *The Seleucid Colonies: Studies in Founding, Administration, and Organization.* Historia Einzelschriften 30. Stuttgart: Franz Steiner, 1978. Scholarly study on Seleucid colonization.

Cribb, Joe and Georgina Herrmann, eds. *After Alexander: Central Asia Before Islam.* Oxford: Oxford University Press, 2007. Superb scholarly study on the archaeology of Central Asia.

Cribionre, R. *Gymnastics of the Mind: Greek Education in Hellenistic and Roman Egypt.* Princeton: Princeton University Press, 2001. Crucial study on the role of education in defining the Greek identity in the Hellenistic world.

Cumont, Franz. *The Mysteries of Mithra,* 2$^{nd}$ ed. rev. Translated by Thomas J. McCormack. New York: Dover Publications, Inc.,1956. Seminal study that proposed the thesis of mystery cults supplanting civic cults in the Hellenistic Age.

————. *Oriental Religions in Roman Paganism*. Translated by Grant Showerman. New York: Dover Publications, Inc, 1956. Sequel to the study on Mithras.

Downey, Glanville. *A History of Antioch in Syria from Seleucus to the Arab Conquest*. Princeton: Princeton University Press, 1961. The classic study on the Seleucid capital's role in the Hellenistic and Roman periods.

Eddy, Samuel K. *The King is Dead: Studies in Near Eastern Resistance, 334–30 B.C.* Lincoln: University of Nebraska Press, 1961. Important study on the Near Eastern reaction to the conquests of Alexander the Great and Macedonian rule.

Erskine, Andrew, ed. *A Companion to the Hellenistic World*. Oxford: Basil Blackwell, 2005. Useful reference work.

Ferguson, W. S. *Hellenistic Athens*. London: Macmillan and Co., Ltd., 1911. The classic study now superceded by Habricht's work.

Finley, M. I. *The Ancient Economy*. Berkeley: University of California Press, 1960. The classic minimalist argument for economic life by a leading British scholar.

Fraser, William A. *Ptolemaic Alexandria*. 3 vols. Oxford: Oxford University Press, 1972. The scholarly account of the city.

Garnsey, Peter. *Famine and Food Supply in the Graeco-Roman World: Responses to Risk and Crisis*. Cambridge: Cambridge University Press, 1988. Important study on the diet and subsistence in the ancient world.

Grainger, John D. *Hellenistic Phoenicia*. Oxford: Oxford University Press, 1991. Learned study of the impact of Hellenization.

————. *Seleuckos Nikator: Constructing a Hellenistic Kingdom.* New York: Routledge, 1990. Modern biography on the king.

Green, Peter. *Alexander to Actium: The Historical Evolution of the Hellenistic Age.* Berkeley: University of California Press, 1993. Controversial account of the limited Greco-Macedonian impact on the Near East.

Habicht, Christian. *The Hellenistic Monarchies: Selected Papers.* Translated by Peregrine Stevenson. Ann Arbor: University of Michigan Press, 2006. Important articles by leading epigraphist and historian.

Hansen, Esther V. *The Attalids of Pergamon.* Ithaca, NY: Cornell University Press, 1947. The classic study of the Attalid dynasty.

Holt, Frank L. *Thundering Zeus: The Making of Hellenistic Bactria.* Berkeley: University of California Press, 1999. Recommended study on Greco-Bactrian kingdom.

Jones, A. H. M. *The Greek City from Alexander to Justinian.* Oxford: Oxford University Press, 1960. Recommended scholarly treatment on the role of Greek cities.

Lund, Helen S. *Lysimachus: A Study in Early Hellenistic Kingship.* New York: Routledge, 1992. The first modern biography.

MacMullen, Ramsay. *Paganism in the Roman Empire.* New Haven: Yale University Press, 1981. Penetrating and controversial study that called into question mystery cults.

Macurdy, G. H. *Hellenistic Queens: A Study of Women-Power in Macedonia, Seleucid Syris and Ptolemaic Egypt.* Baltimore: Johns Hopkins University Press, 1932. Older study on political roles of Macedonian queens.

Pollitt, J. J. *Art in the Hellenistic Age.* Cambridge: Cambridge University Press, 1986. Recommended introduction.

Bibliography

Pomeroy, Sarah. *Women in Hellenistic Egypt: From Alexander to Cleopatra.* New York: Wayne State University Press, 1990. Recommended study on social role of women based on documents of Egypt.

Potter, David. *Prophecy and History in the Crisis of the Roman Empire: A Historical Commentary on the Thirteenth Sibylline Oracle.* Oxford: Oxford University Press, 1991. Scholarly study of the apocalyptic literature of the Near East.

Price, S. R. F. *Rituals and Power: The Roman Imperial Cult in Asia Minor.* Cambridge: Cambridge University Press, 1986. Seminal study on the role of ruler cults and the nature of paganism.

Roller, Lynn E. *In Search of the Mother Goddess: The Cult of Anatolian Cybele.* Berkeley: University of California Press, 1999. Definitive scholarly study.

Rostovtzeff, Michael. *The Social and Economic History of the Hellenistic World.* 3 vols. Oxford: Clarendon Press, 1941. Brilliant synthesis by leading Russian historian who defined the economic role of the Hellenistic world.

Sherwin-White, Susan and Amelie Kuhrt. *From Samarkhand to Sardis: A New Approach to the Seleucid Empire.* Berkeley: University of California Press, 1994. Superb series of essays on the Seleucid Empire.

Shipley, Graham. *The Greek World after Alexander, 323–30 B.C.* New York: Routledge, 2000. The modern narrative account.

Smith, R. R. R. *Hellenistic Royal Portraits.* Oxford: Clarendon Press, 1988. The indispensable scholarly study. Superb study on art and its political uses by leading art historian.

Tarn, W. W. *The Greeks in Bactria and India.* 3rd ed. Revised by Frank L. Holt. Chicago: Ares Publishers, 1984. Classic study revised by Frank Holt, the leading current authority on Bactria.

————. *Hellenistic Civilization*. Rev. ed. Baltimore: Meridian Books, 1961. The classic definition of the Hellenistic world.

Veyne, Paul. *Bread and Circuses: Historical Sociology and Political Pluralism*. Translated and edited by Oswyn Murray and Brian Pierce. Baltimore: Penguin Books, 1992. A controversial but brilliant analysis of the role of patronage.

Walbank, F. W. *The Hellenistic World*. Cambridge, MA: Harvard University Press, 1982. A minimalist view of the Hellenistic world.

————. *Philip V of Macedon*. Cambridge: Cambridge University Press, 1940. Excellent study of this Macedonian king.

Witt, R. E. *Isis in the Graeco-Roman World*. Ithaca, NY: Cornell University Press, 1971. The definitive account of the cult in the Hellenistic world.

**Televised Documentary**
*The Great Commanders: Alexander the Great and the Battle of Issus*. New York: Ambrose Video Publishing Inc., 1993. Available in a set of five other commanders (Julius Caesar, Napoleon, Nelson, Grant, and Zhukov).

Wood, Michael. *In the Footsteps of Alexander the Great*. New York: PBS Home Video, 1998.

**Alexander the Great in Fiction**
Renault, Mary. *Fire from Heaven*, 1969. The youth of Alexander the Great.

————. *The Funeral Games*, 1981. On the successors of Alexander the Great.

————. *The King Must Die*. 1956.

————. *The Last of the Wine*. 1956. Set in Athens during the later Peloponnesian War (414–404 B.C.). The first and finest of Renault's historical novels.

———. *The Mask of Apollo*. 1969. Set in Sicily in the time of Plato and the tyrant Dionysus II. 367–357 B.C. Alexander the Great is introduced at the end of the novel.

———. *The Persian Boy* London: Penguin Books, 1972. The perspective of a fictional eunuch Bagoas on the conquests of Alexander the Great, and source for the movie by Oliver Stone. The least satisfying of Renault's novels.

Note: All Renault's novels are available in reprinted editions from Vintage Books, London, 2001.

### Alexander the Great in Film
*Alexander the Great,* written and directed by Rossen in 1956, with Richard Burton as Alexander and Fredric March as Philip. Available in DVD. Santa Monica: M. G. Entertainment, 2004.

*Alexander*, written and directed by Oliver Stone in 2004, with Colin Farrell as Alexander,

Val Kilmer as Philip, and Angelina Jolie as Olympias. Available in DVD. Burbank: Warner Home Entertainment, 2004.

**Notes**